Leaving Jesus
Revised Edition
James Wood Jr.

New Dominion Publishing
Midland, Virginia

New Dominion Publishing
6137 Beach Road
Midland, Virginia 22728
Leavingjesus.net
James@leavingjesus.net

Revised Edition copyright © 2011, 2012 by James Wood Jr.

ISBN-13: 978-1469995663

ISBN-10: 1469995662

All rights reserved, including but not limited to the right of reproduction in whole or part.

No part of this book may be reproduced in any form by written, oral, or data transmission without the express permission of the author with the exception of short quotes in a review. To obtain permission for any other use contact me at the above address or email.

All Scriptures are taken from the King James Version Bible unless otherwise noted.

Cover design by James Wood Jr.

Edited by David Isaiah Dryden

Also available as an Ebook at Smashwords.com and

an audiobook at www.leavingjesus.net

Dedication

I dedicate this book to God and *my Parents* who gave me life, and to my brother *Rabbi Tovia Singer* for showing me what I couldn't see.

I would like to thank my wonderful wife *Alison* and my children for encouraging me while I wrote this book.

I would also like to thank my friend *David Isaiah Dryden*, who took time out from writing his upcoming book, *The Bitter Root: "Apostle" Paul,* to edit this book.

About the Author

James Wood Jr. is the son of a Southern Baptist Minister and was a committed Christian for 25 years. Years after learning he was of Jewish descent, he entered into the Messianic Jewish movement. Soon after he began realizing there were serious problems with mainline Christianity. After he started learning Hebrew, the questions about his faith in Jesus started piling up. When he discovered that no one could help him with his questions, he embarked on the journey to find the answers himself. What James found was totally unexpected and it resulted in him leaving the Church and Christianity. James shares his uncommon insight into Christianity and the Hebrew Scriptures that have taken him down a road he never expected to travel on.

CONTENTS

INTRODUCTION
  Tell a Lie Often Enough...   7
CHAPTER 1
  The Cycle Starts Again...   8
CHAPTER 2
  Is "Who is the Messiah?" the Right Question?   11
CHAPTER 3
  Sin and Atonement through God's Eyes   18
CHAPTER 4
  Isaiah 53: Linchpin or Nail in the Coffin?   33
CHAPTER 5
  Examining the "Messianic" Prophecies   56
CHAPTER 6
  Vain Genealogies   89
CHAPTER 7
  The Confident God vs. The Bashful God   93
CHAPTER 8
  Paul: Apostle or Pretender Prophet   105
CHAPTER 9
  Satan: God's Servant, Nemesis or...   129
CHAPTER 10
  Crucifying the Resurrection   144
CHAPTER 11
  Will the Real Messiah Step Forward?   189
CHAPTER 12
  Conclusions   197

Also available as an Ebook for all popular Readers at Smashwords.com
For more Leaving Jesus products go to www.leavingjesus.net

INTRODUCTION

Tell a Lie Often Enough...

It is easy to lie to children because they are so trusting. People do this all the time. It starts with Santa Clause, progresses to the Tooth Fairy and may end at the Easter bunny. These lies aren't told to children in order to hurt them. The thought is to give children a good time. Christmas and Easter are supposed to be fun for the children. What harm is a little white lie told to the kids? It's all in fun and it adds a sense of mystery to the holiday. It enhances the lives of the children and adds to the anticipation.

Of course, the parents don't actually believe these lies. They know better. They have been through the entire cycle. They received the lies when they are young. They start to question the lies. They eventually find out the truth. They tell their children the lies. The children receive the lies. The cycle repeats.

The question is, *"What if the parents didn't know they were telling a lie?"* What if parents actually believed the lies they taught their children? Think about the possible harm they could unknowingly do. What if the lie that was being told had been perpetuated for many decades, perhaps even for thousands of years? What if most of society believed this lie? How would you break the cycle of the lie being passed down to the next generation?

This book is about a lie sprinkled with truth that has been twisted. In this book, I will present the problem that this lie has caused and how it could be affecting your life. It is my hope that when you read this book you will be able to learn the truth and, if need be, deliver yourself.

This book is written with two types of people in mind. First, I wrote this book for the Christian, in order to help them understand what they are dealing with when they try to make sense of Jesus and the New Testament. The second type of person is the one who would like to learn how to defend their beliefs against the Christian missionary that uses the Hebrew Scriptures to promote their version of *the messiah*.

CHAPTER 1

The Cycle Starts Again...

I was born into a family that was highly moral but not what I would call Christian. My parents taught me right from wrong but remarkably little about religion. My father was raised in a Mennonite colony, my mother on the outskirts of the colony. My Grandparents were not religious and knew little about the Bible. The result of this was neither of my parents knew much about the Bible either. My parents and grandparents acknowledged the existence of God and Satan but other than that they never discussed their beliefs, if they had any.

When I was about seven, my father decided that we would start attending a Southern Baptist church. I don't know what prompted my father to make this decision. It was soon after my father informed our family that he felt the call to the ministry and would become a pastor. He took some correspondence classes and studied on his own, then with little knowledge of the Bible, took a church near Washington, D.C.

My father is an honest man that has studied hard and knows his New Testament. His beliefs have evolved during his life as a pastor from the main line Southern Baptist beliefs through Pentecostalism finally settling into a form of Messianic Judaism.

These belief systems that my father has progressed through exhibit considerable diversity but they show incredible unity. Of course, I am speaking specifically about my father's beliefs, but this book is actually about the generalities of Christianity. This book is about the way the New Testament presents Jesus as the Messiah and it questions if Christianity is justified in believing that he is.

Universally, Christianity's belief system acknowledges sin, man's depravity, Jesus' messiah-ship and his sacrifice for mankind's salvation. Without doubt, Christian groups would probably disagree with some aspects of these beliefs but one that they all share is the belief that Jesus is the long awaited Messiah. They all base this common belief on the fact that the New Testament clearly states that he is. As a matter of fact, Jesus himself states that he is *The Messiah*.

The belief that Jesus is The Messiah (or the Christ) is the foundation of Christianity thus the name Christianity. Without this binding belief, Christianity would have faded away long ago. Christians might disagree with one another that Jesus is divine, but you will not find any Christians that do not believe that he was *the Messiah*. One point to remember is that Christians not only believe in a messiah, but they believe specifically that Jesus is the Messiah. To the Christian, their primary belief system starts with the fact that Jesus is *The Messiah* and all of their secondary beliefs flow from that. But what if their primary belief is an error? Do Christians consider any facts, or are they actually relying only on their vaporous beliefs?

Personally, I have met many Christians that have told me that they have had a personal experience with Jesus, even a personal relationship. I don't mean that they are saying they have physically seen Jesus or that they have had a vision of him. They insist that they have developed an emotional bond with him that transcends anything physical. A few have even said that they feel that he is more real to them than their spouse or any other relative. When questioned why they believe this, their response is usually the common mantra, *"You just gotta believe!"* For the most part, these Christians are usually unwilling to examine any facts that prove that Jesus is not *The Messiah*. If given a choice, they would prefer their erroneous beliefs to any biblical evidence that would counter them. This is an emotional response.

I want to be brutally honest here. If I ask most Christians if they believe that it is possible to have a personal relationship with George Washington, I know (the opposite of believe) that they would answer, *"no!"* They would probably indicate that the reason would be because George Washington died long ago. But, if I were to ask if they could have a personal relationship with Jesus they would emphatically reply, *"yes!"*

If asked what the difference was between George and Jesus, they would probably say that, *"George had not died for their sins and doesn't live in their heart!"*

Does the Hebrew Bible (what Christians refer to as the Old Testament) actually present the idea that *The Messiah* will come die for man's sins and live in man's heart? If you *"believe"* the Hebrew Bible teaches this idea, and you will not consider any alternative then this book is not for you. But if you are willing to suspend your beliefs in Jesus for even a moment then read on and pray to the God of Abraham, Issac and Jacob and ask him to open your eyes to the truth, whatever it may be.

Generally, Christians believe the following. God created man perfect and sinless and placed him in the Garden of Eden. When man and his wife disobeyed God, they sinned for the first time and immediately inherited a sin nature. After the sin nature had been impressed upon them, in fact, they became only able to sin. It was then, God set in motion his plan to redeem them from their sins and sin nature. Christianity believes that in the third chapter of Genesis, God himself foretells that *"The Messiah"* will come and deliver man from his sin through a veiled innuendo as shown in this Scripture.

And the LORD God said unto the serpent, Because thou hast done this, thou art cursed above all cattle, and above every beast of the field; upon thy belly shalt thou go, and dust shalt thou eat all the days of thy life: And I will put enmity between thee and the woman, and between thy seed and her seed; it shall bruise thy head, and thou shalt bruise his heel. (Genesis 3:14,15)

Christians believe this *messiah* came as Jesus, died upon the cross for the sins of mankind and rose again on the third day. After forty days, he ascended to heaven to sit at God's right hand. Of course, Christians also believe that Jesus will come again, defeat his enemies including Satan and then live with man on Earth forever more. Christians also believe that they will rule with Jesus for all eternity.

Most Christians will tell you that they believe that the New Testament teaches that Jesus is the Messiah and even unbelievers will agree. I have read and studied the Christian Bible for over twenty-five years. I agree that the New Testament does teach that Jesus is the Messiah in unmistakable transparent language. Christians will also tell you that the New Testament gets much of its information directly from the Hebrew

Bible (Christian Old Testament). As a matter of fact, there are at first glance many scriptures that appear to be pulled directly from the Hebrew Bible. Pastors, teachers, lay people, and missionaries alike will tell you that "Jesus is written on every page of the Old Testament."

I was a committed Christian for twenty-five years and agreed with these beliefs. Although this was true, I had come to a turning point. I knew I had to re-evaluate my theology. In this book, I will explain the reasons why I came to understand what the Hebrew Bible actually teaches about the subject of the messiah, and its implications for your eternity.

CHAPTER 2

Is "Who is the Messiah?" the Right Question?

The woman saith unto him, I know that Messias (Messiah) cometh, which is called Christ: when he is come, he will tell us all things. Jesus saith unto her, I that speak unto thee am he. (John 4:25,26)

Jesus' words without any doubt reveal that he believed that he was *The Messiah*. To the average Christian this is proof enough. But to the serious Hebrew Bible Scholar this verse would raise serious questions. We will do a short Bible study to see why this verse raises serious questions in the mind of Hebrew Bible Scholars.

First let's examine the word "messiah." Words mean things. People often pour into words the meaning that they have manufactured in their own mind. More often, they use meanings that someone else has constructed erroneously without their knowledge. True Bible scholars don't have the luxury to allow this. If they did, it would be dishonest and would ultimately lead to an inability to understand the biblical text.

How one understands the Bible shapes your personal world view. One could only imagine how the world has been shaped by world views of those who had no interest in an intense study of God's Word.

Here, I present an analogy. If you want to know if someone is a plumber, then you must know what the word *plumber* means. More importantly, you must know what makes a plumber a plumber. If you learn what the word plumber means, then you can critically examine someone that tries to pass themselves off as a plumber. If they don't do anything that a plumber does, you would question how this person could be a plumber.

This chapter will examine and answer the question, *"Who is the Messiah?"* It is not my intention to name a person whom I believe to be The Messiah but rather to explain the concept. Also, we will determine if Christianity's focus on The Messiah is misplaced. That is not to say that I will not name persons that we can eliminate because they do not fit the requirements of the end-times-king that are found in the Hebrew Bible.

First, we must define the term *messiah*. If you want answers to questions about biblical subjects, the best place to start is the Bible itself. One way people who seriously study the Bible determine what words used in the Hebrew Bible mean is to study their usage, particularly their first usage in the Torah (the books of Moses.)

Before we define the word, here is a fact that you should realize. The English word *Messiah*, a rough transliteration of the Hebrew word *Mashiach (mah-shee'-ahk)*, appears only twice in the King James Bible. Both times the word appears in the ninth Chapter of Daniel. This is the problem, the Hebrew word *Mashiach (mah-shee'-ahk)* is actually found 39 times in the Hebrew Scriptures. The two Scripture references in the

King James Version Bible that use the word *Messiah* found in Daniel, follow.

Know therefore and understand, that from the going forth of the commandment to restore and to build Jerusalem unto **the Messiah** *(Mashiach/Messiah) the Prince shall be seven weeks, and threescore and two weeks: the street shall be built again, and the wall, even in troublous times. And after threescore and two weeks shall* **Messiah** *(Mashiach/Messiah) be cut off, but not for himself: and the people of the prince that shall come shall destroy the city and the sanctuary; and the end thereof shall be with a flood, and unto the end of the war desolations are determined. (Daniel 9:25,26)*

Without getting into the actual translation or language used here, you must realize that the Hebrew word that is translated "Messiah" above is the same Hebrew word that is translated *anointed* everywhere else in the King James Version Bible. The translators rendered *mashiach* as *anointed* except here in Daniel chapter 9 for seemingly no reason. This particular passage in Daniel will be discussed later in chapter 5 of this book.

Following, are the remaining verses that contain the same Hebrew word but translated "anointed."

If the priest that is anointed (Mashiach/Messiah) do sin according to the sin of the people; then let him bring for his sin, which he hath sinned, a young bullock without blemish unto the LORD for a sin offering. (Leviticus 4:3)

And the priest that is anointed (Mashiach/Messiah) shall take of the bullock's blood, and bring it to the tabernacle of the congregation. (Leviticus 4:5)

And the priest that is anointed (Mashiach/Messiah) shall bring of the bullock's blood to the tabernacle of the congregation: (Leviticus 4:16)

And the priest of his sons that is anointed (Mashiach/Messiah) in his stead shall offer it: it is a statute for ever unto the LORD; it shall be wholly burnt. (Leviticus 6:22)

The adversaries of the LORD shall be broken to pieces; out of heaven shall he thunder upon them: the LORD shall judge the ends of the earth; and he shall give strength unto his king, and exalt the horn of his anointed (Mashiach/Messiah).(1 Samuel 2:10)

And I will raise me up a faithful priest, that shall do according to that which is in mine heart and in my mind: and I will build him a sure house; and he shall walk before mine anointed (Mashiach/Messiah) for ever. (1 Samuel 2:35)

Behold, here I am: witness against me before the LORD, and before his anointed (Mashiach / Messiah): whose ox have I taken? or whose ass have I taken? or whom have I defrauded? who have I oppressed? or of whose hand have I received any bribe to blind mine eyes therewith? and I will restore it you. (1 Samuel 12:3)

And he said unto them, The LORD is witness against you, and his anointed (Mashiach/Messiah) is witness this day, that ye have not found ought in my hand. And they answered, He is witness. (1 Samuel 12:5)

And it came to pass, when they were come, that he looked on Eliab, and said, Surely the LORD'S anointed (Mashiach/Messiah) is before him. (1 Samuel 16:6)

And he said unto his men, The LORD forbid that I should do this thing unto my master, the LORD'S anointed (Mashiach/Messiah), to stretch forth mine hand against him, seeing he is the anointed (Mashiach/Messiah) of the LORD. (1 Samuel 24:6)

Behold, this day thine eyes have seen how that the LORD had delivered thee to day into mine hand in the cave: and some bade me kill thee: but mine eye spared thee; and I said, I will not put forth mine hand against my lord; for he is the LORD'S anointed (Mashiach/Messiah). (1 Samuel 24:10)

And David said to Abishai, Destroy him not: for who can stretch forth his hand against the LORD'S anointed (Mashiach/Messiah), and be guiltless? (1 Samuel 26:9)

The LORD forbid that I should stretch forth mine hand against the LORD'S anointed (Mashiach/Messiah): but, I pray thee, take thou now the spear that is at his bolster, and the cruse of water, and let us go. (1 Samuel 26:11)

This thing is not good that thou hast done. As the LORD liveth, ye are worthy to die, because ye have not kept your master, the LORD'S anointed (Mashiach/Messiah). And now see where the king's spear is, and the cruse of water that was at his bolster.

(1 Samuel 26:16)

The LORD render to every man his righteousness and his faithfulness: for the LORD delivered thee into my hand to day, but I would not stretch forth mine hand against the LORD'S anointed (Mashiach/Messiah). (1 Samuel 26:23)

And David said unto him, How wast thou not afraid to stretch forth thine hand to destroy the LORD'S anointed (Mashiach/Messiah)? (2 Samuel 1:14)

And David said unto him, Thy blood be upon thy head; for thy mouth hath testified against thee, saying, I have slain the LORD'S anointed (Mashiach/Messiah).

(2 Samuel 1:16)

Ye mountains of Gilboa, let there be no dew, neither let there be rain, upon you, nor fields of offerings: for there the shield of the mighty is vilely cast away, the shield of Saul, as though he had not been anointed (Mashiach/Messiah) with oil. (2 Samuel 1:21)

But Abishai the son of Zeruiah answered and said, Shall not Shimei be put to death for this, because he cursed the LORD'S anointed (Mashiach/Messiah)? (2 Samuel 19:21)

He is the tower of salvation for his king: and sheweth mercy to his anointed (Mashiach/Messiah), unto David, and to his seed for evermore. (2 Samuel 22:51)

Now these be the last words of David. David the son of Jesse said, and the man who was raised up on high, the anointed (Mashiach/Messiah) of the God of Jacob, and the sweet psalmist of Israel, said, (2 Samuel 23:1)

Saying, Touch not mine anointed (Mashiach/Messiah), and do my prophets no harm. (1Chronicles 16:22)

O LORD God, turn not away the face of thine anointed (Mashiach/Messiah): remember the mercies of David thy servant. (2 Chronicles 6:42)

The kings of the earth set themselves, and the rulers take counsel together, against the LORD, and against his anointed (Mashiach/Messiah), saying, (Psalm 2:2)

Great deliverance giveth he to his king; and sheweth mercy to his anointed

(Mashiach/Messiah), to David, and to his seed for evermore. (Psalm 18:50)

Now know I that the LORD saveth his anointed (Mashiach/Messiah); he will hear him from his holy heaven with the saving strength of his right hand. (Psalm 20:6)

The LORD is their strength, and he is the saving strength of his anointed (Mashiach/Messiah). (Psalm 28:8)

Behold, O God our shield, and look upon the face of thine anointed (Mashiach/Messiah). (Psalm 84:9)

But thou hast cast off and abhorred, thou hast been wroth with thine anointed (Mashiach/Messiah). (Psalm 89:38)

Wherewith thine enemies have reproached, O LORD; wherewith they have reproached the footsteps of thine anointed (Mashiach/Messiah). (Psalm 89:51)

Saying, Touch not mine anointed (Mashiach/Messiah), and do my prophets no harm. (Psalm 105:15)

For thy servant David's sake turn not away the face of thine anointed (Mashiach/Messiah). (Psalm 132:10)

There will I make the horn of David to bud: I have ordained a lamp for mine anointed (Mashiach/Messiah). (Psalm 132:17)

Thus saith the LORD to his anointed (Mashiach/Messiah), to Cyrus, whose right hand I have holden, to subdue nations before him; and I will loose the loins of kings, to open before him the two leaved gates; and the gates shall not be shut. (Isaiah 45:1)

The breath of our nostrils, the anointed (Mashiach/Messiah) of the LORD, was taken in their pits, of whom we said, Under his shadow we shall live among the heathen. (Lamentations 4:20)

Thou wentest forth for the salvation of thy people, even for salvation with thine anointed (Mashiach/Messiah); thou woundedst the head out of the house of the wicked, by discovering the foundation unto the neck. Selah. (Habakkuk 3:13)

This is an all inclusive list of the only scriptures in the Hebrew Bible where the word messiah or *anointed* is to be found. There are no references here to *The Messiah* except in direct reference to Aaron, *the priest that is anointed*, literally *the priest the anointed* in Leviticus 4:3,4:5,4:16 and 6:12. There is no direct reference to the end-times-king who Christians call *The Messiah* to be found anywhere in the Hebrew Bible. Many Christians and Messianic Jews call Jesus, *"Yeshua Ha-Mashiach,"* meaning, *Jesus The Messiah* even though the Hebrew Bible **never** calls this end-times-king, *"The Messiah."* This usage seems to have originated around the time of or slightly before Jesus.

The Hebrew word that is translated *Messiah* is based on a Hebrew word *Mashach* meaning *to smear*. This word is first used in the Hebrew Bible in Genesis. God is speaking to Jacob and uses this word the first time.

I am the God of Bethel, where thou anointedst (mashach) the pillar, and where thou vowedst a vow unto me: now arise, get thee out from this land, and return unto the land of thy kindred. (Genesis 31:13)

This word represents the physical action "to smear" not merely a conceptualized action as Christians use it today. Specifically, in its proper usage throughout the Hebrew Bible means "smear with oil."

In the Hebrew Bible, certain people and even objects were set aside to perform special service for God. These people or objects were anointed with oil as a sign that they were set aside for this service. Objects such as the bread cakes, the Altar, bulls, and even the Tabernacle were all anointed with oil.

Christians seem to believe that there was to be only one messiah thus they refer to him as *"The Messiah."* This concept is flawed. There were *many messiahs* during the time that Israel existed as a nation before the destruction of Jerusalem. There were even some false messiahs afterward.

What was the first thing anointed in the Hebrew Bible? According to the Hebrew Bible, it was a stone pillar as we saw in Genesis 31:13. The first human messiah was Aaron the high priest. His sons followed him in the priesthood and became messiahs also. Aaron's anointing is so important that it is mentioned three times in the Torah (Exodus 28:41; 30:30; 40:13) and David describes it in Psalm 133:2.

There are also others that were anointed. The Hebrew Kings were all messiahs. Saul, David, Solomon and other Jewish kings were all *messiahs*. The kings were all *anointed* either by a prophet or a priest. Even King Cyrus is called, "God's Messiah" in Isaiah 45:1.

Thus saith the LORD to his anointed (Mashiach), to Cyrus, whose right hand I have holden, to subdue nations before him; and I will loose the loins of kings, to open before him the two leaved gates; and the gates shall not be shut; (Isaiah 45:1)

Although, Cyrus wasn't an Israelite, he was a king. Other nations also anointed their kings. This is why the Jewish people call the end-times-king that God will set on his throne in Jerusalem *The Messiah*. Because he is a king means he is a *messiah* or *anointed* but being a *messiah* does not automatically make one a king. This end-times *messiah* is a distinct *messiah* that will rule the entire world.

Christians believe this end-times-king is mentioned in the Hebrew Bible many times. As a matter of fact, some Christians estimate that there are well over three hundred prophecies foretelling of Jesus' role as this *Messiah*.

The following is an introduction of how Christians approach these messianic prophecies. It is in no way a comprehensive attempt to explain the list of prophecies that Christians use to try to prove that Jesus is The Messiah.

Christians actually start very early in the Torah Scriptures with their list of prophecies. Most everyone knows the story of Adam and Eve. They were the first people to sin and that resulted in the entire human race falling. When God confronts them, he passes judgment on them and punishes everyone involved. But God has a peculiar punishment for the serpent, who Christians believe to be Satan (we will discuss the Christian belief pertaining to Satan later in chapter 9.) In the following verses, we see that God dishes out this punishment then makes a statement that Christians see as a prophecy.

And the LORD God said unto the serpent, Because thou hast done this, thou art cursed above all cattle, and above every beast of the field; upon thy belly shalt thou go, and dust shalt thou eat all the days of thy life: And I will put enmity between thee and the *woman, and between **thy seed and her seed**; it shall bruise thy head, and thou shalt bruise his heel. (Genesis 3:14,15)*

Christians say in the passage above, the phrase "her seed" refers to the *virgin birth*. Their reason for saying this is because they believe that it is customary to refer to children as seed of men, not women. They think this is the only reference in the entire Bible to seed coming from a woman. They believe this *seed* must be different. This is a flimsy argument at best. If you think for a moment that this is plausible, you need to reread Genesis. I wonder why Christians haven't found the following verses.

And the angel of the LORD found her (Hagar) by a fountain of water in the wilderness, by the fountain in the way to Shur. And he said, Hagar, Sarai's maid, whence camest thou? and whither wilt thou go? And she said, I flee from the face of my mistress Sarai. And the angel of the LORD said unto her, Return to thy mistress, and submit thyself under her hands. ***And the angel of the LORD said unto her, I will multiply thy seed exceedingly, that it shall not be numbered for multitude.*** *And the angel of the LORD said unto her, Behold, thou art with child, and shalt bear a son, and shalt call his name Ishmael; because the LORD hath heard thy affliction. And he will be a wild man; his hand will be against every man, and every man's hand against him; and he shall dwell in the presence of all his brethren. (Genesis 16:7-12)*

The angel is speaking to Hagar and uses the same basic term referring to **her seed**. This scripture also shows a child being referred to as her (Hagar's) seed. Is this a messianic prophecy? No, of course not. After looking at this passage, why do you suppose that Christians still believe that the statement in Genesis 3 is a prophecy foretelling of a virgin birth? Could it be that they are relying on centuries of misuse of the Hebrew Bible passages because it is the way that it has always been done?

This is only one example of the type of scholarship that has led many people astray from the truth. In chapter 5, I will reveal how many, if not all, of the major New Testament prophetic passages misuse the Hebrew Bible to promote a distorted view of God's Word in order to promote Jesus as the only candidate for the end-times-king. Christians believe that there is utterly no one else that could be *The Messiah*. No one else need apply.

I don't blame the average Christian because they are not trained to study the Bible critically in order to tell when they are being sold a bill of goods. More times than not, when someone comes to make a "decision to accept Jesus" they are told to start their reading with the New Testament, specifically the Gospel of John. This is done in order to immerse them right away into the God-Man doctrine. I have often wondered, if Jesus is on every page of the Hebrew Bible, why don't pastors instruct new believers to start their reading with Genesis? The following verse, which is said to come from the lips of Jesus, follows this line of thinking.

Then he said unto them, O fools, and slow of heart to believe all that the prophets have spoken: Ought not Christ to have suffered these things, and to enter into his glory? ***And beginning at Moses and all the prophets, he expounded unto them in all the scriptures the things concerning himself.*** *(Luke 24:25-27)*

These are supposedly the words of Jesus. He was a man that many Christians believe was God in the flesh. I will discuss this belief and if it is found in the Hebrew Bible later in Chapter 7. One thing has bothered me for a long time about this particular passage. If Jesus had "expounded" (or interpreted) how these Hebrew Bible scriptures were actually pertaining to him then why weren't any of these revelations written down by anyone? Also, many times I had pondered the fact that previous to Jesus all of God's prophets had written down their revelations as a record to be passed down to future generations. It would seem that the only thing written down by Jesus was quickly scattered by the footsteps of his contemporaries. [1]

Revelations from the mouth of a walking, talking man that had been previously deceased would have been an earth-shattering revelation to the average Israelite. But these men never recorded these sayings. Instead, these things were written down much later by men that were desperate to defend their beliefs, namely the authors of the New Testament. As John wrote in his gospel exposing his true intent behind writing his gospel.

*But these are written, that ye might believe that Jesus **is the Christ**, the Son of God; and that believing ye might have life through his name. (John 20:31)*

This verse tells us much about the mindset of the writer if not all of the writers of the New Testament. The concept being delivered here to the reader is that the belief in a person being the anointed is essential to the eternal life of an individual. This sounds very Biblical but let's be sober for a moment. Remember that this is a new concept found in the New Testament and not in the Hebrew Bible. Not even once in the Hebrew Scriptures is there any commandment to believe in the Messiah when he comes. Without doubt nowhere in the Hebrew Scriptures is anyone commanded to believe in an anointed person. Still, the Jews are condemned by Gentiles and some "completed Jews" for not accepting Jesus as their Messiah. I challenge anyone to show me where, in plain language in the Hebrew Bible, anyone is commanded when *"the anointed person"* comes that they must believe that he is *anointed* or they will not have eternal life. I have been challenging people for the last few years and haven't had anyone answer except one person that used his answer to curse me and condemn me to hell. The command to believe in the Messiah actually originates in the pages of the New Testament and is a new concept not based on the Hebrew Bible, whatsoever.

In reality, the question of "Who is the Messiah?" is somewhat unnecessary because it is not our decision and it has little bearing on our justification or righteousness in God's eyes. The next chapter will discuss God's view of sin and its remedy.

---

1   During the episode of the adulteress that was brought to Jesus by the elders, he wrote in the dirt but what was written was not recorded for our benefit.

CHAPTER 3

Sin and Atonement through God's Eyes

"The subject that we are going to deal with tonight from a theological standpoint is most significant and that is the issue of sin and atonement."

Tovia Singer, during his lecture on Sin and Atonement [1]

The subject of Sin and atonement is very important to both Christians and Jews alike. It only happens that it is handled differently by the two parties involved. We will examine this subject from both viewpoints and then answer an important question that may change your life.

The Christian View

What is sin? Christians define sin as a transgression or disobedience of the Law. Of course, there are multiple opinions offered by Christians as to what the Law actually is. Some believe that the Law is the entirety of the *Old Testament*[2]. Others believe it is the five books of Moses or the Torah, while others still believe it is only the Ten Commandments[3]. There is a minority opinion that the Law is superseded by something referred to in the New Testament as the *Law of Christ*. Its elements are unknown, as it is never actually defined in the New Testament. This is the only reference to it in the New Testament.

Bear ye one another's burdens, and so fulfil the law of Christ. (Galatians 6:2)

Occasionally, I will hear someone tell me that the Law is defined in Acts 15 when the Apostles codified the requirements for converts.

Wherefore my sentence is, that we trouble not them, which from among the Gentiles are turned to God: But that we write unto them, that they abstain from pollutions of idols, and from fornication, and from things strangled, and from blood. (Acts 15:19-20)

While Christians hear most of this passage read, rarely do they hear the last verse read.

For Moses of old time hath in every city them that preach him, being read in the synagogues every sabbath day. (Acts 15:21)

This last verse was troubling to me when I was a Christian. What did it actually mean

---
1 Part of the "Let's Get Biblical" lecture series available at www.outreachjudaism.org
2 This is how Christians refer to the Hebrew Scriptures. It shows that they believe that all of the previous covenants that God made have been annulled.
3 Actually referred to in Hebrew and Greek as the *"Ten Words"* and never as the *"Ten Commandments."*

to the Apostles when they sent this letter out? Most Christians are far removed from the thinking of the first Christians. Why would Christians think that they could ignore all of God's Torah or instructions and only concern themselves with theses four requirements? They shouldn't. Were Christians to think that they could ignore the laws that pertained to things such as making sure their weights and measures were correct so they would not defraud their customers when they sold goods in the market? Christians are often not knowledgeable enough to know that the Torah addresses situations that most people think as mundane.

The last verse in the passage is the key to understanding what *Law* the Apostles thought new converts to their new sect of Judaism were supposed to keep. They expected them to learn the entire Torah from what was being taught each Sabbath in the synagogues. I see no mention here about only learning the Ten Commandments in Sunday School or only loving God and your neighbor.

Christians should consider what Jesus would have said about the *Law?* Did Jesus address this subject? Let's see what he said about it.

Think not that I am come to destroy the law, or the prophets: I am not come to destroy, but to fulfil. For verily I say unto you, Till heaven and earth pass, one jot or one tittle shall in no wise pass from the law, till all be fulfilled. Whosoever therefore shall break one of these least commandments, and shall teach men so, he shall be called the least in the kingdom of heaven: but whosoever shall do and teach them, the same shall be called great in the kingdom of heaven. For I say unto you, That except your righteousness shall exceed the righteousness of the scribes and Pharisees, ye shall in no case enter into the kingdom of heaven. (Matthew 5:17-20)

What we see in this passage is that Jesus thought highly of the Law. Christians get the wrong impression sometimes as to what Jesus included in the Law. Jesus did refer to the *commandments.* What exactly did Jesus mean when he used the word *commandments*? Let's see.

And Jesus said unto him, Why callest thou me good? there is none good but one, that is, God. Thou knowest the commandments, Do not commit adultery, Do not kill, Do not steal, Do not bear false witness, Defraud not, Honour thy father and mother. (Mark 10:18,19)

Jesus thought that the commandments consisted of more than only the *Ten Commandments.* Included in this short passage is the commandment *not to defraud.* This command is not in the *Ten Commandments.* I have heard many times preachers say that the commandments Jesus spoke of, only included the ones spoken at Sinai but Jesus seems to disagree. Preachers will, at times, say that the *law* has passed away and we now live in New Testament times. Let me be honest with you. This is a flat out lie. In chapter 4, as well as other places in this book, I will discuss the fact that the New Covenant has not come into being as of yet. For anyone, even Jesus, to say that the New Covenant has been made is incorrect.

Now that we have defined what the New Testament teaches about what the Law is (later we will share God's opinion as to what the law actually is), we will move on to what sin is. According to what we find in the New Testament sin is defined as the following.

Whosoever committeth sin transgresseth also the law: for sin is the transgression of the law. (1 John 3:4)

John (or whoever wrote his epistle) makes it very plain. Sin is breaking the law. It seems very simple doesn't it? Well, it is as long as you don't consider Jesus' words on the subject. Jesus added a little something extra for us to consider.

Ye have heard that it was said by them of old time, Thou shalt not commit adultery: But I say unto you, That whosoever looketh on a woman to lust after her hath committed adultery with her already in his heart. (Matthew 5:27,28)

Jesus is telling us that there is more to sin than the act. I have said enough here but this subject is discussed in more detail in chapter 5 in the section entitled, "Sin vs. Sin Nature."

Now that we have discussed what Christians consider the Law and sin to be we move on to the subject of atonement.

Of course, Christians believe and teach that everything in the Hebrew Scriptures has always been a *foreshadowing* of Jesus and his death on the cross. According to Christians without Jesus' death on the tree there could not be any forgiveness of sins. Christians teach that without the belief in Jesus there is no forgiveness, regardless of the fact that no mention is made of anyone in the Hebrew Scriptures believing anything about Jesus' future sacrifice. Where was the cut-off point? Who was the last person to have the *Old Testament* sacrifices apply to them? Did the *Old Testament* saints obtain salvation or forgiveness by animal blood sacrifices or Jesus' blood sacrifice?

Christians have a different concept in mind when they use the term *salvation* than is presented in the Hebrew Scriptures. *Salvation* in the Hebrew Scriptures is a purely physical one but the New Testament presents what seems to be a different concept about salvation.

And she shall bring forth a son, and thou shalt call his name JESUS: for he shall save his people from their sins. (Matthew 1:21)

This is the hallmark verse the New Testament uses to show Jesus' mission but there are other verses that show some confusion concerning the subject.

And ye shall be hated of all men for my name's sake: but he that endureth to the end shall be saved. (Matthew 10:22)

For God sent not his Son into the world to condemn the world; but that the world through him might be saved. (John 3:17)

He that believeth and is baptized shall be saved; but he that believeth not shall be damned. (Mark 16:16)

And if any man hear my words, and believe not, I judge him not: for I came not to judge the world, but to save the world. (John 12:47)

This last verse doesn't agree with Mark 16:16 where Jesus pronounces damnation on those who don't believe. Of course there is something special about Mark 16:16. In chapter 5, in the section entitled, *"The "These Signs shall Follow" Prophecy,"* I discuss how this verse is part of a passage that is not found in the earliest best manuscripts. Let's continue on in our examination of Christianity's belief system.

Your Sins are Cleansed by the Blood of Jesus or are they?

Most Christians would be quick to tell you about how they were saved. These are some of the mantras that they repeat.

- "I was saved and cleansed by the blood of Jesus."
- "Jesus was the perfect sacrifice."
- "Jesus was the Passover Lamb."

I once believed that these statements were correct but now I almost cringe when I hear them. Why can't Christians realize that these statements don't agree with God's Word as revealed by Moses and the Prophets in the Hebrew Scriptures? It's due to one of two reasons; either it's ignorance or distrust in God. When Christians don't know what the Hebrew Scriptures teach they fall prey to ignorance or deception. I know this from personal experience.

Most Christians believe that Jesus' sacrifice is a perfect fulfillment of the sacrifices in their *"Old Testament."* Let's take a quick look at some of the many verses that are contained in their New Testament.

Jesus' Thoughts on Blood

And he said unto them, This is my blood of the new testament, which is shed for many. (Mark 14:24)

Likewise also the cup after supper, saying, This cup is the new testament in my blood, which is shed for you. (Luke 22:20)

Then Jesus said unto them, Verily, verily, I say unto you, Except ye eat the flesh of the Son of man, and drink his blood, ye have no life in you. Whoso eateth my flesh, and drinketh my blood, hath eternal life; and I will raise him up at the last day. For my flesh is meat indeed, and my blood is drink indeed. He that eateth my flesh, and drinketh my blood, dwelleth in me, and I in him. (John 6:53-56)

What reason would Jesus have to put such an emphasis on his blood? Surely, these statements were shocking to Jews when these words were heard or read in the first century. Why would this be so shocking? We will answer this question in the next section.

One thing that I must stress is, in the passage above Jesus is not speaking figuratively. When the translators used the word, "indeed", they were translating the Greek word "Alethos" which is used frequently in the Greek New Testament to denote something being an actual truth or a reality. Jesus is saying here that his blood is actually a drink and his flesh is actually a meat. Why would he say anything like this? Does the Hebrew Bible ever mention eating the messiah or drinking his blood? This is just about the most disgusting statement that a Jewish rabbi could have uttered.

Where did Jesus get these concepts about blood? Did he get them from the Hebrew Scriptures? We will first familiarize ourselves with the words of the other writers of the New Testament before we can do a complete analysis.

Paul and the Blood

Whom God hath set forth to be a propitiation through faith in his blood, to declare his righteousness for the remission of sins that are past, through the forbearance of God; (Romans 3:25)

Much more then, being now justified by his blood, we shall be saved from wrath through him. (Romans 5:9)

In whom we have redemption through his blood, the forgiveness of sins, according to the riches of his grace; (Ephesians 1:7)

And, having made peace through the blood of his cross, by him to reconcile all things unto himself; by him, I say, whether they be things in earth, or things in heaven. (Colossians 1:20)

It is worth noting that in one passage above *(Romans 3:25)* that Paul makes the statement that Jesus was a *"propitiation through **faith in his blood**, to declare his righteousness for the remission of **sins that are past.**"* Paul is saying here that Jesus is a substitutionary sacrifice for sins that are in the past. How do Christians atone for sins they commit *after* they become a Christian? Evidently, they are to follow what 1 John 1:9 says,

If we confess our sins, he is faithful and just to forgive us our sins, and to cleanse us from all unrighteousness,

If this were true, one would only need to confess the sin and be cleansed of it. This is problematic because if confession of the sin is effective for future sins it should also be sufficient for sins past. Is this telling us that Jesus' blood does not atone for future sins? Could it be that originally Jesus' sacrifice was seen as a way to affect a turning to God and not an actual atonement? There are places where the New Testament writers say that Jesus died only once but there is no passage that indicates he died for the future sins of believers.

Other Writers and Blood

The book of Hebrews is a major source of the theology surrounding Jesus' sacrifice and priesthood. Before I came the full realization of the need to reject the New Testament as a whole, I made the decision that I had to throw out the Book of Hebrews. During this time, I became aware the book of Hebrews had likewise come under attack by a prominent Messianic Rabbi named Monte Judah in an article in his group's publication *"Yavoh."* [4]

*For if the blood of bulls and of goats, and the ashes of an heifer sprinkling the unclean, sanctifieth to the purifying of the flesh: How much more shall the blood of Christ, who through the eternal Spirit offered himself without spot to God, purge your conscience from dead works to serve the living God? And for this cause he is the mediator of the new testament, that by means of death, for the redemption of the transgressions that were under the first testament, they which are called might receive the promise of eternal inheritance. **For where a testament is, there must also of necessity be the death of the testator. For a testament is of force after men are dead: otherwise it is of no strength at all while the testator liveth.**[5] Whereupon neither the first testament was*

---
4   Link: www.leavingjesus.net/articles/Paradigm_of_Hebrews.pdf
5   This particular verse shows that the author of Hebrews completely misunderstands covenants. He has substituted the idea of a last will and testament instead. He is saying here that when a

dedicated without blood. For when Moses had spoken every precept to all the people according to the law, he took the blood of calves and of goats, with water, and scarlet wool, and hyssop, and sprinkled both the book, and all the people, Saying, This is the blood of the testament which God hath enjoined unto you. Moreover he sprinkled with blood both the tabernacle, and all the vessels of the ministry.[6] *And almost all things are by the law purged with blood; and without shedding of blood is no remission. It was therefore necessary that the patterns of things in the heavens should be purified with these; but the heavenly things themselves with better sacrifices than these. For Christ is not entered into the holy places made with hands, which are the figures of the true; but into heaven itself, now to appear in the presence of God for us: Nor yet that he should offer himself often, as the high priest entereth into the holy place every year with blood of others; For then must he often have suffered since the foundation of the world: but now once in the end of the world hath he appeared to put away sin by the sacrifice of himself. (Hebrews 9:13-26)*

For it is not possible that the blood of bulls and of goats should take away sins. (Hebrews 10:4)

Having therefore, brethren, boldness to enter into the holiest by the blood of Jesus. (Hebrews 10:19)

Peter and John on the Blood

But with the precious blood of Christ, as of a lamb without blemish and without spot: (1 Peter 1:19)

But if we walk in the light, as he is in the light, we have fellowship one with another, and the blood of Jesus Christ his Son cleanseth us from all sin. (1 John 1:7)

And from Jesus Christ, who is the faithful witness, and the first begotten of the dead, and the prince of the kings of the earth. Unto him that loved us, and washed us from our sins in his own blood. (Revelation 1:5)

And I said unto him, Sir, thou knowest. And he said to me, These are they which came out of great tribulation, and have washed their robes, and made them white in the blood of the Lamb. (Revelation 7:14)

The Christian Understanding of Jesus' Death and Blood

Jesus' death and blood is presented to be of the ultimate importance in the New Testament. Where did Christians or Jesus get these concepts? Christians and the authors of the New Testament indicate that these ideas come directly from the Hebrew

---

    covenant is made the one making it (in this case God) must die to make it effective. Has he completely forgotten about all of the covenants that God has made with men since creation? Did God die each and every time He made a covenant?

6   The author has a poor memory of what happened at this point in history. Compare Hebrews 9:18-21 with this Exodus 24:6-8 , ***And Moses took half of the blood, and put it in basons; and half of the blood he sprinkled on the altar. And he took the book of the covenant, and read in the audience of the people: and they said, All that the LORD hath said will we do, and be obedient. And Moses took the blood, and sprinkled it on the people, and said, Behold the blood of the covenant, which the LORD hath made with you concerning all these words.*** I don't believe the author had a firm grasp on Hebrew and must have misunderstood this passage when he read it.

Scriptures.

Christians believe that Jesus has become the perfect replacement for their "*Old Testament*" blood sacrifices. What do Christians mean when they say that Jesus is the perfect sacrifice? They mean that all of the elements of the requirements found in the Hebrew Scriptures are transposed onto the life of Jesus. In other words, all of the things that are required of the sacrifices are found in the events of Jesus' life. For instance, Jesus is called "*the lamb of God that takes away the sins of the world*" by John and Paul has the following to say about Jesus.

Purge out therefore the old leaven, that ye may be a new lump, as ye are unleavened. For even Christ our passover is sacrificed for us: (1 Corinthians 5:7)

Christians formulate that the Hebrew Scriptures make the blood sacrifice the most important way to atone for sins both intentional and unintentional. They also believe that instead of relying on animal sacrifices they simply accept that the blood of Jesus was shed on the cross for them.

Consequently, Christians are quick to point out that Jesus must only die once, not every time you sin, because his is an exceedingly better sacrifice. They also believe that the sacrifices are done away with, never to return. This is all because Jesus, being their sinless high priest, has offered his perfect blood in the heavenly tabernacle. The book of Hebrews has Jesus literally required to offer his blood in a physical tabernacle in Heaven as if God must follow rules about atonement that He must actually do in order to forgive his children.

For Christ is not entered into the holy places made with hands, which are the figures of the true; but into heaven itself, now to appear in the presence of God for us: (Hebrews 9:24)

This sounds like the author of Hebrews believed there was an actual physical tabernacle in Heaven that Jesus had to take his physical blood into, to offer it.

*By the which will we are sanctified through the offering of the body of Jesus Christ once for all. And every priest standeth daily ministering and offering oftentimes the same sacrifices, which can never take away sins: But this man, **after he had offered one sacrifice for sins for ever**, sat down on the right hand of God; From henceforth expecting till his enemies be made his footstool. **For by one offering he hath perfected for ever them that are sanctified.** Whereof the Holy Ghost also is a witness to us: for after that he had said before, This is the covenant that I will make with them after those days, saith the Lord, I will put my laws into their hearts, and in their minds will I write them; And their sins and iniquities will I remember no more. Now where remission of these is, there is no more offering for sin. Having therefore, brethren, boldness to enter into the holiest by the blood of Jesus, **By a new and living way**, which he hath consecrated for us, through the veil, that is to say, his flesh. (Hebrews 10:10-20)*

In this short description of what Christians believe I have touched on the most important elements of the subject. But there is one aspect that I have left till last. Christians also believe in a concept that is called *retributive justice*. The idea of *retributive justice* is that for every sin that has been committed there is the need for someone to be punished. Christians believe that the New Testament teaches that although God can forgive freely, it is still necessary for God to pour out his wrath on someone. God cannot punish the one He has forgiven, instead, He chose to punish His son, Jesus, in their place. In other words, God has a rule that must be followed and that rule states that, "Someone must pay for the sin."

Punishing Jesus satisfies the need that God has to punish sin. This process of Jesus being punished for mankind's sins is referred to as "vicarious atonement," which simply means that someone else dies for their sins and not the Christian. Christians believe that God is bound by strict immutable laws that He has imposed on Himself. Conversely, Christians also believe that God is full of grace.

What's God's Opinion about What the Law is?

The first mistake Christians make about the Law is found in the word they use, *Law*. The Hebrew Scriptures use the Hebrew word *Torah*. This word is best translated not as *Law* but *Instruction or Teaching*.

The Christian use of the word *Law* and the way they wield it shows their disrespect for the entire concept as found in God's Word. The Hebrew Scriptures present and maintain concepts and principles easy to understand unlike the New Testament which is full of difficult to understand Pagan confusion and Greek philosophy which is contrary to His *Torah*.

God wants to lovingly teach us how to live with Him and our fellowman in harmony as a father would teach a son to be a good citizen. This is why He gave us a simple set of instructions to learn and follow. He made this instruction easily understandable so we can teach our seed the way to walk, also.

In contrast, Christians would have you believe that God is an intergalactic law officer. He always is waiting in the shadows in order to haul you in and throw you into the lake of fire for the least little infraction of His overbearing set of Laws, that, in the end, you can't keep if you wanted to.

The *"Law"* is actually the set of *instructions* or *teachings* that Moses transmitted to us. Not all of the *Torah* is what one would consider ordinances or statutes. Some are stories that teach us principles and lessons that a simple a *"Thou shalt not" Law* cannot. One example would be the story of the fall of Adam and Eve.

This is one of the major differences between the Hebrew Scriptures and New Testament. The Torah is enough for us. God told us this but The New Testament is actually the body of writings that place the burden on us because it adds to the simple instructions and creates contradictory teachings that leads one astray from the beauty and consistency of the Torah.

What's God's Opinion about Sin and Atonement?

When Christians place their top priority on blood sacrifice, they make a grave error in doing so. Very early in the Torah, God shows us where His emphasis is and explains what type of sacrifice He requires. In an exchange between God and Cain we see in plain language what God really wants from us.

And the LORD said unto Cain, Why art thou wroth? and why is thy countenance fallen? If thou doest well, shalt thou not be accepted? and if thou doest not well, sin lieth at the door. And unto thee shall be his desire, and thou shalt rule over him. (Genesis 4:6-7)

This is simply God telling Cain that he needs to turn to Him, do what is right and not give in to the anger that is driving him. This is the simplest way that God can possibly explain repentance. So from this early point in the Hebrew Bible we see God show that repentance is paramount.

When David sinned in the matter of Bathsheba, he was approached by Nathan the prophet. Nathan confronted David with his sin. David immediately repented and was forgiven by God. David later wrote about this in his Psalms.

Sacrifice and offering thou didst not desire; mine ears hast thou opened: burnt offering and sin offering hast thou not required. (Psalm 40:6)

Deliver me from bloodguiltiness, O God, thou God of my salvation: and my tongue shall sing aloud of thy righteousness. O Lord, open thou my lips; and my mouth shall shew forth thy praise. **For thou desirest not sacrifice; else would I give it: thou delightest not in burnt offering.** *The sacrifices of God are a broken spirit: a broken and a contrite heart, O God, thou wilt not despise. (Psalm 51:14-17)*

What is David saying here? Didn't he know that he had to offer a sacrifice because he had sinned? Didn't he know what Moses taught?

David was very aware of what he had done and he was very aware of what God's requirements were for his forgiveness. David was privy to something that most Christians haven't the foggiest idea about. Sin offerings are only performed for unintentional sin. If someone committed a sin *unknowingly* or *unintentionally* and later they became aware of it, then they were to present a sin offering. In God's economy there is even a special sin offering for the unknown sin, in case Israel had sinned and later did not become aware of it. The sacrifice was to teach one to be more careful and strive harder to avoid committing the sin. Each lamb, goat or turtledove cost the sinner. If a person, or the owner/purchaser of the animals, wasn't going to learn to stop being careless soon they would run out of animals.

The question is, *"What is the purpose of blood sacrifice?"*

Exposing Blood Sacrifice For What It Is and Isn't

Christians believe that every time in the Hebrew Scriptures there is a sacrifice it is for the forgiveness of sin. This is not necessarily the case. Some sacrifices are peace offering and others are done when one actually feels close to God but our subject at hand is blood sacrifice specifically for sin.

I have always wondered where Jesus found his justification for his sacrifice in the Hebrew Scriptures. I have not found anything after over twenty-five years of study but I did find this verse in Hebrews that should really shock you. Most Christians miss this strange statement.

The statement is in Hebrews 10:20, it reads,

*By a **new and living way**, which he hath consecrated for us, through the veil, that is to say, his flesh.*

This is another way of telling us that this is a *new* method of atonement. It signifies a departure from the Torah and its teachings on sin and atonement. In chapter 7, we will see how we are to process new teachings that disagree with God's instructions that are revealed in his Torah.

The following passages will reveal why Jesus' teachings about eating his blood would have been met with astonishment from educated Jews of his time. Of course, later in chapter 5, I will show why his disciples didn't have an adverse reaction to these statements. It was because they were unlearned men. Fishermen were not usually able to read and write in these first century times. They usually became fishermen when they were very young and never learned anything other than their trade. Let's look at the passages that should have had the disciples shutter when Jesus suggested that they eat his blood.

It shall be a perpetual statute for your generations throughout all your dwellings, that ye eat neither fat nor blood. (Leviticus 3:17)

Moreover ye shall eat no manner of blood, whether it be of fowl or of beast, in any of your dwellings. Whatsoever soul it be that eateth any manner of blood, even that soul shall be cut off from his people. (Leviticus 7:26,27)

For the life of the flesh is in the blood: and I have given it to you upon the altar to make an atonement for your souls: for it is the blood that maketh an atonement for the soul. Therefore I said unto the children of Israel, No soul of you shall eat blood, neither shall any stranger that sojourneth among you eat blood. And whatsoever man there be of the children of Israel, or of the strangers that sojourn among you, which hunteth and catcheth any beast or fowl that may be eaten; he shall even pour out the blood thereof, and cover it with dust. For it is the life of all flesh; the blood of it is for the life thereof: therefore I said unto the children of Israel, Ye shall eat the blood of no manner of flesh: for the life of all flesh is the blood thereof:whosoever eateth it shall be cut off. (Leviticus 17:11-13)

It is painfully obvious that this concept of eating blood for atonement is not something a Jewish Rabbi would have taught his disciples. If he had persisted in these teachings, he would have been thrown out of town or much worse. The verses in Leviticus 17 were twisted by the author of Hebrews to say the following in the New Testament.

And almost all things are by the law purged with blood; and without shedding of blood is no remission. (Hebrews 9:22)

This is a total misrepresentation of Leviticus 17, in which God says that the only legitimate use of blood is on the altar, so it is not permissible to eat it. It does not say, however, that blood is the only way to atone for sin. Again, the book of Hebrews scores a failing grade. This is simply a perversion of the Hebrew Scriptures.

When is blood to be used for atonement? First, blood is used only to atone for sin and not just any sin. It is only used to atone for **unintentional** sin. It cannot be used to atone for iniquity as there is no sacrifice for iniquity. Because this chapter is a discussion on sin, the subject of iniquity will have to be done at another time and place.

I cannot share with you any passages that show how blood is used to atone for **intentional** sin because there are none. Remember, I did show in David's Psalms passages[7] that God **did not** require an animal sacrifice for **intentional** sin. There were no sacrifices for *intentional* sin because you weren't being careful in the first place, your intent was to sin.

---

7   *Psalm 40:6 and Psalm 51:14-17*

CHAPTER 3

What did God require of those that had willfully sinned? If the sin was not punishable as a capital offense he wanted repentance and, of course, restitution if it involved a loss to the party who was offended.

Please read this carefully. There is no mention anywhere in the Hebrew Scriptures of the requirement to believe in any messiah, his blood or death for forgiveness of sins. If this is true, why should you believe in Jesus? In chapter 4, in a section entitled, "Dying for Another Person's Sins," I will discuss God's opinion about a person dying for sins committed by someone else.

Although this is true, there is mention of other things that can atone for sins. You must realize that this is the Word of God when you read these passages.

The rich shall not give more, and the poor shall not give less than half a shekel, when they give an offering unto the LORD, to make an atonement for your souls. And thou shalt take the atonement money of the children of Israel, and shalt appoint it for the service of the tabernacle of the congregation; that it may be a memorial unto the children of Israel before the LORD, to make an atonement for your souls. (Exodus 30:15-16)

In this passage, a person can offer money as an atonement.

And he shall bring his trespass offering unto the LORD for his sin which he hath sinned, a female from the flock, a lamb or a kid of the goats, for a sin offering; and the priest shall make an atonement for him concerning his sin. And if he be not able to bring a lamb, then he shall bring for his trespass, which he hath committed, two turtledoves, or two young pigeons, unto the LORD; one for a sin offering, and the other for a burnt offering. And he shall bring them unto the priest, who shall offer that which is for the sin offering first, and wring off his head from his neck, but shall not divide it asunder: And he shall sprinkle of the blood of the sin offering upon the side of the altar; and the rest of the blood shall be wrung out at the bottom of the altar: it is a sin offering. And he shall offer the second for a burnt offering, according to the manner: and the priest shall make an atonement for him for his sin which he hath sinned, and it shall be forgiven him. But if he be not able to bring two turtledoves, or two young pigeons, then he that sinned shall bring for his offering the tenth part of an ephah of fine flour for a sin offering; he shall put no oil upon it, neither shall he put any frankincense thereon: for it is a sin offering. Then shall he bring it to the priest, and the priest shall take his handful of it, even a memorial thereof, and burn it on the altar, according to the offerings made by fire unto the LORD: it is a sin offering.(Leviticus 5:6-12)

This passage starts out having a person offer a lamb or a goat for a sin offering. If the person cannot bring a lamb or a goat because they can't afford it then they can bring two turtle doves or two young pigeons. But what of the person that is poor and cannot afford them? God had thought of this situation also. Fine flour can be offered for a sin offering. Some Christian's heads must feel like they are going to explode when they read this. Flour can't possibly have blood! They must be thinking, "Flour can't possibly atone for sin!" but we have God's Word on it, right here, in black and white. How do some Christians process this? They usually ignore it.

If all this hasn't been enough for a Jesus' blood and death believing Christian to consider that they might be wrong about the shedding of blood being a necessary part of atonement, I submit this passage about jewelry being used as an offering for the atonement of the soul.

And the officers which were over thousands of the host, the captains of thousands, and captains of hundreds, came near unto Moses: And they said unto Moses, Thy servants have taken the sum of the men of war which are under our charge, and there lacketh not one man of us. **We have therefore brought an oblation for the LORD, what every man hath gotten, of jewels of gold, chains, and bracelets, rings, earrings, and tablets, to make an atonement for our souls before the LORD. And Moses and Eleazar the priest took the gold of them, even all wrought jewels. And all the gold of the offering that they offered up to the LORD,** *of the captains of thousands, and of the captains of hundreds, was sixteen thousand seven hundred and fifty shekels.(Numbers 31:48-52)*

What are we to make of these facts we have discussed here in this chapter? Are we to believe after reading these passages that Jesus' blood is the only way to atone for man's sins?

Christians will remind me that the proof of the efficacy of Jesus' atonement is in the proverbial pudding. They will say that not many years after Jesus' sacrifice the Temple was destroyed and the sacrifices stopped, never to be re-instituted. They will point out that even before the Temple was destroyed the scarlet thread that was tied on the scapegoat did not turn white[8] after Jesus was crucified.

Christians will propose that all this was because Jesus' vicarious death was an end to all the sacrifices but was it? There is another possibility.

The New Testament would have us believe that Jerusalem was full of Jesus believing Jews that eventually spread the gospel throughout the world. Could it be that the Jews becoming Jesus followers and violating the command to *not* follow someone that teaches against God's Torah had eventually brought them to ruin. Has God simply kept his word to push them out of the land if they followed the abominations of the nations that occupied the land before them? Remember that the belief in a savior-god-man is spoken about as early as Ezekiel 8:14 and stem back to the times of Nimrod.[9]

What about Jesus' Death on Passover?

Christians are really big about the passover timing but they aren't really interested in what the Passover offering is about. They will often ask, "*Didn't you know that Jesus was the perfect representation of the Passover Lamb?*"

Most Christians don't understand the elements or requirements of the Passover sacrifice. Let's look at the actual passages that tell us about the offering to see what God says about it.

And the LORD spake unto Moses and Aaron in the land of Egypt, saying, This month

---

8 Christians would have you believe that this is actually promised by God to show his acceptance of the sacrifice but it is only discussed in the Talmud.

9 In Ezekiel 8, Tammuz is being weeped over. Tammuz was Semiramis' son who she claimed was conceived without a man being involved (sound familiar?) after Nimrod was killed. Tammuz was killed by a wild boar while hunting in the spring and each spring women would weep for him around the time at that time, while hoping for his rebirth or resurrection. This one of the possible sources for the stories of some of Jesus' life events. Tammuz was worshiped as a saviour-god-man.

shall be unto you the beginning of months: it shall be the first month of the year to you. Speak ye unto all the congregation of Israel, saying, In the tenth day of this month they shall take to them every man a lamb, according to the house of their fathers, a lamb for an house: And if the household be too little for the lamb, let him and his neighbour next unto his house take it according to the number of the souls; every man according to his eating shall make your count for the lamb. Your lamb shall be without blemish, a male of the first year: ye shall take it out from the sheep, or from the goats: And ye shall keep it up until the fourteenth day of the same month: and the whole assembly of the congregation of Israel shall kill it in the evening. And they shall take of the blood, and strike it on the two side posts and on the upper door post of the houses, wherein they shall eat it. And they shall eat the flesh in that night, roast with fire, and unleavened bread; and with bitter herbs they shall eat it. Eat not of it raw, nor sodden at all with water, but roast with fire; his head with his legs, and with the purtenance thereof. And ye shall let nothing of it remain until the morning; and that which remaineth of it until the morning ye shall burn with fire. And thus shall ye eat it; with your loins girded, your shoes on your feet, and your staff in your hand; and ye shall eat it in haste: it is the LORD'S passover. For I will pass through the land of Egypt this night, and will smite all the firstborn in the land of Egypt, both man and beast; and against all the gods of Egypt I will execute judgment: I am the LORD. And the blood shall be to you for a token upon the houses where ye are: and when I see the blood, I will pass over you, and the plague shall not be upon you to destroy you, when I smite the land of Egypt. And this day shall be unto you for a memorial; and ye shall keep it a feast to the LORD throughout your generations; ye shall keep it a feast by an ordinance for ever. (Exodus 12:1-14)

This passage has some interesting elements about the Passover but without the proper background there cannot be a full understanding. First, on the tenth of the month, the lambs (or goats) are taken into the house and kept as a pet would be. The lambs were sacred animals to the Egyptians. They were seen as being divine. To take the animal into the dwelling and keep it as a pet for the children was by itself seen as mocking the Egyptians. The animal was to be physically perfect and without defect but on the fourteenth of the month the sacrifice was slaughtered in front of the house in the street where the Egyptian's could plainly observe it. Then the blood of the animal was put on display by smearing it on the doorposts and the lintel of the door.

This was as if to say to the Egyptians, *"We have brought your gods into our houses, we have treated them as our pets and now we have murdered them! We have dishonored your gods as you have dishonored our God!"*

In the next act of contempt toward the Egyptians and their gods, the sons of Jacob burned their gods. This was to signify that their deities were unable to survive the fire. To add to all of the disrespect and contempt that they had shown the gods of their slave masters, they ate what was left of their gods.

This took a lot of courage on the part of the Hebrews. I am sure that after all of the plagues that had occurred over the past months the Egyptians probably had to think many times about whether or not they would punish them for this sacrilege. Instead, the Egyptians actually voluntarily let the Hebrews plunder them as if they were begging them to leave.

Now, we come to some amazing things that had occurred to me several years ago. First, the Passover sacrifice is not an atonement for sin or what Christians call a sin sacrifice. It has a much deeper meaning than that.

Every plague that God poured out on the Egyptians and their gods showed that the God of Israel was superior to their gods. In the final plague, God showed that the gods that were still remaining were inferior to Him. God would show that he could snuff out their lives at his whim. The lambs represented these gods.

Fast forward to the day when God appeared to the entire nation of Israel. Although the Passover lambs could not survive the fire that the Israelites had subjected them to, the real God of Israel not only survived the fire on the mountain but actually thrived in it. God thrived well enough to actually make a covenant with Israel from the fire. God spoke the *Ten Words* from the fire to not only all of his people but the gentiles that came out of Egypt with them. These Words that God audibly spoke to His new "bride" were a *Ketubah* or a wedding contract. God actually married the nation of Israel while in the fire on Mount Sinai.

Only take heed to thyself, and keep thy soul diligently, lest thou forget the things which thine eyes have seen, and lest they depart from thy heart all the days of thy life: but teach them thy sons, and thy sons' sons; Specially the day that thou stoodest before the LORD thy God in Horeb, when the LORD said unto me, Gather me the people together, and I will make them hear my words, that they may learn to fear me all the days that they shall live upon the earth, and that they may teach their children. And ye came near and stood under the mountain; and the mountain burned with fire unto the midst of heaven, with darkness, clouds, and thick darkness. And the LORD spake unto you out of the midst of the fire: ye heard the voice of the words, but saw no similitude; only ye heard a voice. And he declared unto you his covenant, which he commanded you to perform, even ten commandments; and he wrote them upon two tables of stone. (Deuteronomy 4:9-13)

What a contrast we have here. The many gods of Egypt had been defeated by the ONE God of Israel. The Passover sacrifice symbolizes the rejection of the multitude of the gods of Egypt that Israel had come to revere. The gods of Egypt could not endure the flames but our God performs the most tender-loving act any one could and marries His bride from the midst of Sinai's fire. God didn't die on Passover. God was a champion on that first Passover. He wasn't beaten or whipped. His being wasn't pierced by spikes of iron. Our God was triumphant on that day and He actually overcame the false gods of the heathens.

In contrast on Passover, two thousand years ago, the man who many, believed to be God, could not deliver himself, let alone anyone else and in the final moments "gave up" his ghost and was put in a cold grave. He didn't deliver anyone from their physical enemies and he himself was defeated. Instead of the story Israel tells their children, Christians tell the story of the messiah that was defeated.

This is not my God. None can defeat the God of Israel. In the final analysis of Jesus' actions on Passover, he offered no proof that he was the champion of Passover, the hero that is the subject of the retelling of Passover every year in Jewish synagogues and homes.

Final thoughts on Atonement

In this chapter, I have presented the Christian view of atonement and the opposing opinion offered by God on the matter. If only Christians would put more weight behind the Hebrew Scriptures they would come to the truth. Unfortunately, the entire foundation of the New Testament is built on Jesus' death. As long as Christians process their Bible in this manner they are doomed to fall prey to error after error.

One question that I have not answered is, "If God simply forgives someone, how is God's need to punish someone for their sin satisfied?" One thing I find amazing about the Hebrew Scriptures is this: God has answered just about any question that anyone could possibly think of. This question does not go unanswered by God. This is what God says regarding the punishment of the wicked.

For I have no pleasure in the death of him that dieth, saith the Lord GOD: wherefore turn yourselves, and live ye. (Ezekiel 18:32)

The God of the Hebrew Bible wants people to turn or repent. He doesn't desire for them to die in their sins. Nowhere does God say that someone else must be punished for your sin so he can forgive you. Do Christians think that they can forgive one of their children without having to slay someone else in their place? What makes them more powerful than God when even he doesn't have that ability? Wouldn't that be arrogance on their part? Are you beginning to see how some of these beliefs lead to absurdity?

The New Testament actually says the following.

What if God, wanting to show His wrath and to make His power known, endured with much longsuffering the vessels of wrath prepared for destruction, and that He might make known the riches of His glory on the vessels of mercy, which He had prepared beforehand for glory, (Romans 9:22,23 NKJV)

This passage in my opinion is about election. There is a contrast here between, *"the vessels of wrath prepared for destruction,"* and *"the vessels of mercy."* These are the *elect* and *non-elect* or righteous in Christ and unrighteous in their natural sin nature.[10] This passage is saying that these *vessels of wrath* were created with the intent to be destroyed. This is a perverted picture of the loving God. I have heard Christians speak of this many times even adding comments that they will be glad to see these wicked people judged and thrown into the lake of fire. What a sad commentary about a people and their hatred who profess such love for their fellow Christians.

After considering what God's Words in the Torah and the Prophets teach, I find it almost unbelievable that Christians choose the errors of the New Testament with its conflicts and contradictions. Instead I choose the triumphant God. I hope, as you progress through this book, this will also become your way of thinking. The God of the New Testament, who actually speaks very little, while constantly deferring to Jesus and the Apostles is at odds with what he has said in His Hebrew Scriptures. The God of the Hebrew Scriptures indicated that he would never change his ways, yet the method of atonement and view of sin changes drastically when one migrates from the Hebrew Bible to the New Testament. Which God will you choose?

---

10 I discuss the Christian concept of a sin nature or original sin in chapter 5, in the section entitled, "Sin vs. Sin Nature."

CHAPTER 4

Isaiah 53: Linchpin or Nail in the Coffin?

To Christian missionaries, there is no Scripture more sacred than Isaiah 53. When a missionary says, *"Isaiah 53"* they actually are referring to the passage found in Isaiah 52:13 - Isaiah 53:12. Christians believe that this passage is so convincing that if a person would only read it, they immediately will become a believer in Jesus. They believe it is a direct parallel to Jesus' life and it details his mission to redeem mankind.

This is how the King James Bible presents it.

Behold, my servant shall deal prudently, he shall be exalted and extolled, and be very high. As many were astonished at thee; his visage was so marred more than any man, and his form more than the sons of men: So shall he sprinkle many nations; the kings shall shut their mouths at him: for that which had not been told them shall they see; and that which they had not heard shall they consider. Who hath believed our report? and to whom is the arm of the LORD revealed? For he shall grow up before him as a tender plant, and as a root out of a dry ground: he hath no form nor comeliness; and when we shall see him, there is no beauty that we should desire him. He is despised and rejected of men; a man of sorrows, and acquainted with grief: and we hid as it were our faces from him; he was despised, and we esteemed him not. Surely he hath borne our griefs, and carried our sorrows: yet we did esteem him stricken, smitten of God, and afflicted. But he was wounded for our transgressions, he was bruised for our iniquities: the chastisement of our peace was upon him; and with his stripes we are healed. All we like sheep have gone astray; we have turned every one to his own way; and the LORD hath laid on him the iniquity of us all. He was oppressed, and he was afflicted, yet he opened not his mouth: he is brought as a lamb to the slaughter, and as a sheep before her shearers is dumb, so he openeth not his mouth. He was taken from prison and from judgment: and who shall declare his generation? for he was cut off out of the land of the living: for the transgression of my people was he stricken. And he made his grave with the wicked, and with the rich in his death; because he had done no violence, neither was any deceit in his mouth. Yet it pleased the LORD to bruise him; he hath put him to grief: when thou shalt make his soul an offering for sin, he shall see his seed, he shall prolong his days, and the pleasure of the LORD shall prosper in his hand. He shall see of the travail of his soul, and shall be satisfied: by his knowledge shall my righteous servant justify many; for he shall bear their iniquities. Therefore will I divide him a portion with the great, and he shall divide the spoil with the strong; because he hath poured out his soul unto death: and he was numbered with the transgressors; and he bare the sin of many, and made intercession for the transgressors. (Isaiah 52:13-53:12)

When I was a Christian, I had read this passage many times. At first glance, it looks like it describes Jesus' life perfectly. When this passage is disassembled the similarities all but evaporate. Christians believe because the servant is referred to as a singular entity, it cannot be referring to any group of people. They disagree with the Jews, who believe that these verses are about Israel. Jews contend that Israel is referred to in a singular fashion here as well as in other passages, and some of the same language is used to describe the servant in parallel passages in the Hebrew Bible, yet Christians never use these other passages to point to Jesus.

The Servant: An Overview

The first thing you must realize is that this is not the first or only place the word *servant* is used in Isaiah or in the Hebrew Bible. Sure, Christians know exactly what Isaiah 53 says but do they know about the many other places where Isaiah mentions the servant in singular form or as one person? Let's look at some of these verses.

*But thou, Israel, art my **servant**, Jacob whom I have chosen, the seed of Abraham my friend. Thou whom I have taken from the ends of the earth, and called thee from the chief men thereof, and said unto thee, Thou art my **servant**; I have chosen thee, and not cast thee away. (Isaiah 41:8,9)*

*Who is blind, but my **servant**? or deaf, as my messenger that I sent? who is blind as **he** that is perfect, and blind as the LORD'S **servant**? (Isaiah 42:19)*

Is Jesus blind or deaf?

*Ye are my **witnesses**, saith the LORD, and my **servant** whom I have chosen: that ye may know and believe me, and understand that I am he: before me there was no God formed, neither shall there be after me. (Isaiah 43:10)*

Note that Isaiah actually refers to Israel as God's witnesses (plural) and then God's servant (singular) in the same verse.

Yet now hear, O Jacob my servant; and Israel, whom I have chosen: (Isaiah 44:1)

*Thus saith the LORD that made thee, and formed thee from the womb, which will help thee; Fear not, O Jacob, my **servant**; and thou, Jesurun[1], whom I have chosen. (Isaiah 44:2)*

*Remember these, O Jacob and Israel; for thou art my **servant**: I have formed thee; thou art my servant: O Israel, thou shalt not be forgotten of me. (Isaiah 44:21)*

For Jacob my servant's sake, and Israel mine elect, I have even called thee by thy name: I have surnamed thee, though thou hast not known me. (Isaiah 45:4)

*Go ye forth of Babylon, flee ye from the Chaldeans, with a voice of singing declare ye, tell this, utter it even to the end of the earth; say ye, The LORD hath redeemed his **servant** Jacob. (Isaiah 48:20)*

*And said unto me, Thou art my **servant**, O Israel, in whom I will be glorified. (Isaiah 49:3)*

These verses are all describing Israel, not Jesus. Don't think that Isaiah is the only one that uses this method for referring to Israel. The following verses are from Jeremiah where he speaks of Israel in the Singular form.

---

1 Jesurun is another term for righteous Israel.

*Is Israel a servant? is **he** a homeborn slave? why is **he** spoiled? The young lions roared upon **him**, and yelled, and they made **his** land waste: **his** cities are burned without inhabitant. (Jeremiah 2:14,15)*

*Therefore fear thou not, O my **servant** Jacob, saith the LORD; neither be dismayed, O Israel: for, lo, I will save thee from afar, and thy seed from the land of their captivity; and Jacob shall return, and shall be in rest, and be quiet, and none shall make **him** afraid. (Jeremiah 30:10)*

*But fear not thou, O my **servant** Jacob, and be not dismayed, O Israel: for, behold, I will save thee from afar off, and thy seed from the land of their captivity; and Jacob shall return, and be in rest and at ease, and none shall make **him** afraid. (Jeremiah 46:27)*

*Fear thou not, O Jacob my **servant**, saith the LORD: for I am with thee; for I will make a full end of all the nations whither I have driven thee: but I will not make a full end of thee, but correct thee in measure; yet will I not leave thee wholly unpunished. (Jeremiah 46:28)*

I am not finished yet. Here are still more verses from the prophet Ezekiel.

*Thus saith the Lord GOD; When I shall have gathered the house of Israel from the people among whom they are scattered, and shall be sanctified in them in the sight of the heathen, then shall they dwell in their land that I have given to my **servant** Jacob. (Ezekiel 28:25)*

*And they shall dwell in the land that I have given unto Jacob my **servant**, wherein your fathers have dwelt; and **they** shall dwell therein, even **they**, and **their** children, and **their** children's children for ever: and my servant David shall be **their** prince for ever. (Ezekiel 37:25)*

In this last verse, Ezekiel switches from a singular servant to using plural personal pronouns in reference to the servant. Remember, this is The King James Version and not a Jewish translation that I am quoting these verses from. Now that we have established conclusively that the *major* prophets were inspired to refer to Israel in the singular form, let's get back to the text of Isaiah 53.

Picking Isaiah 53 Apart

The best way for me to show you that Isaiah 53 has nothing to do with Jesus is to go through the entire passage section by section. I will discuss the translation problems, which are many, and then compare and contrast Israel and Jesus. I will also show other passages that speak of the same subject. Before I start, I want to step backwards a little bit and get a little more context. We will go back to verse 1 of Chapter 52.

Awake, awake; put on thy strength, O Zion; put on thy beautiful garments, O Jerusalem, the holy city: for henceforth there shall no more come into thee the uncircumcised and the unclean. Shake thyself from the dust; arise, and sit down, O Jerusalem: loose thyself from the bands of thy neck, O captive daughter of Zion. For thus saith the LORD, Ye have sold yourselves for nought; and ye shall be redeemed without money. For thus saith the Lord GOD, My people went down aforetime into Egypt to sojourn there; and the Assyrian oppressed them without cause. Now therefore, what have I here, saith the LORD, that my people is taken away for nought? they that rule over them make them to howl, saith the LORD; and my name continually every day is blasphemed. Therefore my people shall know my name: therefore they shall know in that day that I am he that doth speak: behold, it is I. How beautiful upon the mountains are the feet of him that bringeth good tidings, that publisheth peace; that bringeth good tidings of good, that publisheth salvation; that saith unto Zion, Thy God reigneth! Thy watchmen shall lift up the voice; with the voice together shall they sing: for they shall see eye to eye, when the LORD shall bring again Zion. Break forth into joy, sing together, ye waste places of Jerusalem: for the LORD hath comforted his people, he hath redeemed Jerusalem. The LORD hath made bare his holy arm in the eyes of all the nations; and all the ends of the earth shall see the salvation of our God. Depart ye, depart ye, go ye out from thence, touch no unclean thing; go ye out of the midst of her; be ye clean, that bear the vessels of the LORD. For ye shall not go out with haste, nor go by flight: for the LORD will go before you; and the God of Israel will be your rereward. (Isaiah 52:1-12)

First, we can see here that these verses present a future time when Jacob will be delivered from the nations. This is speaking of a physical salvation not a spiritual one. First we must ask, "Who is speaking here?"

This is God speaking. He is saying that he will come and deliver them and immediately flowing out of these verses we see the rest of the passage that follows.

Behold, my servant shall deal prudently, he shall be exalted and extolled, and be very high. As many were astonished at thee; his visage was so marred more than any man, and his form more than the sons of men: (Isaiah 52:13,14)

God is referring to the same servant that He had earlier in Isaiah. What God is saying here is because Israel has been delivered they will prosper. They will be lifted up and be the topic of every conversation. The phrase, *"my servant shall deal prudently"* is easier to understand if you consider how the Hebrew behind this phrase is used in other verses in the Hebrew Bible. The Hebrew word behind this is *yashkil* which means to *act intelligently* or to *prosper* or to *succeed*. It is also translated *understand* or *instruct*. Its meaning is somewhat ambiguous, but it doesn't scream, *"This is about Jesus!"* God also says that many were amazed at Israel and that he was considered ugly by men more than any other people. In other words, he, Israel was despised. We can see this in our modern times. God uses the plural *sons of men,* not simply *man* in this verse.

Christians say that this is speaking of Jesus during his trial, when he was whipped. Surely Jesus wasn't whipped to the point so that he was *"marred"* more than any other man, was he? Is this truly fulfilled in the gospels? Jesus was beaten[2], but it does not say that he was beaten more than any other man.

One thing to understand about prophecy is that we can never know for sure what some prophecies mean with 100% accuracy until it has come to pass. We will not know with surety what some of this passage means. We will look, however, for an overall view from the parts that are easily understood. From those parts, we can form the picture of what this passage portrays. One should never think that an artist could paint a picture with one brushstroke on a blank canvas. With that in mind, let me say that it will be obvious to you, after we have gone through this passage, there will be no doubt that it does not point to Jesus when basing one's conclusions on the text and context instead of what one believes the text should say.

---

2 In one gospel account we will see that Jesus was not beaten but only struck several times.

CHAPTER 4

So shall he sprinkle many nations; the kings shall shut their mouths at him: for that which had not been told them shall they see; and that which they had not heard shall they consider. (Isaiah 52:15)

God is still speaking here. Israel will shake up many nations because what will happen will be totally unexpected. Their delivery from their enemies will shake up the whole world. The world leaders will all be dumbfounded and aghast. Their unbelief in the fact that God has favored Israel will cause them to put their hands over their mouths. They will realize that they have to consider that all they have believed about Israel is wrong. They will be forced to rethink their world view concerning Israel.

Christians say that this is speaking about Jesus somehow. Perhaps they think that this is when Jesus returns and the rulers of the nations are shocked to see him. The thing to consider here, is that people that are non-Christians even talk about Jesus returning. Muslims expect Jesus to return to help their Maudi kill the Christians and the Jews. They believe that Jesus will be praying to Allah for him to give strength to the Maudi, so he can complete the mission to destroy his enemies.

What a surprise it will be when God raises Israel to prominence in the world scene, when no one actually is expecting Him to do it. If everyone previously had considered what they were going to experience, there would be no shock in what they were observing.

Now, we are going to listen to a different speaker and their thoughts about the subject of this passage.

Who hath believed our report? and to whom is the arm of the LORD revealed. (Isaiah 53:1)

Now, God is no longer speaking. These are the Kings (Rulers) speaking from the previous verse. One must realize that these chapter divisions are not part of the original text. The Kings are doubting if others would believe what they are seeing. What are they seeing? If we look back to the last chapter, we see the event that is transpiring is that God has delivered Israel. This is what they mean by the phrase, *"the arm of the LORD."* It is the physical salvation of Israel being accomplished by their God.

The LORD hath made bare his holy arm in the eyes of all the nations; and all the ends of the earth shall see the salvation of our God. (Isaiah 52:10)

This is language similar to that used in the Torah (The Books of Moses). When Israel was in slavery in Egypt, they were delivered when God bared his stretched out arm.

*And remember that thou wast a servant in the land of Egypt, and that **the LORD thy God brought thee out thence through a mighty hand and by a stretched out arm**: therefore the LORD thy God commanded thee to keep the sabbath day. (Deuteronomy 5:15)*

Let's continue to the next part of the passage.

For he shall grow up before him as a tender plant, and as a root out of a dry ground: he hath no form nor comeliness; and when we shall see him, there is no beauty that we should desire him. (Isaiah 53:2)

The Prophet is saying that the servant sprouted up from nothing and looked as if he would not survive. This describes Israel perfectly. At times, it seemed that Israel would vanish from the face of the Earth. They were attacked, captured, and many times carted off to other lands. Despite these things, God preserved them. There was nothing remarkable about their appearance to attract anyone to them. There have been many people that have expressed their disgust at the appearance of the Jews even to the point where they compared them to pigs and dogs. Some others have compared them to apes. The speaker is saying that they are not attracted to them any more than any other people. Still, there is nothing that speaks of any messiah or Jesus up to this point in the passage.

He is despised and rejected of men; a man of sorrows, and acquainted with grief: and we hid as it were our faces from him; he was despised, and we esteemed him not. (Isaiah 53:3)

This is how the nations see Israel. They hated Israel. They rejected them. Israel was seen as a man that had nothing but troubles. Now, this is where Christian translations have hidden what the Hebrew actually says. The phrase, "acquainted with grief" is translated poorly to hide something that Christians would say can't be speaking about Jesus. This phrase should be translated *has known sickness* or *has experienced illness*. In other words, he is *sickly*. Remember, whether correct or incorrect these are the views of the nations, not necessarily the view of truth through the eyes of God Himself.

You must realize, Christians believe that Jesus could never have been sick or ill. His body was not subject to frailties and disease, because he was not sinful. He was perfect. Why would the translators try to hide this obvious meaning of the word and instead render it with an ambiguous word like grief?

Surely he hath borne our griefs, and carried our sorrows: yet we did esteem him stricken, smitten of God, and afflicted. (Isaiah 53:4)

What we see here is, the nations admit that they had poured out their griefs and sorrows on the servant, but they used the excuse that it was God's will that Israel was stricken and afflicted. Perhaps they were thinking that it was God's method of punishing them for killing the Son of God. They were only helping God punish the Jews for wrong doing. Christians, of course, believe that this is Jesus bearing their sins for forgiveness. Now you may agree but after reading the dissection of the next verse you might want to re-examine your thinking.

But he was wounded for our transgressions, he was bruised for our iniquities: the chastisement of our peace was upon him; and with his stripes we are healed. (Isaiah 53:5)

This verse is translated improperly. Rabbi Singer calls this a *"theological crime scene."* [3] If the Word of God is so important to Christians then why do they feel compelled to change it?

In Hebrew, as well as in English, prepositions play a particularly pivotal role in the meaning of the passage. A single preposition can steer the whole passage in the wrong direction. Say for instance that the translators rendered a verse as, *"he was killed for the sword"* instead of *"he was killed by the sword."* The two phrases have the same subject, object, and verb, but the proposition is different. This changes the meaning of the verse. If you translate a preposition incorrectly, you can cause a verse to convey an

---

3 Let's Get Biblical Video Series –

altogether different thought than the author intended.

This is exactly what has happened here. Hebrew is different from English in that prepositions are not separate words but are prefixes that are attached to the Hebrew object. In this verse, the translator has rendered the preposition incorrectly. This was done purposefully. If the preposition had been translated properly, this passage would be of no consequence to Christians. This is the verse translated properly.

*But he is being wounded **because of** our transgressions, he is being bruised **because of** our iniquities: the chastisement of our peace was upon him; and with his stripes we **were** healed. (Isaiah 53:5)*

This translation paints a wholly different picture, doesn't it? Suddenly, the idea of Jesus being sacrificed for your sins has no foundation in this verse. Notice the phrase "was wounded" in the KJV should be translated as a continuing action and not as a completed action. The same mistake was made with the phrase "was bruised." Also, notice that the source of the common refrain "we are healed" reads "we were healed" and is in the past tense. As Rabbi Tovia Singer would ask, "How do you play with my Bible?"

Many Christians believe that you can translate Hebrew in any manner you would like to as long as you do it their way. Christians will disagree and argue with the rabbis about the Hebrew, but they will not argue with the Chinese restaurant owner about what their Chinese menu actually says. I wonder why Christians impose their beliefs on the text and will not rely on the Jewish translation. Is it that they believe the rabbis actually realize it is speaking about Jesus in these text passages, but the rabbis want only to deny that Jesus is the Messiah? Or, is it that Christians start with their belief in Jesus and they are willing to "reverse engineer" the entire Hebrew Bible to make him fit into it?

Dying for Another Person's Sins

Let's step back for a moment from this text and examine the idea of someone dying for another person's sins. Can someone else die for your sins? Can you die for another person's sins? These questions were addressed more than once in the Hebrew Bible. Let's look at these Scriptures briefly.

And Moses returned unto the LORD, and said, Oh, this people have sinned a great sin, and have made them gods of gold. Yet now, if thou wilt forgive their sin--; and if not, blot me, I pray thee, out of thy book which thou hast written. And the LORD said unto Moses, Whosoever hath sinned against me, him will I blot out of my book. (Exodus 32:31-33)

Moses has realized that Israel has displeased God and offers himself as a sacrifice for them. God rejects his offer and informs him that whoever sins against him is responsible for their own sins and adds no qualifiers. This is not the only scripture that answers the question of someone giving their life for another in order to *"save someone from their sins."* Even though Israel had the Torah and specifically this scripture, they forgot this truth. The prophet Ezekiel was used to remind Israel that no man can die for another person's sin. He also taught them that sin is not passed down from one generation to the next.

The word of the LORD came unto me again, saying, What mean ye, that ye use this proverb concerning the land of Israel, saying, The fathers have eaten sour grapes, and the children's teeth are set on edge? As I live, saith the Lord GOD, ye shall not have occasion any more to use this proverb in Israel. Behold, all souls are mine; as the soul of the father, so also the soul of the son is mine: the soul that sinneth, it shall die. But if a man be just, and do that which is lawful and right, And hath not eaten upon the mountains, neither hath lifted up his eyes to the idols of the house of Israel, neither hath defiled his neighbour's wife, neither hath come near to a menstruous woman, And hath not oppressed any, but hath restored to the debtor his pledge, hath spoiled none by violence, hath given his bread to the hungry, and hath covered the naked with a garment; He that hath not given forth upon usury, neither hath taken any increase, that hath withdrawn his hand from iniquity, hath executed true judgment between man and man, Hath walked in my statutes, and hath kept my judgments, to deal truly; he is just, he shall surely live, saith the Lord GOD. If he beget a son that is a robber, a shedder of blood, and that doeth the like to any one of these things, And that doeth not any of those duties, but even hath eaten upon the mountains, and defiled his neighbour's wife, Hath oppressed the poor and needy, hath spoiled by violence, hath not restored the pledge, and hath lifted up his eyes to the idols, hath committed abomination, Hath given forth upon usury, and hath taken increase: shall he then live? he shall not live: he hath done all these abominations; he shall surely die; his blood shall be upon him. Now, lo, if he beget a son, that seeth all his father's sins which he hath done, and considereth, and doeth not such like, That hath not eaten upon the mountains, neither hath lifted up his eyes to the idols of the house of Israel, hath not defiled his neighbour's wife, Neither hath oppressed any, hath not withholden the pledge, neither hath spoiled by violence, but hath given his bread to the hungry, and hath covered the naked with a garment, That hath taken off his hand from the poor, that hath not received usury nor increase, hath executed my judgments, hath walked in my statutes; he shall not die for the iniquity of his father, he shall surely live. As for his father, because he cruelly oppressed, spoiled his brother by violence, and did that which is not good among his people, lo, even he shall die in his iniquity. Yet say ye, Why? doth not the son bear the iniquity of the father? When the son hath done that which is lawful and right, and hath kept all my statutes, and hath done them, he shall surely live. The soul that sinneth, it shall die. The son shall not bear the iniquity of the father, neither shall the father bear the iniquity of the son: the righteousness of the righteous shall be upon him, and the wickedness of the wicked shall be upon him. But if the wicked will turn from all his sins that he hath committed, and keep all my statutes, and do that which is lawful and right, he shall surely live, he shall not die. All his transgressions that he hath committed, they shall not be mentioned unto him: in his righteousness that he hath done he shall live. Have I any pleasure at all that the wicked should die? saith the Lord GOD: and not that he should return from his ways, and live? But when the righteous turneth away from his righteousness, and committeth iniquity, and doeth according to all the abominations that the wicked man doeth, shall he live? All his righteousness that he hath done shall not be mentioned: in his trespass that he hath trespassed, and in his sin that he hath sinned, in them shall he die. Yet ye say, The way of the Lord is not equal. Hear now, O house of Israel; Is not my way equal? are not your ways unequal? When a righteous man turneth away from his righteousness, and committeth iniquity, and dieth in them; for his iniquity that he hath done shall he die. Again, when the wicked man turneth away from his wickedness that he hath committed, and doeth that which is lawful and right, he shall save his soul alive. Because he considereth, and turneth away from all his transgressions that he hath committed, he shall surely live, he shall not die. Yet saith the house of Israel, The way of the Lord is not equal. O house of Israel, are not my ways equal? are not your ways unequal? Therefore I will judge you, O house of Israel, every one according to his ways, saith the Lord GOD. Repent, and turn yourselves from all your transgressions; so iniquity shall not be your ruin. Cast away from you all your transgressions, whereby ye have transgressed; and make you a new heart and a new spirit: for why will ye die, O house of Israel? For I have no pleasure in the death of him that dieth, saith the Lord GOD: wherefore turn yourselves, and live ye. (Ezekiel 18:1-32)

Many people reading this will question if this actually has anything to do with Jesus dying for mankind's sins. This passage starts with God asking a question concerning a false doctrine, presented as a proverb, being circulated amongst the people of Israel. This false doctrine is based on two premises. The first premise is that a man can inherit guilt from someone else, and the second is that someone can die for another person's sins.

Using impeccable logic, God lays out every possibility of someone either inheriting sin from someone else or someone sacrificing themselves for another. God's unwavering decision is that neither wickedness or righteousness cannot be imputed to another person. Each person dies or lives because of their own actions not someone else's. These are God's words being given to Israel through a holy prophet, not the words of a theologian sitting in a seminary.

The hallmark of Christianity is that Jesus bore our iniquity and died for us all. This idea is foreign to the Hebrew Bible. Christians are under the false impression that the New Covenant presents this *new truth* and replaces God's own words concerning this false doctrine. If you are a Christian that has not thoroughly studied the Hebrew Bible, you may have been deceived by this teaching, as I was.

In the book of Jeremiah, we are given a description of what things will be like when the New Covenant is finally given by God to Israel. Of course, if you are a Christian you have probably read in the New Testament that Jesus has already instituted the New Covenant. Although we will discover that Jesus did not initiate the New Covenant, the point I want to make will surprise you as much as it did me. We will now examine the passage in Jeremiah that describes what happens when the New Covenant is given by God.

In those days they shall say no more, The fathers have eaten a sour grape, and the children's teeth are set on edge. But every one shall die for his own iniquity: every man that eateth the sour grape, his teeth shall be set on edge. Behold, the days come, saith the LORD, that I will make a new covenant with the house of Israel, and with the house of Judah: Not according to the covenant that I made with their fathers in the day that I took them by the hand to bring them out of the land of Egypt; which my covenant they brake, although I was an husband unto them, saith the LORD: But this shall be the covenant that I will make with the house of Israel; After those days, saith the LORD, I will put my law in their inward parts, and write it in their hearts; and will be their God, and they shall be my people. (Jeremiah 31:29-33)

In this passage, the first thing we notice is that the formerly mentioned false doctrine, identified as a proverb, is associated with the phrase, *"But every one shall die for his own iniquity."* This means that the idea of someone dying for someone else's sin is incorrect. At first glance, this seems out of place. If I were a Christian, I would be asking, *"Why is this statement here?"* Doesn't this disagree with the entire basis of the reason of Jesus dying on the cross? Shouldn't there be a statement here indicating that once and for all mankind will understand that the messiah came and died for mankind's sins, dispelling the Old Testament idea that each man needs to die for his own sins? Instead, what we have here in the same passage describing the New Covenant is a statement saying someone can't die for someone else's sins.

Additionally, the Jeremiah passage here also shows us some more information about something pertaining to the New Covenant that will surprise you. Most people stop reading when they get to the end of verse 33 of Jeremiah Chapter 31. God makes a statement in the next verse that shocks most Christians when they think about it for a few minutes after reading it. We are going to look at verse 34 in a few seconds but consider this thought first.

How much money do you think Christian churches as a whole spent last year teaching the world about God? Well, the actual amount doesn't matter but the fact that they spent any money is the problem. The reason why this is a problem will become evident when you read verse 34.

And they shall teach no more every man his neighbour, and every man his brother, saying, Know the LORD: for they shall all know me, from the least of them unto the greatest of them, saith the LORD: for I will forgive their iniquity, and I will remember their sin no more. (Jeremiah 31:34)

This verse indicates that after God renews his covenant that **all** will know him. After Jesus *gave* the New Covenant to his disciples, did all men come to know God? How many times have you observed people worshiping other gods or realized that they didn't know anything about the God of Israel? Obviously, there is a real problem with the current situation of all men not knowing the God of Israel. The fact is that the New Covenant or what should actually be referred to as the Renewed Covenant has not been instituted yet. Most Christians will try to argue with me when I point this out, but the fact remains that God's Word is clear here. There is no mention anywhere that this covenant will be given earlier or more than once. Can you believe that Jesus had the power to establish the covenant even though it didn't result in fulfilling Jeremiah's prophecy? I can't.

Let us return to our analysis of Isaiah 53. We last looked at verse 5, so we will continue on. Remember the kings of the nations are still speaking here..

All we like sheep have gone astray; we have turned every one to his own way; and the LORD hath laid on him the iniquity of us all. (Isaiah 53:6)

We see in this passage that the kings have realized that they have been doing their own thing not following God's way. They have done wrong to inflict pain and suffering upon Israel by oppressing them. They laid their iniquities on Israel by sinning against them as a bricklayer lays bricks on a foundation.

He was oppressed, and he was afflicted, yet he opened not his mouth: he is brought as a lamb to the slaughter, and as a sheep before her shearers is dumb, so he openeth not his mouth. (Isaiah 53:7)

The speaker is painting an accurate picture of Israel. How many times was Israel persecuted yet did nothing about it? Even today Israel takes it on the chin almost unceasingly and yet they rarely even return fire. Rockets rain down on Israel, yet they essentially do nothing. There are parallel passages that echo this thought in Scripture.

Yea, for thy sake are we killed all the day long; we are counted as sheep for the slaughter. (Psalm 44:22)

Christians believe that verse 5 has to be about Jesus. They believe that Jesus remained silent and offered no defense to the charges against him. This is not the case. Let me show you how I know.

The New Testament contains four books referred to as the Gospels. There are three synoptic[4] gospels and John. Let's look at each of the accounts in order to see if Jesus keeps his silence and offers no defense at his trial. The first gospel is Matthew. Let's see what he has to say.

Now the chief priests, and elders, and all the council, sought false witness against Jesus, to put him to death; But found none: yea, though many false witnesses came, yet found they none. At the last came two false witnesses, And said, This fellow said, I am able to destroy the temple of God, and to build it in three days. And the high priest arose, and said unto him, Answerest thou nothing? what is it which these witness against thee? But Jesus held his peace. And the high priest answered and said unto him, I adjure thee by the living God, that thou tell us whether thou be the Christ, the Son of God. **Jesus saith unto him, Thou hast said: nevertheless I say unto you, Hereafter shall ye see the Son of man sitting on the right hand of power, and coming in the clouds of heaven.** *Then the high priest rent his clothes, saying, He hath spoken blasphemy; what further need have we of witnesses? behold, now ye have heard his blasphemy. What think ye? They answered and said, He is guilty of death... When the morning was come, all the chief priests and elders of the people took counsel against Jesus to put him to death: And when they had bound him, they led him away, and delivered him to Pontius Pilate the governor... And Jesus stood before the governor: and the governor asked him, saying, Art thou the King of the Jews? And Jesus said unto him,* **Thou sayest.** *And when he was accused of the chief priests and elders, he answered nothing. Then said Pilate unto him, Hearest thou not how many things they witness against thee? And he answered him to never a word; insomuch that the governor marvelled greatly. Now at that feast the governor was wont to release unto the people a prisoner, whom they would. And they had then a notable prisoner, called Barabbas. Therefore when they were gathered together, Pilate said unto them, Whom will ye that I release unto you? Barabbas, or Jesus which is called Christ? For he knew that for envy they had delivered him. When he was set down on the judgment seat, his wife sent unto him, saying, Have thou nothing to do with that just man: for I have suffered many things this day in a dream because of him. But the chief priests and elders persuaded the multitude that they should ask Barabbas, and destroy Jesus. The governor answered and said unto them, Whether of the twain will ye that I release unto you? They said, Barabbas. Pilate saith unto them, What shall I do then with Jesus which is called Christ? They all say unto him, Let him be crucified. And the governor said, Why, what evil hath he done? But they cried out the more, saying, Let him be crucified. When Pilate saw that he could prevail nothing, but that rather a tumult was made, he took water, and washed his hands before the multitude, saying, I am innocent of the blood of this just person: see ye to it. (Matthew 26:59-66,27:1,2,11-24)*

---

4   Synoptic means *common view.*

Matthew's account shows that Jesus doesn't say much, but he does not meet the expectations of *openeth not his mouth*. Let's move on to Mark.

And they led Jesus away to the high priest: and with him were assembled all the chief priests and the elders and the scribes. And Peter followed him afar off, even into the palace of the high priest: and he sat with the servants, and warmed himself at the fire. And the chief priests and all the council sought for witness against Jesus to put him to death; and found none. For many bare false witness against him, but their witness agreed not together. And there arose certain, and bare false witness against him, saying, We heard him say, I will destroy this temple that is made with hands, and within three days I will build another made without hands. But neither so did their witness agree together. And the high priest stood up in the midst, and asked Jesus, saying, Answerest thou nothing? what is it which these witness against thee? But he held his peace, and answered nothing. Again the high priest asked him, and said unto him, Art thou the Christ, the Son of the Blessed? **And Jesus said, I am: and ye shall see the Son of man sitting on the right hand of power, and coming in the clouds of heaven.** *Then the high priest rent his clothes, and saith, What need we any further witnesses? Ye have heard the blasphemy: what think ye? And they all condemned him to be guilty of death.... And straightway in the morning the chief priests held a consultation with the elders and scribes and the whole council, and bound Jesus, and carried him away, and delivered him to Pilate. And Pilate asked him, Art thou the King of the Jews? And he answering said unto him,* **Thou sayest it**. *And the chief priests accused him of many things: but he answered nothing. And Pilate asked him again, saying, Answerest thou nothing? behold how many things they witness against thee. But Jesus yet answered nothing; so that Pilate marvelled. Now at that feast he released unto them one prisoner, whomsoever they desired. And there was one named Barabbas, which lay bound with them that had made insurrection with him, who had committed murder in the insurrection. And the multitude crying aloud began to desire him to do as he had ever done unto them. But Pilate answered them, saying, Will ye that I release unto you the King of the Jews? For he knew that the chief priests had delivered him for envy. But the chief priests moved the people, that he should rather release Barabbas unto them. And Pilate answered and said again unto them, What will ye then that I shall do unto him whom ye call the King of the Jews? And they cried out again, Crucify him. Then Pilate said unto them, Why, what evil hath he done? And they cried out the more exceedingly, Crucify him. And so Pilate, willing to content the people, released Barabbas unto them, and delivered Jesus, when he had scourged him, to be crucified. (Mark 14:53-64, 15:1-15)*

Mark's Gospel also does not have Jesus remaining silent before his accusers. Take notice that the two accounts differ slightly. Luke is touted by Christians as being an investigative reporter. Let's see if Luke's report shows Jesus as being totally silent as a lamb before his shearer.

And the men that held Jesus mocked him, and smote him. And when they had blindfolded him, they struck him on the face, and asked him, saying, Prophesy, who is it that smote thee? And many other things blasphemously spake they against him. And as soon as it was day, the elders of the people and the chief priests and the scribes came together, and led him into their council, saying, Art thou the Christ? tell us. And he said unto them, **If I tell you, ye will not believe: And if I also ask you, ye will not answer me, nor let me go. Hereafter shall the Son of man sit on the right hand of the power** *of God. Then said they all, Art thou then the Son of God? And he said unto them, Ye say that I am. And they said, What need we any further witness? for we ourselves have heard of his own mouth. And the whole multitude of them arose, and led him unto Pilate. And they began to accuse him, saying, We found this fellow perverting the nation, and forbidding to give tribute to Caesar, saying that he himself is Christ a King. And Pilate asked him, saying, Art thou the King of the Jews? And he answered him and said,* **Thou sayest it.** *Then said Pilate to the chief priests and to the people, I find no fault in this man. And they were the more fierce, saying, He stirreth up the people, teaching throughout all Jewry, beginning from Galilee to this place. When Pilate heard of Galilee, he asked whether the man were a Galilaean. And as soon as he knew that he belonged unto Herod's jurisdiction, he sent him to Herod, who himself also was at Jerusalem at that time. And when Herod saw Jesus, he was exceeding glad: for he was desirous to see him of a long season, because he had heard many things of him; and he hoped to have seen some miracle done by him. Then he questioned with him in many words; but he answered him nothing. And the chief priests and scribes stood and vehemently accused him. And Herod with his men of war set him at nought, and mocked him, and arrayed him in a gorgeous robe, and sent him again to Pilate. And the same day Pilate and Herod were made friends together: for before they were at enmity between themselves. And Pilate, when he had called together the chief priests and the rulers and the people, Said unto them, Ye have brought this man unto me, as one that perverteth the people: and, behold, I, having examined him before you, have found no fault in this man touching those things whereof ye accuse him: No, nor yet Herod: for I sent you to him; and, lo, nothing worthy of death is done unto him. I will therefore chastise him, and release him. (For of necessity he must release one unto them at the feast.) And they cried out all at once, saying, Away with this man, and release unto us Barabbas: (Who for a certain sedition made in the city, and for murder, was cast into prison.) Pilate therefore, willing to release Jesus, spake again to them. But they cried, saying, Crucify him, crucify him. And he said unto them the third time, Why, what evil hath he done? I have found no cause of death in him: I will therefore chastise him, and let him go. And they were instant with loud voices, requiring that he might be crucified. And the voices of them and of the chief priests prevailed. And Pilate gave sentence that it should be as they required. (Luke 22:63-23:24)*

Luke doesn't proclaim that Jesus remains silent either. So far, three out of the four gospels show that Jesus didn't remain silent. At each of his two trials, he does speak in a limited way to his accusers. We have examined all of the synoptic gospels, now we move on to the last occasion that we have of showing that Jesus was like a lamb in John.

And led him away to Annas first; for he was father in law to Caiaphas, which was the high priest that same year. Now Caiaphas was he, which gave counsel to the Jews, that it was expedient that one man should die for the people... The high priest then asked Jesus of his disciples, and of his doctrine. Jesus answered him, **I spake openly to the world; I ever taught in the synagogue, and in the temple, whither the Jews always resort; and in secret have I said nothing. Why askest thou me? ask them which heard me, what I have said unto them: behold, they know what I said.** *And when he had thus spoken, one of the officers which stood by struck Jesus with the palm of his hand, saying, Answerest thou the high priest so? Jesus answered him,* **If I have spoken evil, bear witness of the evil: but if well, why smitest thou me?** *Then led they Jesus from Caiaphas unto the hall of judgment: and it was early; and they themselves went not* *into the judgment hall, lest they should be defiled; but that they might eat the passover. Pilate then went out unto them, and said, What accusation bring ye against this man? They answered and said unto him, If he were not a malefactor, we would not have delivered him up unto thee. Then said Pilate unto them, Take ye him, and judge him according to your law. The Jews therefore said unto him, It is not lawful for us to put any man to death: That the saying of Jesus might be fulfilled, which he spake, signifying what death he should die. Then Pilate entered into the judgment hall again, and called Jesus, and said unto him, Art thou the King of the Jews? Jesus answered him,* **Sayest thou this thing of thyself, or did others tell it thee of me?** *Pilate answered, Am I a Jew? Thine own nation and the chief priests have delivered thee unto me: what hast thou done? Jesus answered,* **My kingdom is not of this world: if my kingdom were of this world, then would my servants fight, that I should not be delivered to the Jews: but now is my kingdom not from hence.** *Pilate therefore said unto him, Art thou a king then? Jesus answered,* **Thou sayest that I am a king. To this end was I born, and for this cause came I into the world, that I should bear witness unto the truth. Every one that is of the truth heareth my voice.** *Pilate saith unto him, What is truth? And when he had said this, he went out again unto the Jews, and saith unto them, I find in him no fault at all. But ye have a custom, that I should release unto you one at the passover: will ye therefore that I release unto you the King of the Jews? Then cried they all again, saying, Not this man, but Barabbas. Now Barabbas was a robber. Then Pilate therefore took Jesus, and scourged him. And the soldiers platted a crown of thorns, and put it on his head, and they put on him a purple robe, And said, Hail, King of the Jews! and they smote him with their hands. Pilate therefore went forth again, and saith unto them, Behold, I bring him forth to you, that ye may know that I find no fault in him. Then came Jesus forth, wearing the crown of thorns, and the purple robe. And Pilate saith unto them, Behold the man! When the chief priests therefore and officers saw him, they cried out, saying, Crucify him, crucify him. Pilate saith unto them, Take ye him, and crucify him: for I find no fault in him. The Jews answered him, We have a law, and by our law he ought to die, because he made himself the Son of God. When Pilate therefore heard that saying, he was the more afraid; And went again into the judgment hall, and saith unto Jesus, Whence art thou? But Jesus gave him no answer. Then saith Pilate unto him, Speakest thou not unto me? knowest thou not that I have power to crucify thee, and have power to release thee? Jesus answered,* **Thou couldest have no power at all against me, except it were given thee from above: therefore he that delivered me unto thee hath the greater sin.** *And from thenceforth Pilate sought to release him: but the Jews cried out, saying, If thou let this man go, thou art not Caesar's friend: whosoever maketh himself a king speaketh against Caesar. When Pilate therefore heard that saying, he brought Jesus forth, and sat down in the judgment seat in a place that is called the Pavement, but in the Hebrew, Gabbatha. And it was the preparation of the passover, and about the sixth hour: and he saith unto the Jews, Behold your King! But they cried out, Away with him, away with him, crucify him. Pilate saith unto them, Shall I crucify your King? The chief priests answered, We have no king but Caesar. Then delivered he him therefore unto them to be crucified. And they took Jesus, and led him away. (John 18:13,14;18:19-23;18:28-19:16)*

No doubt you can see now that Jesus is clearly defending himself. He even goes to the point of saying that his kingdom is not of this earth. Is this an attempt to avert charges of insurrection? Also, Jesus' denying his kingdom being an earthly one clearly disagrees with the Hebrew Bible's teaching of the end-times-king who will sit on David's throne.

If Jesus' kingdom is not of this world then how can he rule here? This goes against everything that defines the real end-times-king. Jesus also says that he always spoke openly, but many times he did speak in secret and told some not to tell of his actions.

And Jesus went out, and his disciples, into the towns of Caesarea Philippi: and by the way he asked his disciples, saying unto them, Whom do men say that I am? And they answered, John the Baptist: but some say, Elias; and others, One of the prophets. And he saith unto them, But whom say ye that I am? And Peter answereth and saith unto him, Thou art the Christ. And he charged them that they should tell no man of him. (Mark 8:27:30)

If this is an example of Jesus *speaking openly*, then we have misunderstood Jesus somehow. Jesus knew that if he had said publicly that he was The Messiah then people would know that he was announcing his plans to sit on the throne. By doing this, he would become a threat to Herod and Rome. John's portrayal of Jesus' trial certainly doesn't prove Jesus as a meek lamb silent before his shearers. Either John's gospel is not true, or Isaiah 53:7 isn't about Jesus. You can't have it both ways.

Let's look at the next verse in Isaiah 53.

He was taken from prison and from judgment: and who shall declare his generation? for he was cut off out of the land of the living: for the transgression of my people was he stricken. (Isaiah 53:8)

Was Jesus in prison? Jesus was taken from the garden and then to Herod then immediately to Pilate. When does it ever say that he was in prison? If any of the gospel writers thought that Isaiah 53:8 was a portrait of Jesus, and he had been in prison for any amount of time they surely would have mentioned it.

I will admit that Jesus was taken from judgment but what does the phrase *who shall declare his generation* mean in relation to him? This phrase could also be translated, *who would meditate about his being severed from the land of the living?* In other words, *who would even think twice that he was ejected from the land of the living?* What is the land of the living? Does this mean that he was killed or separated from the living? Not necessarily. This phrase, *land of the living* is not unique to this passage. It can mean *being alive* or *the land of Israel*.

Here is a passage about Israel being cut off.

Then he said unto me, Son of man, these bones are the whole house of Israel: behold, they say, Our bones are dried, and our hope is lost: we are cut off for our parts. (Ezekiel 37:11)

The following verse shows a reference to the land of the living.

When I shall bring thee down with them that descend into the pit, with the people of old time, and shall set thee in the low parts of the earth, in places desolate of old, with them that go down to the pit, that thou be not inhabited; and I shall set glory in the land of the living; (Ezekiel 26:20)

This verse is about the destruction of Tyrus. When Tyrus is destroyed then God will bring glory back to Israel. Even Christian commentators such as John Gill, Albert Barnes and Adam Clarke bear witness that the reference here to *the land of the living* means Israel.

CHAPTER 4   48

Let me remind you that this is the kings of the nations speaking. The thoughts portrayed here may or may not be correct but are view from the eyes of these rulers.

Let's assume that these kings could be correct in some of their views. The next statement is probably the most problematic for Christians. The phrase, *"For the transgression of my people was he stricken"* is not properly translated. The Hebrew text should be translated, *"For a transgression of my people a plague on them."* The Hebrew word that the King James translated as *him* is *lamo*. It means *them*, as in a group of people, not *him*. If this passage is talking about Jesus, they are speaking about him in the plural.

"You can speak about a nation in the singular but you don't talk about one person in the plural. That doesn't make sense at all. Checkmate."

- Tovia Singer during lecture "Isaiah 53 – Part 2"

Let's proceed to verse 9. This is another verse where the speaker switches between singular and plural references to the subject at hand. God does this more than once. We had already discussed where God had spoken in dual terms in the same verse in Isaiah 43.

*Ye are my **witnesses**, saith the LORD, and my **servant** whom I have chosen: that ye may know and believe   me, and understand that I am he: before me there was no God formed, neither shall there be after me. (Isaiah 43:10)*

Isaiah 53:9 is another verse like this one.

And he made his grave with the wicked, and with the rich in his death; because he had done no violence, neither was any deceit in his mouth. (Isaiah 53:9)

There are many words here in verse 9 that seem to play together but when we look closely, we will see that they don't play so nicely. Words such as *grave* and *wicked*, *rich* and *death* seem as if they belong together in the story of Jesus but they are truly strange bed-partners. Let's take this verse at face value and compare it to information we can get from the gospels. Let's examine it phrase by phrase.

"And he made his grave with the wicked," sounds like a phrase we have heard from one of the gospels. Let's see if we can find a similar phrase in one of the gospels.

When the even was come, there came a rich man of Arimathaea, named Joseph, who also himself was Jesus' disciple: He went to Pilate, and begged the body of Jesus. Then Pilate commanded the body to be delivered. And when Joseph had taken the body, he wrapped it in a clean linen cloth, And laid it in his own new tomb, which he had hewn out in the rock: and he rolled a great stone to the door of the sepulchre, and departed. (Matthew 27:57-60)

There is something seriously wrong here. Isaiah 53:9 indicates that the servant made his grave with the wicked. Mathew's gospel says that it was a rich man named Joseph of Arimathaea that gave his tomb to be the burial place of Jesus. Let's look at what the gospels say if Joseph was a wicked man or not.

When the even was come, there came a rich man of Arimathaea, named Joseph, who also himself was Jesus' disciple: (Matthew 27:57)

Joseph of Arimathaea, an honourable counsellor, which also waited for the kingdom of

God, came, and went in boldly unto Pilate, and craved the body of Jesus. (Mark 15:43)

And, behold, there was a man named Joseph, a counsellor; and he was a good man, and a just:(The same had not consented to the counsel and deed of them;) he was of Arimathaea, a city of the Jews: who also himself waited for the kingdom of God. (Luke 23:50, 51)

And after this Joseph of Arimathaea, being a disciple of Jesus, but secretly for fear of the Jews, besought Pilate that he might take away the body of Jesus: and Pilate gave him leave. He came therefore, and took the body of Jesus. (John 19:38)

These verses don't seem to relay any information to make us conclude that Joseph of Arimathaea was wicked. To the contrary, the previous verses indicate that Joseph was a good, just and honorable disciple of Jesus. It does tell us something that we wouldn't expect to see here. In Matthew 27:57 it does use one of the words we were examining earlier, "rich." We are expecting to find that someone wicked was related to his grave or burial. Instead, we find a rich righteous disciple burying Jesus. Let's examine the phrase in the verse to clarify our understanding.

"And with the rich in his death" is the next phrase in the verse. We will examine this phrase on two levels. First, we will look at it at face value.

Did Jesus die with the rich? Let's look at the gospel accounts to see what the writers say. I can't show long passages here because there isn't much information in the gospels but it does answer the question at hand.

Then were there two thieves crucified with him, one on the right hand, and another on the left. (Matthew 27:38)

And with him they crucify two thieves; the one on his right hand, and the other on his left. And the scripture was fulfilled, which saith, And he was numbered with the transgressors. (Mark 15:27,28)

And there were also two other, malefactors, led with him to be put to death. (Luke 23:32)

Where they crucified him, and two other with him, on either side one, and Jesus in the midst. (John 19:19)

It should be obvious that none of the gospel writers recorded anything about Jesus dying with the rich. Although that is true, we must look at this phrase on a different level. There is a word in this phrase that is translated incorrectly. The Hebrew word behind the English word "death" is unique and found only here in the Hebrew Bible. It is *b'mah-tov* and it should be translated *deaths*, as in more than one death. Did Jesus die more than one death?

No, what we see here is that the servant was treated as two different types of people that have to be careful with their lives: the wicked and the rich. These two types of people are always looking over their shoulder. The wicked are always expecting to be caught and punished, while the rich are always careful not to be robbed and killed. When I first heard this revelation from Rabbi Singer, it was if a brick had fallen from the sky onto my head. It was definitely a eye opener.

Let's continue on to see if there are more surprises.

CHAPTER 4 50

The next phrase we must investigate is, *"because he had done no violence."* Jesus is viewed by many as a pacifist but do the gospel writers portray him that way?

And the Jews' passover was at hand, and Jesus went up to Jerusalem, And found in the temple those that sold oxen and sheep and doves, and the changers of money sitting: And when he had made a scourge of small cords, he drove them all out of the temple, and the sheep, and the oxen; and poured out the changers' money, and overthrew the tables; And said unto them that sold doves, Take these things hence; make not my Father's house an house of merchandise. And his disciples remembered that it was written, The zeal of thine house hath eaten me up. (John 2:13-17)

To some Christians, this might seem like a small point but this passage portrays Jesus doing violence. If John had honestly thought that Jesus was the servant found in Isaiah 53 then why would he show Jesus being violent here in this passage? If Christians want to be dogmatic about Isaiah 53 being about Jesus, they must also be willing to deal with Isaiah's phrase, *"he had done no violence."*

While any one of the conclusions that I come to here in this examination of Isaiah 53 may not seem enough by itself to prove that Isaiah was not speaking of Jesus, the entire examination should be more than enough to prove Isaiah was speaking of Israel.

The last phrase in this verse that remains to look at is, *"neither was any deceit in his mouth."* You are probably thinking that this could not be speaking about the Jews. Many people have a prejudice about the Jews. They have preconceptions about Jewish businessmen being dishonest in their dealings. Perhaps the common image of the crooked Jewish lawyer comes to their mind whenever they consider the Jewish people. These statements could be a reference to the righteous remnant. Perhaps God makes other statements like this in the Hebrew Bible. In a parallel passage that describes Israel when her salvation comes we read the following.

In that day shalt thou not be ashamed for all thy doings, wherein thou hast transgressed against me: for then I will take away out of the midst of thee them that rejoice in thy pride, and thou shalt no more be haughty because of my holy mountain. I will also leave in the midst of thee an afflicted and poor people, and they shall trust in the name of the LORD. **The remnant of Israel shall not do iniquity, nor speak lies; neither shall a deceitful tongue be found in their mouth:** *for they shall feed and lie down, and none shall make them afraid. Sing, O daughter of Zion; shout, O Israel; be glad and rejoice with all the heart, O daughter of Jerusalem. The LORD hath taken away thy judgments, he hath cast out thine enemy: the king of Israel, even the LORD, is in the midst of thee: thou shalt not see evil any more. In that day it shall be said to Jerusalem, Fear thou not: and to Zion, Let not thine hands be slack. The LORD thy God in the midst of thee is mighty; he will save, he will rejoice over thee with joy; he will rest in his love, he will joy over thee with singing. I will gather them that are sorrowful for the solemn assembly, who are of thee, to whom the reproach of it was a burden. Behold, at that time I will undo all that afflict thee: and I will save her that halteth, and gather her that was driven out; and I will get them praise and fame in every land where they have been put to shame. At that time will I bring you again, even in the time that I gather you: for I will make you a name and a praise among all people of the earth, when I turn back your captivity before your eyes, saith the LORD. (Zephaniah 3:11-20)*

This is plain language that follows the same thought pattern about the servant in

Isaiah's passage. So, the question is, *"Does this verse still scream 'Jesus?"*

There are only a few verses left and our study of this amazing passage will be finished. This is now God speaking through Isaiah.

Yet it pleased the LORD to bruise him; he hath put him to grief: when thou shalt make his soul an offering for sin, he shall see his seed, he shall prolong his days, and the pleasure of the LORD shall prosper in his hand. (Isaiah 53:10)

The Rabbis teach that if God loves someone, He tests them. This teaching is consistent with the Hebrew Bible. God tested Abraham to the point where He had him prepare to sacrifice his own flesh and blood. God tested Job to see if he would serve and love Him in diversity and sickness. You must understand that God already knew what Job would ultimately do. The test was for the benefit of Job himself. The test for Israel as a whole was in the form of the exile and persecution from the world. With all that God put Israel through, the remnant remained faithful while the unfaithful failed God's tests.

This verse does have its own translation problem. The phrase, *"when thou shalt make his soul an offering for sin"* is mistranslated. The Hebrew word translated *an offering for sin* is *ahsham*. The concept of *ahsham* is closely related to guilt itself and not necessarily an actual offering. This use of ahsham is ambiguous and probably has nothing to do with what Christians would consider a offering or sacrifice. This explains why the Jewish translation reads, *"if his soul acknowledges guilt"* and makes no reference to an offering. This might be rendered *"if he (the servant) realizes that he is guilty."*

One other problem is the word *if* in the following phrase, *"**if** thou shalt make his soul an offering for sin."* The translators rendered this as *"when"* and not *"if"* because they didn't want to cast any doubt whether Jesus would offer himself as our sacrifice or not. To present any question of Jesus' not following through dying on the cross would undo the possibility of this passage being about Jesus. This is a dishonest way of promoting their Christian belief.

It is obvious that the Christian's use of the Hebrew Bible, even how they translate it, flows out of their belief in Jesus, and not in order to convey the truth of God's Word, wherever it may lead. Do Christians actually believe that they can translate the Hebrew Scriptures in whatever manner that supports their belief in Jesus? This verse, only being one example, answers this question indubitably. They do not respect the words of the prophets, they simply change them to preach their "Christian Gospel."

To understand the concept of the making the affliction of one's own soul an atonement you must keep a couple of things in mind. The first being one principle we have already addressed. A man can only die for his own sins and not someone else's.

The second principle that we addressed is that blood is not the only way to atone for one's sin. God Himself speaks about Israel's suffering atoning for their sins.

Comfort ye, comfort ye my people, saith your God. Speak ye comfortably to Jerusalem, and cry unto her, that her warfare is accomplished, that her iniquity is pardoned: for she hath received of the LORD'S hand double for all her sins. (Isaiah 40:1,2)

Here, God tells Israel that her iniquity is forgiven because she was punished twice over for her sins. Notice that there is no mention of Jesus or any sacrifice but the wrath of God that was poured out on her by the nations has atoned for her sins. Whenever Israel walked away from God's ways, God used the nations to afflict them in an attempt to get them to repent. This is God's economy. You might be tempted to think that it is not fair or even righteous for God to do this, but this is how God deals with Israel. So you will have to take it up with him, if you have any objections.

So how does this relate to Isaiah 53:10? Israel had wandered from God's ways and was exiled from the Land of Israel. The verse here is speaking of the deal that God will make with Israel in order to achieve this atonement. If Israel will admit and accept that she has sinned; If she realizes the exile and punishment administered was because of that sin then her sins will be forgiven and she will be rewarded. The rewards are that the servant will see seed and his days will be lengthened. For anyone reading this that would still make the claim that this verse or Isaiah 53 is about Jesus, you want to pay close attention to the next section.

Physical Children or...

God promises that Israel will see seed or have offspring. What this means is that she will continue to live on by having children. The Hebrew word behind this word *seed* is *zer'-ah*. It means *physical seed*. These are some verses where *zerah* is used.

And God said, Let the earth bring forth grass, the herb yielding seed, and the fruit tree yielding fruit after his kind, whose seed is in itself, upon the earth: and it was so. (Genesis 1:11)

And I will put enmity between thee and the woman, and between thy seed and her seed ; it shall bruise thy head, and thou shalt bruise his heel. (Genesis 3:15)

And the LORD appeared unto Abram, and said, Unto thy seed will I give this land: and there builded he an altar unto the LORD, who appeared unto him. (Genesis 12:7)

And Abram said, Behold, to me thou hast given no seed: and, lo, one born in my house is mine heir. (Genesis 15:3)

This Hebrew word *zerah* is used 205 times in the Hebrew Bible. Each and every time it always refers to physical seed of either plants, animals or human. There are many Christians that have been taught that this word can mean *disciple* but anyone teaching this is in error.

Recorded in the Torah in the book of Genesis is a conversation between God and Abraham.

After these things the word of the LORD came unto Abram in a vision, saying, Fear not, Abram: I am thy shield, and thy exceeding great reward. And Abram said, Lord GOD, what wilt thou give me, seeing I go childless, and the steward of my house is this Eliezer of Damascus? And Abram said, Behold, to me thou hast given no seed: and, lo, one born in my house is mine heir. And, behold, the word of the LORD came unto him, saying, This shall not be thine heir; but he that shall come forth out of thine own bowels shall be thine heir. And he brought him forth abroad, and said, Look now toward heaven, and tell the stars, if thou be able to number them: and he said unto him, So shall thy seed be. And he believed in the LORD; and he counted it to him for righteousness. (Genesis 15:1-6)

This is where we see God actually remove any dispute to the fact that *zerah* can only mean *physical seed* or *children*. Abraham erroneously thinks that God has not given him seed or children but instead is going to pass his inheritance to his *disciple* or *steward* named Eliezar. God addresses his thinking and sets him straight. The question that begs to be asked is, *"How can Isaiah 53:10 be about Jesus if he never had physical children?"* This verse is beginning not to scream "Jesus!", but it is actually beginning to whimper, if not sob, instead.

Verse 10 contains an additional statement about another reward the servant will receive if he makes his soul's suffering an offering is, *"he shall prolong his days."* In many Christian minds, this verse is still speaking about Jesus. Consider these points.

Christians believe that Jesus is God himself. The question I have for them is, *"How could God prolong his own days?"* God had no beginning and has no end. It is ludicrous to consider that He could shorten or lengthen his lifetime. How can this be speaking of an eternal being?

God cannot be speaking about lengthening the lifetime of an eternal being but if He is speaking of Israel then this verse certainly makes sense. Perhaps this is a reference to the passages that speak of the resurrection in Daniel 12.

And many of them that sleep in the dust of the earth shall awake, some to everlasting life, and some to shame and everlasting contempt. And they that be wise shall shine as the brightness of the firmament; and they that turn many to righteousness as the stars for ever and ever. (Daniel 12:2,3)

Perhaps this is referring to the Jewish people continuing to be a nation forever as God states many times in the Hebrew Bible. Here is a passage that describes Israel and their continuing into eternity after the Messianic Age has begun.

And say unto them, Thus saith the Lord GOD; Behold, I will take the children of Israel from among the heathen, whither they be gone, and will gather them on every side, and bring them into their own land: And I will make them one nation in the land upon the mountains of Israel; and one king shall be king to them all: and they shall be no more two nations, neither shall they be divided into two kingdoms any more at all: Neither shall they defile themselves any more with their idols, nor with their detestable things, nor with any of their transgressions: but I will save them out of all their dwellingplaces, wherein they have sinned, and will cleanse them: so shall they be my people, and I will be their God. And David my servant shall be king over them; and they all shall have one shepherd: they shall also walk in my judgments, and observe my statutes, and do them. And they shall dwell in the land that I have given unto Jacob my servant, wherein your fathers have dwelt; and they shall dwell therein, even they, and their children, and their children's children for ever: and my servant David shall be their prince for ever. Moreover I will make a covenant of peace with them; it shall be an everlasting covenant with them: and I will place them, and multiply them, and will set my sanctuary in the midst of them for evermore. My tabernacle also shall be with them: yea, I will be their God, and they shall be my people. And the heathen shall know that I the LORD do sanctify Israel, when my sanctuary shall be in the midst of them for evermore. (Ezekiel 37:21-28)

It seems that we are forced to accept the fact that you are dealing with God prolonging the days of the people of Israel and not His own days. We have one more part of this verse to deal with before we move on to the next.

The phrase, *"the pleasure of the LORD shall prosper in his hand,"* is speaking about the success the servant will have in fulfilling the will of God. It has always been God's will for Israel to be a light to the world. This would be accomplished by spreading the Torah to all men.

*And many people shall go and say, Come ye, and let us go up to the mountain of the LORD, to the house of the God of Jacob; and he will teach us of his ways, and we will walk in his paths: for out of Zion shall go forth **the law**, and the word of the LORD from Jerusalem. (Isaiah 2:3)*

O LORD, my strength, and my fortress, and my refuge in the day of affliction, the Gentiles shall come unto thee from the ends of the earth, and shall say, Surely our fathers have inherited lies, vanity, and things wherein there is no profit. Shall a man make gods unto himself, and they are no gods? (Jeremiah 16:20,21)

Thus saith the LORD of hosts; In those days it shall come to pass, that ten men shall take hold out of all languages of the nations, even shall take hold of the skirt of him that is a Jew, saying, We will go with you: for we have heard that God is with you. (Zechariah 8:23)

All these passages take place after the Messianic Age has come into reality. This is the success that Israel will have. When God delivers Israel and shows his unwavering support of them, the nations will realize their error and cling to Israel and their God. Whatever God wants Israel to do, she will succeed and it will please God.

Let's look at verse 11.

He shall see of the travail of his soul, and shall be satisfied: by his knowledge shall my righteous servant justify many; for he shall bear their iniquities. (Isaiah 53:11)

This is where we come to the most exciting part of this entire chapter. This is the answer to whether or not the servant steps up to the plate and fulfills his part of the *bargain*. Does the servant realize that God has put him through all that He had in order to purify him? Israel answers the call and does as God wishes. Israel is satisfied with God's decision to afflict her to bring her to the place she is at today.

Israel will teach the world the Torah or what Christians call *"the Law."* It is the Torah that converts men's hearts.

The law (Torah) of the LORD is perfect, converting the soul: the testimony of the LORD is sure, making wise the simple. (Psalm 19:7)

Then will I teach transgressors thy ways; and sinners shall be converted unto thee. (Psalm 51:13)

If Isaiah 53 were about Jesus you would be reading, *"**by his blood** shall my righteous servant justify many; for he shall bear their iniquities,"* but that is **not to be found anywhere in this passage**. Instead you see that Israel's knowledge of God's true nature and his Words convert the world.

Israel obeys and goes on to fulfill her destiny to be a priestly nation and bears the iniquities of the entire world just as Aaron the High Priest bore the iniquities of the Tabernacle. Now we come to the last verse in the passage.

Therefore will I divide him a portion with the great, and he shall divide the spoil with the strong; because he hath poured out his soul unto death: and he was numbered with the transgressors; and he bare the sin of many, and made intercession for the transgressors. (Isaiah 53:12)

In this verse, we see God continues to bless Israel by giving the resources of the world to them. God makes them great in the eyes of the entire world because they have suffered much at the hands of the nations even to the point of death. Israel was oppressed in the gas chambers, the pogroms and persecutions throughout the ages. Israel was treated like a criminal in the past. Even today, when they defend themselves in their own homeland, they are treated as if they are unjustified in doing so. Israel has borne the reproach of the nations. God will remove this reproach and restore them to a peaceful respected people.

And I will raise up for them a plant of renown, and they shall be no more consumed with hunger in the land, neither bear the shame of the heathen any more. (Ezekiel 34:29)

The sins of the nations were heaped on Israel meaning that they were sinned and transgressed against as well as ridiculed by the nations. It seems that every time the world economy suffers Israel is somehow blamed and at times, even during the plagues, Israel was seen as the source. Despite this, the Jews remained faithful to God and prayed for the nations, acting as intercessors between God and their enemy nations.

Putting Jesus in his place but not in Isaiah

This portrait of the Servant in Isaiah 53 matches the one painted in the rest of Isaiah and the rest of the prophets. It is painfully clear that this beautiful passage has been hijacked and used by Christians to fortify their belief in Jesus. Christians have a theory that throughout the rest of Isaiah the Servant is in no doubt Israel but in this lone passage Isaiah is speaking about Jesus. If this theory is examined logically as I have done, one can only conclude that the theory is wrong. This passage does not point to Jesus in any way.

If the theory that this passage is about Jesus were correct, then it would be correct on all points not only a few, or only one. One might argue that some of the ambiguous verses could possibly pertain to Jesus, but that would be arguing from verses that are ambiguous against verses that are clear. Is this a wise thing to do? Christian apologists seem more than willing to tweak unclear verses like the ones found in Isaiah 53 in an attempt to help God make the connection. They don't expect the average Christian to do their homework and examine any of the other prophetic writings that are parallels to Isaiah 53. I wonder how many souls they have damaged by misrepresenting only half of the facts to the myriads of Christians that trust their words.

Christians should rather rely on the passages which clearly show us what the end-times-king will be like. What I discovered to be strange, when I was in the Messianic movement, is that almost none of those involved were concerned with the passages that clearly concerned the end-times-king. Rather they were captivated by the ambiguous passages that sound as if they might point to Jesus. In the next chapter, we will examine some of those passages which seemingly point to him.

This passage is not about Jesus. We must look elsewhere to find a true portrait of this first century rabbi that many look to as a way to God even though they shouldn't.

CHAPTER 5

Examining the "Messianic" Prophecies

When I became interested in learning Hebrew, I had several people in my messianic congregation ask me to listen to some audio lectures that Rabbi Tovia Singer had produced. The lectures were about how the messianic prophecies found in the Hebrew Bible were used in the New Testament. I wasn't interested in the least. It was probably five years later after I had left the messianic movement that I was doing some research on the Internet and I came across Rabbi Singer's website.[1] I actually was afraid to look around the site. I found the download page where his lectures were located. I downloaded the files and when the gravity of the situation struck me, I was terrified as to what I might hear when I listened to them. So I put them aside.

For about a month, I seriously pondered what I was considering. I was a truly committed Christian getting ready to listen to what *"some Jewish Rabbi"* had to think about Jesus. I honestly had no idea what to expect. I was afraid to listen to the lectures because I was sure that Singer knew more about the Hebrew Bible than I did, and to be honest that really frightened me.

I bought an audio player then I started listening to the first lecture. I went to bed at my usual time and settled in to listen. What I heard literally changed my life forever. Singer proposed that the New Testament misused the Hebrew Scriptures to prove that Jesus was the messiah. My question was, *"Could Singer prove what he proposed?"* The answer was a resounding, *"Yes!"* The remainder of this chapter shows what the authors of the New Testament did to promote their belief about Jesus over the obvious and clear meaning of the Hebrew Scriptures.

The easiest way to accomplish my goal is to focus on only the most commonly recognized prophecies in the New Testament. There are many prophecies that the New Testament writers used to try to convince the reader that Jesus was The Messiah. We will examine only those which Christians maintain the reliability of the New Testament hangs on.

The Virgin Birth *"Prophecy"*

Every Christian has heard that Jesus was virgin born. There are twenty-seven books in the New Testament. Although almost every Christian will tell you that Christianity stands or falls on the belief of the virgin birth, the virgin birth is mentioned only in two of of the New Testament books. Although the Bible never tells us why *The Messiah* must be born of a virgin, Christians have formulated a complete, systematic theology to justify it.

---

1 http://www.outreachjudaism.org

CHAPTER 5

Most Christians don't notice the Apostle Paul doesn't mention the virgin birth even in passing. Actually, Paul hardly says anything about the actual life of Jesus although he does say that he was "made of a woman under the law" in Galatians 4:4. The phrase, *"under the law"* seems to imply that his conception was within the norms of the Torah or, in other words, an ordinary conception that was *legal*. If the idea of Jesus' virgin birth were the hinge pin of the Christian faith, then it is strange that it isn't mentioned in Paul's writings. Never once is the connection made between his miraculous conception and his supposed sinless nature. Only in the Epistle of Hebrews is the idea of Jesus' absence of sin discussed and only briefly. Most scholars believe that Hebrews was not written by Paul. If that is true, then Paul never mentions either the virgin birth or Jesus' lack of sin or sin nature.

Let's now examine the actual passages that are found in the New Testament pertaining to the *virgin birth* of Jesus.

First, we will look at Matthew's account.

Now the birth of Jesus Christ was on this wise: When as his mother Mary was espoused to Joseph, before they came together, she was found with child of the Holy Ghost. Then Joseph her husband, being a just man, and not willing to make her a public example, was minded to put her away privily. But while he thought on these things, behold, the angel of the Lord appeared unto him in a dream, saying, Joseph, thou son of David, fear not to take unto thee Mary thy wife: for that which is conceived in her is of the Holy Ghost. And she shall bring forth a son, and thou shalt call his name JESUS: for he shall save his people from their sins. Now all this was done, that it might be fulfilled which was spoken of the Lord by the prophet, saying, **Behold, a virgin shall be with child, and shall bring forth a son, and they shall call his name Emmanuel**, *which being interpreted is, God with us. Then Joseph being raised from sleep did as the angel of the Lord had bidden him, and took unto him his wife: And knew her not till she had brought forth her firstborn son: and he called his name JESUS. (Matthew 1:18-25)*

Now, let's look at Luke's account.

And in the sixth month the angel Gabriel was sent from God unto a city of Galilee, named Nazareth, **To a virgin** *espoused to a man whose name was Joseph, of the house of David; and the virgin's name was Mary. And the angel came in unto her, and said, Hail, thou that art highly favoured, the Lord is with thee: blessed art thou among women. And when she saw him, she was troubled at his saying, and cast in her mind what manner of salutation this should be. And the angel said unto her, Fear not, Mary: for thou hast found favour with God. And, behold, thou shalt conceive in thy womb, and bring forth a son, and shalt call his name JESUS. He shall be great, and shall be called the Son of the Highest: and the Lord God shall give unto him the throne of his father David: And he shall reign over the house of Jacob for ever; and of his kingdom there shall be no end. Then said Mary unto the angel, How shall this be, seeing I know not a man? And the angel answered and said unto her, The Holy Ghost shall come upon thee, and the power of the Highest shall overshadow thee: therefore also that holy thing which shall be born of thee shall be called the Son of God. (Luke 1:26-35)*

Matthew's Gospel is intended to persuade Hebrew readers to accept Jesus as the Messiah. To do this, Matthew uses the Hebrew Scriptures to show what he believes to be the direct relationship between the life of Jesus and the Messiah. He uses the Hebrew Bible to lay out what he sees as prophecy relating to Jesus. The author believes that Mary is approached by an angel and is told that she will be impregnated by the Holy Spirit and maintain her virginity. Matthew presents us with a supposed prophetic fulfillment. This prophecy is being brought to us courtesy of Isaiah. Every Christian has heard this prophecy, *"Behold, a virgin shall be with child, and shall bring forth a son, and they shall call his name Emmanuel"*. It is recited at Christmas plays and during Sunday sermons, but the average Christian has not studied the context of the Isaiah prophecy.

Let's look at the passage in context in the Christian King James Bible.

And it came to pass in the days of Ahaz the son of Jotham, the son of Uzziah, king of Judah, that Rezin the king of Syria, and Pekah the son of Remaliah, king of Israel, went up toward Jerusalem to war against it, but could not prevail against it. And it was told the house of David, saying, Syria is confederate with Ephraim. And his heart was moved, and the heart of his people, as the trees of the wood are moved with the wind. Then said the LORD unto Isaiah, Go forth now to meet Ahaz, thou, and Shearjashub thy son, at the end of the conduit of the upper pool in the highway of the fuller's field; And say unto him, Take heed, and be quiet; fear not, neither be fainthearted for the two tails of these smoking firebrands, for the fierce anger of Rezin with Syria, and of the son of Remaliah. Because Syria, Ephraim, and the son of Remaliah, have taken evil counsel against thee, saying, Let us go up against Judah, and vex it, and let us make a breach therein for us, and set a king in the midst of it, even the son of Tabeal: Thus saith the Lord GOD, It shall not stand, neither shall it come to pass. For the head of Syria is Damascus, and the head of Damascus is Rezin; and within threescore and five years shall Ephraim be broken, that it be not a people. And the head of Ephraim is Samaria, and the head of Samaria is Remaliah's son. If ye will not believe, surely ye shall not be established. Moreover the LORD spake again unto Ahaz, saying, Ask thee a sign of the LORD thy God; ask it either in the depth, or in the height above. But Ahaz said, I will not ask, neither will I tempt the LORD. And he said, Hear ye now, O house of David; Is it a small thing for you to weary men, but will ye weary my God also? Therefore the Lord himself shall give you a sign; **Behold, a virgin shall conceive, and bear a son, and shall call his name Immanuel.** *Butter and honey shall he eat, that he may know to refuse the evil, and choose the good. For before the child shall know to refuse the evil, and choose the good, the land that thou abhorrest shall be forsaken of both her kings. (Isaiah 7:1-25)*

Now briefly, let's look at some of the translation errors in this passage. The word that Christians immediately home in on is *"virgin."* The Hebrew word used is *ha-al-mah*. Christians will argue that the Hebrew word always translates into *virgin*. Let's get beyond the meaning of the Hebrew *ha-al-mah* for just a moment and look at the broader picture.

If *al'mah* truly meant *virgin*, the word *ha-al-mah* would not actually literally translate to *a virgin*. It would actually translate as **the virgin**. When speaking Hebrew, to show that a definite article is attached to a noun you add a single Hebrew letter *Hay* (equivalent to the English letter *H*) to the beginning of the noun. This *Hay* or *Hayhiyadim* in Hebrew indicates that the identity of the subject of interest is known to the persons involved. What Isaiah is saying here is that Ahaz and he both know who this young girl is. Now realize that the problem here in this translated passage is that the woman being spoken of is not *the virgin* but *the young girl*. This is seen by the fact that every Hebrew word related to the word "al-mah" refers only to youth and never to virginity (1 Samuel 17:56; 20:22; Isaiah 54:4; Job 20:11). Also in the Torah of Moses, whenever virginity is important to the subject matter of the text, it uses another Hebrew word "betulah" or forms of it (e.g., Leviticus 21:10-14; Deuteronomy 22:13-21) and never just al-mah.

But if you don't believe this, then try to answer the following simple question.

"*Who was the virgin that Isaiah and Ahaz both knew that conceived miraculously and bore a son during their lifetimes?*"

Some would answer that this child was born seven hundred years later, as Jesus. The words of the prophecy say that **before** this child becomes old enough to know right from wrong **Rezin** and **Pekah** would be **eliminated**. In 2 Kings 15:30, Pekah was slain. In 2 Kings 16:9, Rezin was also killed, fulfilling the prophecy seven hundred years before Jesus was born.

And Hoshea the son of Elah made a conspiracy against Pekah the son of Remaliah, and smote him, and slew him, and reigned in his stead, in the twentieth year of Jotham the son of Uzziah. (2Kings 15:30)

And the king of Assyria hearkened unto him: for the king of Assyria went up against Damascus, and took it, and carried the people of it captive to Kir, and slew Rezin. (2Kings 16:9)

Sin vs. Sin Nature

Why does Christianity require their savior to be *virgin born*? Why is this so crucial? Christians believe that Jesus' birth is unique and because he had no human father he was not tainted by a sin nature because they believe that sin is passed down from a male, not a female parent. This in Christian theology makes Jesus the solitary individual fit to be sacrificed for mankind's forgiveness. This idea stems from the requirements of an animal sacrifice. When an animal was chosen by someone it had to be without blemish. Christians superimpose this physical requirement onto their messiah and equate it to the sinless nature of Jesus. The idea of a virgin-born demi-god existed long before Christianity in other pagan religions.

Christians treat sin as a genetic disorder instead of the act of disobedience or defiance toward God. Also in the New Testament, Jesus elevated thoughts of committing sin to be the same level as the actual committing of the sin. This occurred when Jesus equated lust in a person's heart to be equal to the act of actually committing adultery.

Ye have heard that it was said by them of old time, Thou shalt not commit adultery: But I say unto you, That whosoever looketh on a woman to lust after her hath committed adultery with her already in his heart. (Matthew 5:27,28)

Please don't misunderstand me. One of the Ten Commandments is, "Thou shalt not covet thy neighbor's wife," but the sin of adultery carries the death penalty while coveting has no attached penalty. For Jesus to have equalized the two is clearly "adding to the words of this Torah (law)." Adding to or taking away from the words of the Torah is a sin.

The problem is that Jesus eliminated objectivity and replaced it with subjectivity. What actually constitutes an act of lust? Is it thinking about having a non-marital or extra-marital relationship for one second? How about contemplating it for one minute?

Would one have to plan on how to carry out the act for an hour? Anyone would know when they have sinned by committing the physical act of adultery, but one man's passing thought about another man's wife could become another man's full fledged adultery if we remove the objectivity of the physicality of the actual act. Of course, this is in keeping with Paul's subjective attitude that one man's sin may not be another man's sin.

If we support this kind of reasoning, we would never know when we are sinning or when we are being righteous. By doing this, we would have actually lost the meaning of sin. Although Paul had postulated that it may be permitted for one person to eat meat offered to idols (even after the Jerusalem Council had determined it was not) he would probably agree with what John wrote.

Whosoever committeth sin transgresseth also the law: for sin is the transgression of the law. (1 John 3:4)

The *sin nature* is tremendously valuable to Christianity. Without it, there would be no need for *The Messiah* to come and die for mankind's sin in the first place. But if sin is actually a nature that is inherited by children and through no fault of their own they become sinful at birth, then why would it be right for a just God to punish us for something we have no control over? Wouldn't a just God owe us forgiveness if we had no choice but to sin?

Final Thoughts on The Isaiah 7 Passage

Here is another question that you must ask yourself.

"Having found out what a 'messiah' actually is, is there anything in the entirety of the Isaiah 7 passage would bring you to think of a person anointed with oil?"

The following are basic questions (along with answers), to help you understand what is going on in this passage that isn't an actual messianic prophecy.

To answer this I will use Isaiah's own words.

What is the sign to prove to Ahaz?

Then said the LORD unto Isaiah, Go forth now to meet Ahaz, thou, and Shearjashub thy son, at the end of the conduit of the upper pool in the highway of the fuller's field; **(1)And say unto him, Take heed, and be quiet; fear not, (2)neither be fainthearted for the two tails of these smoking firebrands, for the fierce anger of Rezin with Syria, and of the son of Remaliah.** *Because Syria, Ephraim, and the son of Remaliah, have taken evil counsel against thee, saying, Let us go up against Judah, and vex it, and let us make a breach therein for us, and set a king in the midst of it, even the son of Tabeal: Thus saith the Lord GOD, It shall not stand, neither shall it come to pass.*

What is the sign that Isaiah says is to be given to Ahaz?

*Behold, a virgin shall conceive, and bear a son, and shall call his name Immanuel. Butter and honey shall he eat, that he may know to refuse the evil, and choose the good. **(TIMEFRAME)** For before the child shall know to refuse the evil, and choose the good, **(ACTUAL SIGN)** the land that thou abhorrest shall be forsaken of both her kings.*

This sign will confirm Ahaz has (1) no need to be afraid or (2) be fainthearted regarding these two kings, Rezin and Pekah. Although they have besieged Jerusalem God is with them (Immanuel) or on their side, despite Ahaz's wickedness. God is being faithful to Jerusalem for the house of David's sake in order to protect them. The two kings are going to be eliminated in a way in order to prove to Ahaz that God has not abandoned His children. But you must understand the child's birth is only related to the prophecy and not the actual sign itself. Besides, what use is a sign if you can't see it? The Christian makes a mistake in their reasoning that the virgin conceiving is the sign. Do Christians believe that Ahaz observed this female during the mysterious conception? I doubt that.

If Christians believe that this passage is about a sign to show that Jesus is The Messiah, then they have derived their reason for believing from a source other than the Hebrew Bible. Isaiah clearly defined in this passage the sign was to be the two kings were going to be eliminated. This was to prove there is no reason to fear that God had abandoned them, even though their situation appeared exceedingly grim.

To add the final nail to the coffin, the eighth chapter of Isaiah may tell us who this child was. Christianity, it seems has no interest in reading what follows the Isaiah 7 passage. Isaiah has this to say about his children.

Behold, I and the children whom the LORD hath given me are for signs and for wonders in Israel from the LORD of hosts, which dwelleth in mount Zion. (Isaiah 8:18)

Let's look at this scripture in context.

Moreover the LORD said unto me, Take thee a great roll, and write in it with a man's pen concerning Mahershalalhashbaz. And I took unto me faithful witnesses to record, Uriah the priest, and Zechariah the son of Jeberechiah. **And I went unto the prophetess; and she conceived, and bare a son.** *Then said the LORD to me, Call his name Mahershalalhashbaz.* **For before the child shall have knowledge to cry, My father, and my mother, the riches of Damascus and the spoil of Samaria shall be taken away before the king of Assyria.** *The LORD spake also unto me again, saying, Forasmuch as this people refuseth the waters of Shiloah that go softly, and rejoice in Rezin and Remaliah's son; Now therefore, behold, the Lord bringeth up upon them the waters of the river, strong and many, even the king of Assyria, and all his glory: and he shall come up over all his channels, and go over all his banks: And he shall pass through Judah; he shall overflow and go over, he shall reach even to the neck; and the stretching out of his wings shall fill the breadth of thy land,* **O Immanuel.** *Associate yourselves, O ye people, and ye shall be broken in pieces; and give ear, all ye of far countries: gird yourselves, and ye shall be broken in pieces; gird yourselves, and ye shall be broken in pieces. Take counsel together, and it shall come to nought; speak the word, and it shall not stand: for God is with us. For the LORD spake thus to me with a strong hand, and instructed me that I should not walk in the way of this people, saying, Say ye not, A confederacy, to all them to whom this people shall say, A confederacy; neither fear ye their fear, nor be afraid. Sanctify the LORD of hosts himself; and let him be your fear, and let him be your dread. And he shall be for a sanctuary; but for a stone of stumbling and for a rock of offence to both the houses of Israel, for a gin and for a snare to the inhabitants of Jerusalem. And many among them shall stumble, and fall, and be broken, and be snared, and be taken. Bind up the testimony, seal the law among my disciples. And I will wait upon the LORD, that hideth his face from the house of Jacob, and I will look for him.* **Behold, I and the children whom the LORD** *hath given me are for signs and for wonders in Israel from the LORD of hosts, which dwelleth in mount Zion. (Isaiah 8:1-18)*

In this Isaiah 8 passage, we encounter the almost exact same language found in Isaiah 7. Both the time frame and events match the description in the previous chapter. Isaiah's wife may be the young woman that is being spoken about. She isn't a virgin, because one of her children accompanied Isaiah when he spoke to King Ahaz. Also in verse 8, the name *Immanuel* is referenced again.

For those who raise the point that the name used in this passage pertaining to Isaiah's child not being Immanuel; this is my response:

Hebrew culture was unlike most cultures that exist today. The concept of names is understood in a different light. What follows are two Scriptures that show the unusual way names are used.

In his days Judah shall be saved, and Israel shall dwell safely: and this is his name whereby he shall be called, THE LORD OUR RIGHTEOUSNESS. (Jeremiah 23:6)

In those days shall Judah be saved, and Jerusalem shall dwell safely: and this is the name wherewith she shall be called, The LORD our righteousness. (Jeremiah 33:16)

In these passages the same type of language that Isaiah used in Isaiah 7:14 is echoed. Someone in Jeremiah 23:6 and in the instance of Jeremiah 33:16, a thing is being called what many would consider a name of God. Judah and Jerusalem are both being called *"The LORD our righteousness."*

It would be ridiculous to think that suddenly Judah (or Israel) and Jerusalem have both become the Almighty himself, there must be something unusual going on in these passages. In the case of Isaiah 7:14 you are seeing a tribute to God being given by someone being named with the attributes of God. It is the same type of tribute being shown in these passages.

Many times in the Hebrew Scriptures people had God's name embedded in their personal names. Biblical names that end with "iah" such as *Hezekiah (God is strong)* contain the name of God but Christians don't believe that all of these people are God. Why would anyone believe that someone named *Immanuel (God with us)* would be God?

The thought in the Christian mind that when Jesus was conceived suddenly God was now manifest among humankind. The fact is that this is not the idea being conveyed by Isaiah in the seventh chapter. The question at the time was, "Had God suddenly abandoned the sons of Jacob?" Isaiah is trying to convince King Ahaz, as well as all of Judah, that God had not abandoned them. To show them, God will fulfill this prophecy.

As a tribute to Himself, God tells us that this child's mother will call his name *Immanuel*. If Christians were to follow the logic that they use with Isaiah 7:14, they would have to deduce that Jerusalem will become God when she becomes known as, "The LORD our righteousness" but I have never heard any Christian reason in that manner.

The beauty of the Hebrew Bible is God often supplies another view of the same prophecy, or its fulfillment. The tragedy occurs when Christians don't study carefully enough to discover it. Often, they do find it but choose to ignore it because it doesn't fit into their view of Jesus. So, it is dropped, or should I say shoved, off their radar screen.

The reference to Isaiah's child *Mahershalalhashbaz* in chapter 8 is of no consequence to Christians. They never consider this could be the second *name* (or second tribute to God) of the same child, in 7:14. This name *Mahershalalhashbaz* could have been used to illustrate another aspect of Israel's profit from the fulfillment of the same prophecy.

I can't say that *Mahershalalhashbaz* is definitely Immanuel. Perhaps the events that would happen in *Mahershalalhashbaz*'s life reflect the life of Immanuel so much that the fulfillment of the prophecy must have happened in *Mahershalalhashbaz's* lifetime. Either way, if he is Immanuel or not, Christians are in trouble with the prophecy in chapter 8, so it is ignored.

There is another instance of a child being born in a passage that Christians also try to hijack to make a messianic prophecy. Because the following prophecy shares elements with the one in 7:14, I will discuss it briefly.

The "A Child is Born to Us" Prophecy

I was once a member in a messianic congregation. The congregation was actually named after one of the phrases in this passage that follows.

For unto us a child is born, unto us a son is given: and the government shall be upon his shoulder: and his name shall be called Wonderful, Counsellor, The mighty God, The everlasting Father, The Prince of Peace. Of the increase of his government and peace there shall be no end, upon the throne of David, and upon his kingdom, to order it, and to establish it with judgment and with justice from henceforth even for ever. The zeal of the LORD of hosts will perform this. (Isaiah 9:6-7)

Like the previous prophecy we examined in Isaiah 7:14, this passage is quoted in Christmas pageants and plays every year. This passage also involves the birth and naming of a male child.

Christians, of course, believe this is Jesus. At first glance it appears as if this prophecy could be about the birth of someone that would be considered to be God. This is mainly because of the elements of the passage that concern the naming of the one being born. There is one major problem with this thinking. Although the passage seems to be about a future event because of the phrase *"and his name shall be called Wonderful, Counsellor, The mighty God, The everlasting Father, The Prince of Peace."*

Although this seems to be the case there is an important phrase that Christians seem to be blind to. The words, *"For unto us a child is born, unto us a son is given,"* is almost never analyzed. Even the verse in the King James Version Bible clearly shows that there would be a problem using this verse to point to Jesus birth in the first century. This is mainly because the male child being spoken about has already been born.

How do we know this? I hate to be blunt but to any thinking person that honestly reads this text should be able to see why. The English and Hebrew both say, *"is born"* **not** *"will be born"* or *"shall be born."* If you knew my wife were pregnant and I called you on the phone and I said to you, "My child is born," would you ask me, "when is your child going to be born?" No, you would realize that my child was born some time before our conversation took place.

Christians that unabashedly adhere to the thought that this prophecy is pointing to Jesus don't see it this way. They cannot possibly separate the fact that this child has already been born from the names that this child will be called in the future because they start with Jesus and walk backwards into this prophecy. Who says that fundamentalist Christians aren't Liberals at heart? I certainly don't.

This Hebrew word, *yalad,* used here, is in the *pual perfect* tense or what we would simply call the *passive past* tense. It is related to someone already born. This, coupled with what we learned about the Hebrew concept of names in the last prophecy we examined, leads one to logically conclude the following: This prophecy does not point to Jesus but someone that was born in the time of Isaiah and certainly not God in the flesh.

This person was going to be highly revered and seen as a life that was a tribute to God Himself because of his great courage and righteousness thus the many names that he would be called. This child is thought by many scholars to have been the one that grew up to become King Hezekiah. He actually fits the bill unlike Jesus that was not born in the time of Isaiah but many centuries later.

Christians ignore Hezekiah because they fail to adhere to any logical examination of these passages in order to determine if they are actually prophetic of Jesus or not. The following section discusses what constitutes an actual prophecy.

What is prophecy? How can we tell if it really is a prophecy?

Generally, in simple terms a prophecy tells someone that something will happen in the future. If I told you that I was prophetically speaking to you about something I had done earlier today, yesterday or last month, you would probably think I was irrational or that I didn't understand what prophecy was. Unfortunately, this is exactly the way Christians think, but often they do it unknowingly. They discard actual prophecy and substitute a concept they refer to as, "prophetically speaking."

Here is an example of actual prophecy.

Behold, the days come, saith the LORD, that I will make a new covenant with the house of Israel, and with the house of Judah: (Jeremiah 31:31)

In this verse, there is no doubt that this language is future. The event has not happened yet. This is an actual utterance of God through the Prophet Jeremiah that tells of something that has not occurred yet. This is an actual prophecy. It contains elements that are common with other prophecies.

   Here are the elements:

1. It is presented as a statement from God Himself.
2. It is to happen in the future.
3. It contains a description of an event.
4. It contains a subject performing the action.
5. It most often contains an object receiving the action. This object is often

implied and not explicit.

These are the elements of authentic prophecy. The following is an example of a passage that is "prophetically speaking" and not an actual prophecy. We will examine this so-called prophecy by looking for the *elements* we discussed above.

The "They have Pierced My Hands and Feet" Prophecy

For dogs have compassed me: the assembly of the wicked have inclosed me: **they pierced my hands and my feet.** *(Psalm 22:16)*

I could not begin to count the times that I have seen or heard this prophecy used by Christians in an attempt to prove that Jesus is *The Messiah*. The thought is that because crucifixion was not yet invented this language must be a prediction of *the messiah*. What is prophecy? How can we tell if it truly is a prophecy?

This is from a Psalm of David. The text that is *prophetically speaking* is located approximately in the middle of the psalm.

Let's look at our elements to see which ones it contains:

1. Is it presented to be a statement from God Himself?

    No, it is not. These are the words of David and not God. David was called a King. God even called him a priest but He never called him a prophet.

2. Is it set to happen in the future?

    No, the statements here are presented as past and present not future.

3. Does it contain a description of an event?

    Yes, these are actions of David's enemies.

4. Does it contain a subject performing the action.

    Yes, an unnamed enemy of David.

5. Does it contains an object receiving the action. This object is often implied and not explicit.

    Yes, David.

Because this verse fails the first two element tests, we would have to conclude that this is not a prophecy. Christians believe, even if this is not an actual prophecy, it is still speaking about Jesus because these actions also happened to him. What in this passage would make anyone to believe that it will also be a future event happening to Jesus? There is no justification in Christians believing that this has anything to do with the end-times-king, let alone Jesus. This will become quite clear after we consider the real problem with this verse.

What else is going on here that is not immediately apparent to the naked eye? There is a terrible translation problem in this verse. The phrase, *"they pierced my hands and feet"* should be translated *"like a lion at my hands and feet."*

The word in question is pronounced *cah'-ah-ree* and means *like a lion*. The root word is *ari* meaning *lion*. In Hebrew when you want to indicate that something is *like or similar* to something, the writer simply inserts a Hebrew letter called a K*aph* (equivalent to the English letter K) in front of the noun. The noun in question does not mean *pierce*; it means *like a lion*. I cannot stress this enough. It is impossible for this word to mean anything other than *"like a lion."*

I have used various pieces of software to assist in the study of the Bible. One popular version shows that this Hebrew word is not *cah'-ah-ree* but is *cah'-rah*. Instead of giving the Strong's number[2] of the Hebrew word *ah-ree* (*cah'-ah-ree* is *ah-ree* with the Kaph prefix) he supplies the number for the Hebrew word *cah'-rah*, a word that is not found anywhere in the Hebrew text of this verse. This word *cah'-rah* means *dig*. I am not exactly sure how a Roman soldier would *dig someone's hands and feet*. According to the software this Hebrew word *cah'-rah* means *dig* in twelve places, *make* in two places, *open* in one place, and *pierce* in one place but, truth be known, it is not found in Psalm 22:16.

David wrote many of the Psalms and this word *cah'-rah* is found other places in David's writings. Here are the Scriptures.

*He **made** a pit, and digged it, and is fallen into the ditch which he made. (Psalm 7:15)*

*Sacrifice and offering thou didst not desire; mine ears hast thou **opened**: burnt offering and sin offering hast thou not required. (Psalm 40:6)*

*They have prepared a net for my steps; my soul is bowed down: they have **digged** a pit before me, into the midst whereof they are fallen themselves. Selah. (Psalm 57:6)*

*That thou mayest give him rest from the days of adversity, until the pit be **digged** for the wicked. (Psalm 94:13)*

*The proud have **digged** pits for me, which are not after thy law. (Psalm 119:85)*

One curious thing to note is that David is using the word *cah'-rah* as if the pit is already there and dirt in the pit is being removed. This would account for usage in Psalm 40:6 of the word in relation to his ears being opened. Symbolically, his ears were plugged preventing him from listening to God. David states that God opened or removed *cah'-rah* whatever was in his ears. The meaning of *cah'-rah* is always presented as removing something but not here. The word *cah'-rah* is used in this instance by dishonest Christians to mean *driving a nail*. This is intellectual dishonesty. Amazingly, Christians wonder why learned Jews don't take their scholarship seriously.

David is painting a picture here of his enemies attacking him as if they were a lion biting at his hands and feet. There are other verses where the same Hebrew word *cah'-ah-ree* or *like a lion* is used.

*He couched, he lay down **as a lion**, and as a great lion: who shall stir him up? Blessed is he that blesseth thee, and cursed is he that curseth thee. (Numbers 24:9)*

*I reckoned till morning, that, **as a lion**, so will he break all my bones: from day even to night wilt thou make an end of me. (Isaiah 38:13)*

*There is a conspiracy of her prophets in the midst thereof, **like a roaring lion** ravening the prey; they have devoured souls; they have taken the treasure and precious things; they have made her many widows in the midst thereof. (Ezekiel 22:25)*

---

2 James Strong authored an *Exhaustive Concordance of the Bible*. It is organized in a fashion that assigns each Hebrew and Greek word found in the Bible an individual number.

The previous verses are all from the King James Bible and with the exception of Psalm 22:16 (not shown) this Hebrew word is always translated as 'like a lion." David used this image of a lion many times in his writings. Here are some other verses where he did. Strangely enough, two of the verses, Psalms 22 verses 13 and 21 are only words away from the 'prophecy' at hand.

Lest he tear my soul like a lion, rending it in pieces, while there is none to deliver. (Psalm 7:2)

He lieth in wait secretly as a lion in his den: he lieth in wait to catch the poor: he doth catch the poor, when he draweth him into his net. (Psalm 10:9)

Like as a lion that is greedy of his prey, and as it were a young lion lurking in secret places. (Psalm 17:12)

They gaped upon me with their mouths, as a ravening and a roaring lion. (Psalm 22:13)

Save me from the lion's mouth: for thou hast heard me from the horns of the unicorns. (Psalm 22:21)

Thou shalt tread upon the lion and adder: the young lion and the dragon shalt thou trample under feet.(Psalm 91:13)

When David was young he killed a lion in order to protect his flock. It should be easy to see why David had a fascination with lions. David still saw the lion as his enemy and this is why he used it often as a symbol of his adversaries. This has nothing to do with the Jesus of the New Testament.

Other Prophecies of the New Testament Authors

The "My Son out of Egypt" Prophecy

In Matthew 2 the author presents a prophecy and its fulfillment. Let's examine the is verse in context.

When they had heard the king, they departed; and, lo, the star, which they saw in the east, went before them, till it came and stood over where the young child was. When they saw the star, they rejoiced with exceeding great joy. And when they were come into the house, they saw the young child with Mary his mother, and fell down, and worshipped him: and when they had opened their treasures, they presented unto him gifts; gold, and frankincense, and myrrh. And being warned of God in a dream that they should not return to Herod, they departed into their own country another way. And when they were departed, behold, the angel of the Lord appeareth to Joseph in a dream, saying, Arise, and take the young child and his mother, and flee into Egypt, and be thou there until I bring thee word: for Herod will seek the young child to destroy him. When he arose, he took the young child and his mother by night, and departed into Egypt: **And was there until the death of Herod: that it might be fulfilled which was spoken of the Lord by the prophet, saying, Out of Egypt have I called my son.** *(Matthew 2:9-15)*

What Matthew shows us is presented as a prophecy about Jesus. This is being done in order to convince us that Jesus must be the Messiah, the son of God. Jesus is taken to safety to escape a dangerous King Herod. This is because the *Slaughter of the*

Innocents occurs soon after Jesus' birth so this is done to protect baby Jesus. Although this horrible act of Herod is recorded by Matthew, there is no historical evidence that this event ever occurred.[3]

What Matthew is actually doing is partially quoting the Prophet Hosea in Hosea 11:1.

When Israel was a child, then I loved him, and called my son out of Egypt. (Hosea 11:1)

This is not a prophecy about any messiah. It is a retelling about Israel coming out of Egypt. Matthew had no reason according to this passage in Hosea to tie this to the end-times-king. There is another scripture in the Torah that backs up this thought. In Exodus God calls Israel his son in a conversation with Moses.

And thou shalt say unto Pharaoh, Thus saith the LORD, Israel is my son, even my firstborn:(Exodus 4:22)

This is God's view of whom he considers his firstborn son. There is nothing here about a messianic end-times-king. Christians such as the author of Matthew took liberties with the Hebrew Scriptures and started using them to play a game that will not end well with many unsuspecting players.

The *"Called a Nazarene"* Prophecy

Of course, Matthew got a little more bolder. In order to provide more details about Jesus' life, Matthew tries to validate Jesus as the messiah but does something a little unorthodox. This is a prophecy that Matthew tells us about in an attempt to prove that Jesus certainly must be the messiah.

*And he came and dwelt in a city called Nazareth: that it might be fulfilled which was spoken by the prophets, He **shall be called a Nazarene.** (Matthew 2:23)*

This is a compelling prophecy. Matthew doesn't tell us which of the prophets gives us this information, but he is sure it points to Jesus. But there is one problem with this prophecy. It is bogus. It is not found anywhere in the Hebrew Bible. Matthew made this one up. Many Christians want to address this problem by introducing the thought that Matthew is saying that Jesus will take the Nazarite vow but according to Numbers Jesus did not. This is the description of the vow.

And the LORD spake unto Moses, saying, Speak unto the children of Israel, and say unto them, When either man or woman shall separate themselves to vow a vow of a Nazarite, to separate themselves unto the LORD: He shall separate himself from wine and strong drink, and shall drink no vinegar of wine, or vinegar of strong drink, neither shall he drink any liquor of grapes, nor eat moist grapes, or dried. All the days of his separation shall he eat nothing that is made of the vine tree, from the kernels even to the husk. All the days of the vow of his separation there shall no razor come upon his head: until the days be fulfilled, in the which he separateth himself unto the LORD, he shall be holy, and shall let the locks of the hair of his head grow. All the days that he separateth himself unto the LORD he shall come at no dead body. He shall not make himself unclean for his father, or for his mother, for his brother, or for his sister, when

---

3 None of the historians that lived in or around the time of Jesus recorded anything about the Slaughter of the Innocents. The only record of this event is contained in Matthew's Gospel.

they die: because the consecration of his God is upon his head. All the days of his separation he is holy unto the LORD. And if any man die very suddenly by him, and he hath defiled the head of his consecration; then he shall shave his head in the day of his cleansing, on the seventh day shall he shave it. And on the eighth day he shall bring two turtles, or two young pigeons, to the priest, to the door of the tabernacle of the congregation: And the priest shall offer the one for a sin offering, and the other for a burnt offering, and make an atonement for him, for that he sinned by the dead, and shall hallow his head that same day. And he shall consecrate unto the LORD the days of his separation, and shall bring a lamb of the first year for a trespass offering: but the days that were before shall be lost, because his separation was defiled. And this is the law of the Nazarite, when the days of his separation are fulfilled: he shall be brought unto the door of the tabernacle of the congregation: And he shall offer his offering unto the LORD, one he lamb of the first year without blemish for a burnt offering, and one ewe lamb of the first year without blemish for a sin offering, and one ram without blemish for peace offerings, And a basket of unleavened bread, cakes of fine flour mingled with oil, and wafers of unleavened bread anointed with oil, and their meat offering, and their drink offerings. And the priest shall bring them before the LORD, and shall offer his sin offering, and his burnt offering: And he shall offer the ram for a sacrifice of peace offerings unto the LORD, with the basket of unleavened bread: the priest shall offer also his meat offering, and his drink offering. And the Nazarite shall shave the head of his separation at the door of the tabernacle of the congregation, and shall take the hair of the head of his separation, and put it in the fire which is under the sacrifice of the peace offerings. And the priest shall take the sodden shoulder of the ram, and one unleavened cake out of the basket, and one unleavened wafer, and shall put them upon the hands of the Nazarite, after the hair of his separation is shaven: And the priest shall wave them for a wave offering before the LORD: this is holy for the priest, with the wave breast and heave shoulder: and after that the Nazarite may drink wine. This is the law of the Nazarite who hath vowed, and of his offering unto the LORD for his separation, beside that that his hand shall get: according to the vow which he vowed, so he must do after the law of his separation. (Numbers 6:1-21)

This vow is only temporary. If Jesus had taken this vow for life, he certainly did not keep it. He would not be allowed to drink vinegar or wine, cut his hair, or touch dead bodies. He would be required to offer a sin offering. Does this fit the pattern of his life as indicated in the New Testament? It is hard to understand how anyone could accept this vow as the explanation for this prophetic deception.

We are faced here with a difficult decision. Do we reject this verse in Matthew and accept the rest of his gospel or do we toss out all of Matthew? Remember, the New Testament is supposed to be perfect and infallible. If this were the only place where the New Testament fails in this manner, it should make Christians pause and think for a second, but there is much more as we will see later.

The *"Look upon Me Whom They have Pierced"* Prophecy

And again another scripture saith, They shall look on him whom they pierced. (John 19:37)

I think that most Christians have tunnel vision. I know that when I first looked at these prophecies, I did. I have to admit that I thought that I saw Jesus also. It had to be Jesus.

Who else could it have been? This prophecy is an example of one of the places where it is evident that tunnel vision plays a part in Christianity. Although the usual problems exist with this passage, there is something else going on here. This is the verse that Christians use as the source of this prophecy fulfillment.

And I will pour upon the house of David, and upon the inhabitants of Jerusalem, the spirit of grace and of supplications: and they shall look upon me whom they have pierced, and they shall mourn for him, as one mourneth for his only son, and shall be in bitterness for him, as one that is in bitterness for his firstborn. (Zechariah 12:10)

This verse is at the center of the tunnel. If you compare the verse in John with the verse in Zechariah you will also notice that John has changed a couple of words.

John's version: *they shall look on **him** whom they pierced. (John 19:37)*

Zechariah's version: *they shall look upon **me** whom they have pierced. (Zechariah 12:10)*

He does this to shoehorn the prophecy into the life of Jesus. He shares with the reader as little information as possible about the prophecy. Let's look at this verse in context. If there is a center there must be fringes.

The burden of the word of the LORD for Israel, saith the LORD, which stretcheth forth the heavens, and layeth the foundation of the earth, and formeth the spirit of man within him. Behold, I will make Jerusalem a cup of trembling unto all the people round about, when they shall be in the siege both against Judah and against Jerusalem. And in that day will I make Jerusalem a burdensome stone for all people: all that burden themselves with it shall be cut in pieces, though all the people of the earth be gathered together against it. In that day, saith the LORD, I will smite every horse with astonishment, and his rider with madness: and I will open mine eyes upon the house of Judah, and will smite every horse of the people with blindness. And the governors of Judah shall say in their heart, The inhabitants of Jerusalem shall be my strength in the LORD of hosts their God. In that day will I make the governors of Judah like an hearth of fire among the wood, and like a torch of fire in a sheaf; and they shall devour all the people round about, on the right hand and on the left: and Jerusalem shall be inhabited again in her own place, even in Jerusalem. The LORD also shall save the tents of Judah first, that the glory of the house of David and the glory of the inhabitants of Jerusalem do not magnify themselves against Judah. In that day shall the LORD defend the inhabitants of Jerusalem; and he that is feeble among them at that day shall be as David; and the house of David shall be as God, as the angel of the LORD before them. And it shall come to pass in that day, that I will seek to destroy all the nations that come against Jerusalem. **And I will pour upon the house of David, and upon the inhabitants of Jerusalem, the spirit of grace and of supplications: and they shall look upon me whom they have pierced, and they shall mourn for him, as one mourneth for his only son, and shall be in bitterness for him, as one that is in bitterness for his firstborn.** *In that day shall there be a great mourning in Jerusalem, as the mourning of Hadadrimmon in the valley of Megiddon. And the land shall mourn, every family apart; the family of the house of David apart, and their wives apart; the family of the house of Nathan apart, and their wives apart; The family of the house of Levi apart, and their wives apart; the family of Shimei apart, and their wives apart; All the families that remain, every family apart, and their wives apart. (Zechariah 12:1-13)*

CHAPTER 5

We see this verse is situated amongst a number of prophecies. How did John pick out this particular one from the ones here?

This passage is describing a particular time. Is this the past? If it were we would be able to recognize the fulfillment of these surrounding prophecies. Here are the questions we need to ask:

1. Was Israel delivered from their enemies in the time of Jesus?
2. Were the Jewish People strong and mighty in or around Jesus' time?
3. Were all of the nations that had come against Jerusalem destroyed in Jesus' time?
4. Did all of Israel mourn for Jesus?

The answers to all these questions are an energetic, *"No!"* Christians believe that John is justified when he reaches into his hat among all of the prophecies in this entire chapter and pulls out this one rabbit. We can't know what John was thinking, but we can probably take an educated guess why he did this. He did it to promote the belief in Jesus.

And many other signs truly did Jesus in the presence of his disciples, which are not written in this book: But these are written, that ye might believe that Jesus is the Christ, the Son of God; and that believing ye might have life through his name. (John 20:30,31)

We are now going to discuss the translation problem we find in the verse. We will set John's prophecy aside because he doesn't give us much to work with. We will use Zechariah's passage to illustrate the Christian alterations that were made in the process of translation.

And I will pour upon the house of David, and upon the inhabitants of Jerusalem, the spirit of grace and of supplications: and they shall look upon me whom they have pierced, and they shall mourn for him, as one mourneth for his only son, and shall be in bitterness for him, as one that is in bitterness for his firstborn.

The troubling section of the passage is:

...and they shall look upon me whom they have pierced, and they shall mourn for him, as one mourneth for his only son, and shall be in bitterness for him, as one that is in bitterness for his firstborn.

What Christian translators have done with this passage should be considered a crime. Not only have they ignored all of the prophecies surrounding this passage, ones that clearly show no relation to fulfillment in or around the time of Jesus, but they also altered the prophecy to obscure its actual meaning resulting in deceiving the reader. Often, this is how most of the Christian translators work. When they find a passage in the Hebrew Bible they think betrays the New Testament they simply change it to support what the New Testament says. This is what they have done here.

The John 19:37 verse twists and distorts the Zechariah 12:10 passage so the Christian translators back annotate the Zechariah verse in an effort to fix this problem.

I once was employed in the electronics industry. I designed printed circuit boards. When we supplied the final circuit board design to the customer often they would make small changes to our design. They would add or remove connections. When we received the final set of changes we would alter the original schematics so the customer could update their documentation. This is called "back annotation." This is what has been done here. What John saw as the execution of this prophecy did not actually match what the prophet wrote so the translators changed the original prophecy in Zechariah 12:10.

But what does the prophecy actually say in Zechariah 12:10?

According to Uri Yosef, a Hebrew scholar, Zechariah 12:10 doesn't say what Christian translators indicate. In this brief quote he explains how the commonly mistranslated Hebrew *et ash-er'* should be rendered:

"(et asher) must be read as, 'because of' or 'concerning or 'regarding [something]' or simply 'because' or 'that which', but not simply as 'whom' or 'the one', which are common in Christian translations. The particular translation depends on the context of the specific passage. The following example demonstrates this in another passage which has a grammatical structure similar to Zechariah 12:10B(i): [4]

1 Samuel 30:23 – And David said, "You will not do so, my brothers, CONCERNING THAT WHICH [(et asher)] the L-rd has given us, and He watched over us, and delivered the troop that came against us into our hand.

That the KJV and several other Christian "Old Testament" versions translate this passage in a manner that is close to being correct:

<u>*1 Samuel 30:23(KJV)*</u> *– Then said David, Ye shall not do so, my brethren, with that which the LORD hath given us, who hath preserved us, and delivered the company that came against us into our hand."*

We can now get a better idea how this should be translated. This is what it should look like.

*And I will pour upon the house of David, and upon the inhabitants of Jerusalem, the spirit of grace and of supplications: and they shall look upon me **because of** whom they have pierced, and they shall mourn for him, as one mourneth for his only son, and shall be in bitterness for him, as one that is in bitterness for his firstborn.*

In addition, we are pointed to an event that has happened in the past in order to help us understand what this situation is like. The reference to the event is included in the Zechariah 12 passage.

In that day shall there be a great mourning in Jerusalem, as the mourning of Hadadrimmon in the valley of Megiddon. (Zechariah 12:11)

What is this verse referring to? It is referring to an event that happened in the time of King Josiah.

Nevertheless Josiah would not turn his face from him, but disguised himself, that he might fight with him, and hearkened not unto the words of Necho from the mouth of God, and came to fight in the valley of Megiddo. And the archers shot at king Josiah;

---

[4] The entire article is available at http://thejewishhome.org/counter/Zech12_10.pdf

and the king said to his servants, Have me away; for I am sore wounded. His servants therefore took him out of that chariot, and put him in the second chariot that he had; and they brought him to Jerusalem, and he died, and was buried in one of the sepulchres of his fathers. And all Judah and Jerusalem mourned for Josiah. And Jeremiah lamented for Josiah: and all the singing men and the singing women spake of Josiah in their lamentations to this day, and made them an ordinance in Israel: and, behold, they are written in the lamentations. (2 Chronicles 35:22-25)

The event spoken about in Zechariah 12 will be like the one that occurred when Josiah was killed. The entire nation mourned for Josiah. This type of mourning did not occur in the time of Jesus. As a matter of fact, it seems that only after fifty days had passed, when Pentecost occurred, the men that gathered didn't seem affected by the events that had occurred only weeks earlier. Some were even unaware of the events that had occurred.

It seems like everything was back to normal, and despite John's view that this prophecy had been fulfilled, Jerusalem had not been delivered from her enemies. There is no evidence that this prophecy was ever fulfilled in John's lifetime. This cannot be about Jesus.

The "Messiah must Suffer and Die" Prophecy

And said unto them, Thus it is written, and thus it behoved Christ to suffer, and to rise from the dead the third day: (Luke 24:46)

But those things, which God before had shewed by the mouth of all his prophets, that Christ should suffer, he hath so fulfilled. (Acts 3:18)

That Christ should suffer, and that he should be the first that should rise from the dead, and should shew light unto the people, and to the Gentiles.(Acts 26:23)

Anyone that has read the New Testament knows that it says Jesus suffered and died a horrible death. The New Testament makes the claim in several places that Jesus told the disciples that the Hebrew Scriptures foretold that he (the Messiah) would suffer, die and rise from the dead on the *third day*. This is the complete passage found in Luke.

*But they were terrified and affrighted, and supposed that they had seen a spirit. And he said unto them, Why are ye troubled? and why do thoughts arise in your hearts? Behold my hands and my feet, that it is I myself: handle me, and see; for a spirit hath not flesh and bones, as ye see me have. And when he had thus spoken, he shewed them his hands and his feet. And while they yet believed not for joy, and wondered, he said unto them, Have ye here any meat? And they gave him a piece of a broiled fish, and of an honeycomb. And he took it, and did eat before them. And he said unto them, These are the words which I spake unto you, while I was yet with you, that all things must be fulfilled, which were written in the law of Moses, and in the prophets, and in the psalms, concerning me. Then opened he their understanding, that they might understand the scriptures, And said unto them, Thus it is written, and thus it **behoved** Christ to suffer, and to rise from the dead the third day: And that repentance and remission of sins should be preached in his name among all nations, beginning at Jerusalem. And ye are witnesses of these things. (Luke 24:36-48)*

Here we see Jesus tell his disciples about two prophecies.

1. It benefited Christ to suffer.

2. Christ will rise from the dead the third day.

Aside from the strange way that he speaks about himself in the third person, what he says seems logical but is this actually correct? Does the Hebrew Bible contain these specific prophecies? What are we to make of this phrase, " *and thus it **behoved** Christ to suffer?"* Isn't it supposed to benefit the world that Christ suffered?

We have previously discussed Isaiah 53 and found it lacking any prophecies of Jesus' suffering and death. Because of this we are forced to look to other parts of the Hebrew Bible. Even if we did include Isaiah 53, which still isn't a messianic prophecy, it still says absolutely nothing about being raised again in 3 days.

After looking in several Christian Bibles, I was surprised to see the only cross references to this passage are to other statements in Luke. There is no cross reference to any Hebrew Bible passage foretelling of any suffering or resurrection of any messiah. Could this be a dead end like the 'Nazarene prophecy?"

There is one prophecy in the Hebrew Bible that does mention someone that will be raised on the third day. Let's look at it and see who it is speaking of.

Come, and let us return unto the LORD: for he hath torn, and he will heal us; he hath smitten, and he will bind us up. After two days will he revive us: in the third day he will raise us up, and we shall live in his sight. Then shall we know, if we follow on to know the LORD: his going forth is prepared as the morning; and he shall come unto us as the rain, as the latter and former rain unto the earth. (Hosea 6:1-3)

This has nothing to do with the *messiah*. It contains only plural pronouns and is speaking of a group of people. This is the only passage that remotely resembles anything that speaks of a resurrection on the third day. Could Jesus have been confused? And if so, why? Could Luke have not been able to read Hebrew well enough to understand that this passage was about a group and not a singular person? We may never know for sure.

What is going on here? What would cause someone to write down a prophecy reference that doesn't exist? Luke indicates that he investigated all these things carefully. He was a gentile and probably had not been exposed to the Hebrew Bible or misread the Hebrew as I mentioned previously. Maybe he actually believed that there were prophecies that corresponded to the words of Jesus.

I ask you to verify what I am reporting to you. Read your Hebrew Bible to see if I am telling you the truth. Get the tools you need to search the Scriptures to verify what I am saying. There are many free tools available on the Internet to help you. [5] I challenge you.

The "Thirty Pieces of Silver" Prophecy

Jesus had 12 disciples but one would ultimately betray him. Of course, nothing important seems to happen in Jesus' life without being foretold by a prophet. When Judas betrays Jesus he does it for a measly thirty pieces of silver. This is how it

---

5   *Online Bible* is available at http://www.OnlineBible.net and there is another excellent program that is called *Interlinear Scripture Analyzer* at http://www.scripture4all.org/ Both are free.

Then one of the twelve, called Judas Iscariot, went unto the chief priests, And said unto them, What will ye give me, and I will deliver him unto you? And they covenanted with him for thirty pieces of silver. And from that time he sought opportunity to betray him. (Matthew 26:14-16)

Rise, let us be going: behold, he is at hand that doth betray me. And while he yet spake, lo, Judas, one of the twelve, came, and with him a great multitude with swords and staves, from the chief priests and elders of the people. Now he that betrayed him gave them a sign, saying, Whomsoever I shall kiss, that same is he: hold him fast. And forthwith he came to Jesus, and said, Hail, master; and kissed him. And Jesus said unto him, Friend, wherefore art thou come? Then came they, and laid hands on Jesus, and took him. (Matthew 26:46-50)

Then Judas, which had betrayed him, when he saw that he was condemned, repented himself, and brought again the thirty pieces of silver to the chief priests and elders, Saying, I have sinned in that I have betrayed the innocent blood. And they said, What is that to us? see thou to that. And he cast down the pieces of silver in the temple, and departed, and went and hanged himself. And the chief priests took the silver pieces, and said, It is not lawful for to put them into the treasury, because it is the price of blood. And they took counsel, and bought with them the potter's field, to bury strangers in. Wherefore that field was called, The field of blood, unto this day. Then was fulfilled that which was spoken by Jeremy the prophet, saying, And they took the thirty pieces of silver, the price of him that was valued, whom they of the children of Israel did value; And gave them for the potter's field, as the Lord appointed me. (Matthew 27:3-10)

If I had written this Gospel, I would be embarrassed to have handled God's Word this way. In these passages we see Judas, one of Jesus' disciples, obtains money, specifically *thirty pieces of silver* but just giving these details isn't good enough for Matthew. He has to show that there is a prophecy that corresponds to this story. The following passage is what Matthew thinks is a foretelling of this situation involving the thirty pieces of silver.

And I said unto them, If ye think good, give me my price; and if not, forbear. So they weighed for my price thirty pieces of silver. And the LORD said unto me, Cast it unto the potter: a goodly price that I was prised at of them. And I took the thirty pieces of silver, and cast them to the potter in the house of the LORD. (Zechariah 11:12,13)

First, Matthew gets the prophet wrong. It is not Jeremiah, it is Zechariah. The only things that the two passages share is a few words. There is no mention of a messiah, betrayal or a field in the original. There is a potter but no potter's field. They do share the phrase of "thirty pieces of silver" but even the word "pieces" is added and not actually found in the Hebrew underlying the English. Strangely, the Hebrew word translated as 'potter' is actually a verb meaning to create or form and not necessarily about a potter. The authors of the King James tweaked the text to make it fit Matthew's fabrication. This qualifies as another *"back annotation."*

This passage has nothing to do with Judas or Jesus. This passage is poetic prose about false shepherds and the true shepherd that God will raise up. It has nothing to do with Matthew's story. Again, it is another dead end prophecy found in the New Testament.

CHAPTER 5

The "A Bone of Him shall not be Broken" Prophecy

Amongst the gospel writers, John stands alone in the fact that he identifies Jesus with the Passover Lamb. This is a very important theme to John. He sees Jesus a the *lamb of God*. The word *lamb* or its plural *lambs* only appears four times in the gospels and three of those times are in John's gospel. This association is so important to John that he has Jesus die on a different day than in the other gospels. He sees to it that Jesus dies on the day before the passover, the same day that the lambs are slaughtered.

In some ways, John is like Matthew because he finds prophecies that Jesus is required to fulfill. This is one such prophecy.

The Jews therefore, because it was the preparation, that the bodies should not remain upon the cross on the sabbath day, (for that sabbath day was an high day,) besought Pilate that their legs might be broken, and that they might be taken away. Then came the soldiers, and brake the legs of the first, and of the other which was crucified with him. But when they came to Jesus, and saw that he was dead already, they brake not his legs: But one of the soldiers with a spear pierced his side, and forthwith came there out blood and water. And he that saw it bare record, and his record is true: and he knoweth that he saith true, that ye might believe. For these things were done, that the scripture should be fulfilled, **A bone of him shall not be broken.** *(John 19:31-36)*

The fundamental statement we are concerned with is "A bone of him shall not be broken." I have looked for this statement in the Hebrew Bible, and it is nowhere to be found. The fact is that John has done a little slight of hand here to accomplish his goal. The Passover is when the Jewish People celebrate their exodus from Egypt. In Exodus, God gave clear instructions how the passover lamb or goat is to be treated. One of the requirements that God gave is that the passover lamb's bones were not to be broken. John somehow without any reason has applied this to the messiah. This is the passage that shows the requirement.

And the LORD said unto Moses and Aaron, This is the ordinance of the passover: There shall no stranger eat thereof: But every man's servant that is bought for money, when thou hast circumcised him, then shall he eat thereof. A foreigner and an hired servant shall not eat thereof. In one house shall it be eaten; thou shalt not carry forth ought of the flesh abroad out of the house; **neither shall ye break a bone thereof.** *All the congregation of Israel shall keep it. And when a stranger shall sojourn with thee, and will keep the passover to the LORD, let all his males be circumcised, and then let him come near and keep it; and he shall be as one that is born in the land: for no uncircumcised person shall eat thereof. One law shall be to him that is homeborn, and unto the stranger that sojourneth among you. Thus did all the children of Israel; as the LORD commanded Moses and Aaron, so did they. And it came to pass the selfsame day, that the LORD did bring the children of Israel out of the land of Egypt by their armies. (Exodus 12:43-51)*

And the LORD spake unto Moses, saying, Speak unto the children of Israel, saying, If any man of you or of your posterity shall be unclean by reason of a dead body, or be in a journey afar off, yet he shall keep the passover unto the LORD. The fourteenth day of the second month at even they shall keep it, and eat it with unleavened bread and bitter herbs. They shall leave none of it unto the morning, **nor break any bone of it:** *according to all the ordinances of the passover they shall keep it. But the man that is clean, and is not in a journey, and forbeareth to keep the passover, even the same soul* *shall be cut off from among his people: because he brought not the offering of the LORD in his appointed season, that man shall bear his sin. And if a stranger shall sojourn among you, and will keep the passover unto the LORD; according to the ordinance of the passover, and according to the manner thereof, so shall he do: ye shall have one ordinance, both for the stranger, and for him that was born in the land. (Numbers 9:9-14)*

These are commands not prophecies. Additionally, in some Bibles there is a cross reference to another verse in Psalms.

He keepeth all his bones: not one of them is broken. (Psalm 34:20)

These are the words of David. He is saying that even after he dies, God will take care of him, and in the resurrection he will be made whole. Again, we see that Christians use verses as they wish. If it's not John or the other gospel writers twisting the words of the Hebrew Bible, it's a Bible publisher. These verses don't pass the prophecy test I outlined earlier, meaning they have nothing to do with the end-times-king. This association must be made by John because of his belief that the Passover sacrifice is a sin sacrifice but there is nothing in the Hebrew Bible to make one believe that it is. What is the Passover, if it is not a sin sacrifice? The answer to that question is beyond the scope of this chapter. We have already discussed the subject of what the Passover sacrifice actually is in chapter 3, "*Sin and Atonement through God's Eyes.*"

The "This Day is this Scripture Fulfilled in your Ears" Prophecy

Many Christians don't know or accept that Jesus was a Jewish Rabbi. The New Testament tells us that Jesus could read and write but most poor people could not. Most prophets were educated by priests as in Samuel's case or were in the royal family as Isaiah was. They were schooled in reading and writing, but there is no record of Jesus having such training.[6] There are even statements in the New Testament to the fact that the men from Galilee were *unlearned*, as we will see in a later chapter. Most people's thinking is influenced by the time they live in. They believe that because all children are taught to read, write and do arithmetic in their present day society, they must have in Jesus' time also. In the following verse, we see that other Galilean's in Jesus' day were unlearned.

Now when they saw the boldness of Peter and John, and perceived that they were unlearned and ignorant men, they marvelled; and they took knowledge of them, that they had been with Jesus. (Acts 4:13)

This is not the main point I will be making, but it is worth mentioning.

And he taught in their synagogues, being glorified of all. And he came to Nazareth, where he had been brought up: and, as his custom was, he went into the synagogue on the sabbath day, and stood up for to read. And there was delivered unto him the book of the prophet Esaias. And when he had opened the book, he found the place where it was written, **The Spirit of the Lord is upon me, because he hath anointed me to preach the gospel to the poor; he hath sent me to heal the brokenhearted, to preach deliverance to the captives, and recovering of sight to the blind, to set at liberty them**

---

[6] There is a story in Luke 2:42-52 of Jesus being in the Temple talking to the doctors but no other evidence that he received formal teaching.

that are bruised, To preach the acceptable year of the Lord. And he closed the book, and he gave it again to the minister, and sat down. And the eyes of all them that were in the synagogue were fastened on him. And he began to say unto them, This day is this scripture fulfilled in your ears. And all bare him witness, and wondered at the gracious words which proceeded out of his mouth. And they said, Is not this Joseph's son? And he said unto them, Ye will surely say unto me this proverb, Physician, heal thyself: whatsoever we have heard done in Capernaum, do also here in thy country. And he said, Verily I say unto you, No prophet is accepted in his own country. (Luke 4:15-24)

In this passage, Jesus opens the Isaiah Scroll and reads what we now know as Isaiah 61 verses 1 and 2. At least that is what Jesus tries to pass it off as. Jesus doesn't actually read the verses from the Hebrew Scroll, his words come from the Greek Septuagint. Here are the words of Isaiah.

The Spirit of the Lord GOD is upon me; because the LORD hath anointed me to preach good tidings unto the meek; he hath sent me to bind up the brokenhearted, to proclaim liberty to the captives, and the opening of the prison to them that are bound; To proclaim the acceptable year of the LORD, and the day of vengeance of our God; to comfort all that mourn; (Isaiah 61:1,2)

The Septuagint contains the phrase, *"and recovering of sight to the blind,"* while the Hebrew text does not. The problem with this is that it was impossible for Jesus to have read from the Septuagint. Only highly educated people knew how to read Greek in Jesus' time. Whoever wrote Luke read the Greek Septuagint and not the Hebrew Scriptures, that is why he and most other New Testament authors quoted from the Greek Septuagint. According to the trustworthy historical writings we have today, we have not reason to believe that the Rabbis had anything except the Torah which had been translated into Greek. (i.e. the books of Moses)

While much mystery surrounds the origins of our modern day version of the Septuagint it is quite evident that it differs in many ways from the version that was originally translated for Ptolemy. Josephus tells us:

I found, therefore, that the second of the Ptolemies was a king who was extraordinarily diligent in what concerned learning, and the collection of books; that he was also peculiarly ambitious to procure a translation of our law, and of the constitution of our government therein contained, into the Greek tongue. Now Eleazar the high priest, one not inferior to any other of that dignity among us, did not envy the forenamed king the participation of that advantage, which otherwise he would for certain have denied him, but that he knew the custom of our nation was, to hinder nothing of what we esteemed ourselves from being communicated to others. Accordingly, I thought it became me both to imitate the generosity of our high priest, and to suppose there might even now be many lovers of learning like the king; for he did not obtain all our writings at that time; ***but those who were sent to Alexandria as interpreters, gave him only the books of the law****, while there were a vast number of other matters in our sacred books.*

- Josephus from the 'Antiquities of the Jews'

The Modern Greek Septuagint seems to be a product of the Christian community, which didn't exist until after Jesus' death and resurrection. Many Christians believe that the rabbis translated the Hebrew Scriptures into Greek, but they only translated the Torah or the five books of Moses, as indicated by Josephus. There is reason to believe that the *Neviim* or *The Prophets* and the other books of the Hebrew Scripture were not translated before Jesus' death. Strangely enough; according to modern scholarship even the Torah portion of the Septuagint, we have today, isn't the version that was completed by Ptolemies II. That version has been lost.

The strangest thing about the New Testament is that many of its authors quote from the Septuagint but why would Jesus himself quote from it? Wasn't Jesus *"The Word?"* Didn't he know the words that he supposedly gave to Isaiah? Could Jesus have been unaware that there are significant differences between the words of the Hebrew and the Greek texts? If he were ignorant of this, what does that make you think about his being God in the flesh?

The real question should be,

"If God gave the Hebrews his words to preserve and teach to the nations, in order for them to know him, why would he move the writers of the New Testament to change them or use the corrupted Greek Septuagint?"

The prophecies that I have discussed so far have been ones that were used to make others believe that Jesus was the Messiah, but this next set of prophecies will be different. I am going to discuss the prophecies Jesus and the writers of the New Testament gave about future events.

The Prophecies of Jesus

The *"I Come Quickly"* Prophecies

Jesus' words are often repeated today. People find comfort in Jesus' words when they come on hard times. The most popular sayings seem to be his promises of his imminent return. He promised to return again and collect his followers. Christians seem to dwell on these prophecies more now than ever before because Christians believe, *"Things have never been this bad before!"* Most Christians have never scrutinized Jesus' foretelling abilities to see how he actually scored as a prophet. These are some of his most well known prophetic utterances. I will begin with what he said about his return.

First, the actual sayings of Jesus:

Verily I say unto you, There be some standing here, which shall not taste of death, till they see the Son of man coming in his kingdom. (Matthew 16:28)

And he said unto them, Verily I say unto you, That there be some of them that stand here, which shall not taste of death, till they have seen the kingdom of God come with power. (Mark 9:1)

But I tell you of a truth, there be some standing here, which shall not taste of death, till they see the kingdom of God. (Luke 9:27)

Behold, I come quickly: hold that fast which thou hast, that no man take thy crown. (Revelations 3:11)

Behold, I come quickly: blessed is he that keepeth the sayings of the prophecy of this book. (Revelations 22:7)

And, behold, I come quickly; and my reward is with me, to give every man according as his work shall be.(Revelations 22:12)

He which testifieth these things saith, Surely I come quickly. Amen. Even so, come,

CHAPTER 5

Lord Jesus. *(Revelations 22:20)*

Now, the sayings of other writers in the New Testament:

*The Revelation of Jesus Christ, which God gave unto him, to shew unto his servants things **which must shortly come to pass**; and he sent and signified it by his angel unto his servant John: (Revelations 1:1)*

Truth is objective. Either something is true or not. Either these prophecies came true in the time line presented, or they did not. It is that simple. All these prophecies describe a day of fulfillment as coming to occur frightfully soon. Jesus says that some of his disciples wouldn't die before they have seen his kingdom come in power. Did this happen? Were these prophecies fulfilled? One detail worth noting, directed especially to those who insist that Jesus gave up being fully God while he was in human flesh is the following.

The book of Revelations was written much later, supposedly, after Jesus has ascended to Heaven and when he has regained his full Godhood. If you look at the last verse, Revelations 1:1, it is said that this book is a revelation that God gave to Jesus to give to his servants. It is not information that emanated from Jesus himself: God gave it to him. If Jesus were fully God and all-knowing then why must God have given him the revelation? The New Testament writers can't make up their minds if Jesus is fully God or not, even after his ascension to heaven.

Ask yourself this question that I asked myself, "Did Jesus come into his kingdom while his disciples were living?" No, but plenty of explanations are offered to explain this one away. Many Christian pastors note that when he was on the Mount of Transfiguration he came into his kingdom. Did anything actually change afterward? Did Jesus govern any kingdom or people[7] in any greater way after he came down from the mountain? I don't think so.

The thing I noticed about Christianity is that they *spiritualize* mostly everything. They do this to explain away why their prophecies haven't actually materialized in the physical world.

In this case, Jesus doesn't become a real king that rules over Israel as prophesied, instead he becomes a *spiritual king* that rules over the hearts of men. You can't observe this happening with your eyes. No one can. You must accept this by faith. Faith is the mysterious power of belief in something you cannot view or experience in anticipation of it becoming real.

To tell you the truth, as I see it, this is like children playing "make believe." This is part of the hidden liberalism of Christianity. They interpret the scriptures as they see fit: relying on their own beliefs and oral traditions, instead of the understandable reading of the Hebrew Bible. This resulted in the erroneous understanding that lead to the belief that Jesus was the king of the Universe. They read a particular passage in the Hebrew Bible and if the meaning doesn't fall in line with their belief in Jesus, then they must reinterpret the passage to match their belief.

---

7   To be an effective governor one must have a people that obey your commands or laws. Most of Jesus' followers lay claims to the fact that they are under no law and that their actions have no bearing on the fact if they are righteous or not. Their righteousness is a foreign one. It belongs to their king. This creates a dilemma and actually makes the validity of Jesus government depend on his obedience to his own laws.

In the examination of these specific prophecies, you probably noticed that I didn't list any scriptures from John's gospel. This may seem to be an unrelated passage, but look closely at it and it might raise some intriguing questions.

Then Peter, turning about, seeth the disciple whom Jesus loved following; which also leaned on his breast at supper, and said, Lord, which is he that betrayeth thee? Peter seeing him saith to Jesus, Lord, and what shall this man do? Jesus saith unto him, If I will that he tarry till I come, what is that to thee? follow thou me. Then went this saying abroad among the brethren, that that disciple should not die: yet Jesus said not unto him, He shall not die; but, If I will that he tarry till I come, what is that to thee? This is the disciple which testifieth of these things, and wrote these things: and we know that his testimony is true. And there are also many other things which Jesus did, the which, if they should be written every one, I suppose that even the world itself could not contain the books that should be written. Amen. (John 21:20-25)

Could this be related to the other passages that speak of people remaining alive until Jesus returned? What are we to make of it? Let's look a little deeper.

One must keep in mind, this conversation took place after the resurrection. Supposedly, at this point the disciples had realized that Jesus was God. Evidently, Peter has a question about what the *disciple that Jesus loved* would do. This passage seems to dangle out in the middle of nowhere. It seems out of place. Just before this passage, there are verses that discuss the manner in which Peter would die. From this, we can deduce what Peter is actually asking Jesus. Peter is asking how the disciple that Jesus loved will die.

Basically, Jesus is telling Peter that it is none of Peter's concern. Jesus is saying that it has no bearing on Peter's commitment to Jesus if the disciple that Jesus loves is allowed to live until his second coming.

What follows is a very strange admission for a writer of the New Testament to pen. It appears that there was a misunderstanding resulting from Jesus' words here and a rumor developed and spread widely that this particular disciple would not die. Is the author trying to counter this rumor?

When I first introduced this examination of the *I come quickly* section, I listed the passages that illustrated Jesus saying that there were disciples that would still be alive when he came into his kingdom or when he became king. What I didn't reveal was that immediately following these statements Jesus went to a mountain top with a select few disciples where they witnessed him speak to Moses and Elijah and Jesus being glorified. This occurs before Jesus' resurrection. These are the passages.

Verily I say unto you, There be some standing here, which shall not taste of death, till they see the Son of man coming in his kingdom. And after six days Jesus taketh Peter, James, and **John** *his brother, and bringeth them up into an high mountain apart, And was transfigured before them: and his face did shine as the sun, and his raiment was white as the light. And, behold, there appeared unto them Moses and Elias talking with him. Then answered Peter, and said unto Jesus, Lord, it is good for us to be here: if thou wilt, let us make here three tabernacles; one for thee, and one for Moses, and one for Elias. While he yet spake, behold, a bright cloud overshadowed them: and behold a voice out of the cloud, which said, This is my beloved Son, in whom I am well pleased; hear ye him. And when the disciples heard it, they fell on their face, and were sore afraid. And Jesus came and touched them, and said, Arise, and be not afraid. And when* *they had lifted up their eyes, they saw no man, save Jesus only. And as they came down from the mountain, Jesus charged them, saying, Tell the vision to no man, until the Son of man be risen again from the dead. (Matthew 16:28-17:9)*

And he said unto them, Verily I say unto you, That there be some of them that stand here, which shall not taste of death, till they have seen the kingdom of God come with power. And after six days Jesus taketh with him Peter, and James, and John, and leadeth them up into an high mountain apart by themselves: and he was transfigured before them. And his raiment became shining, exceeding white as snow; so as no fuller on earth can white them. And there appeared unto them Elias with Moses: and they were talking with Jesus. And Peter answered and said to Jesus, Master, it is good for us to be here: and let us make three tabernacles; one for thee, and one for Moses, and one for Elias. For he wist not what to say; for they were sore afraid. And there was a cloud that overshadowed them: and a voice came out of the cloud, saying, This is my beloved Son: hear him. And suddenly, when they had looked round about, they saw no man any more, save Jesus only with themselves. And as they came down from the mountain, he charged them that they should tell no man what things they had seen, till the Son of man were risen from the dead. And they kept that saying with themselves, questioning one with another what the rising from the dead should mean. (Mark 9:1-10)

But I tell you of a truth, there be some standing here, which shall not taste of death, till they see the kingdom of God. And it came to pass about an eight days after these sayings, he took Peter and John and James, and went up into a mountain to pray. And as he prayed, the fashion of his countenance was altered, and his raiment was white and glistering. And, behold, there talked with him two men, which were Moses and Elias: Who appeared in glory, and spake of his decease which he should accomplish at Jerusalem. But Peter and they that were with him were heavy with sleep: and when they were awake, they saw his glory, and the two men that stood with him. And it came to pass, as they departed from him, Peter said unto Jesus, Master, it is good for us to be here: and let us make three tabernacles; one for thee, and one for Moses, and one for Elias: not knowing what he said. While he thus spake, there came a cloud, and overshadowed them: and they feared as they entered into the cloud. And there came a voice out of the cloud, saying, This is my beloved Son: hear him. And when the voice was past, Jesus was found alone. And they kept it close, and told no man in those days any of those things which they had seen. And it came to pass, that on the next day, when they were come down from the hill, much people met him. (Luke 9:27-37)

Supposedly, Jesus had twelve disciples. Peter, James, and John were among them. They were his inner circle and were present when Jesus was glorified on the mountain top. John wrote his gospel but unbeknownst to most Christians John doesn't cover this story in his gospel. Although it is common to all of the other gospels, John doesn't include the statement about those being alive when Jesus returns or the "Story of the Transfiguration" or make any allusions to either. Instead, he discounted the rumor that was circulated that he wouldn't die before Jesus returned. He doesn't offer any alternative. He doesn't tell us that there is the possibility that other disciples will remain alive till the return of Jesus. His silence is deafening.

I could understand that John doesn't mention some of the stories found in the other Gospels. This is one of the two times when God speaks audibly in the New Testament. John also doesn't mention God speaking audibly when Jesus is baptized. One would think that John would mention something that the Jews would have considered as crucial as this. Consider this. John missed his opportunity to record when God spoke audibly from the sky, and he did it, twice. Could it be that John had no need for another God to speak from the sky because God was already here in the flesh?

What we see when we examine this set of *"I Come Quickly"* prophecies is the fact that these will never be fulfilled because every man that lived in Jesus time has died and Jesus has not returned. Either the Christian scholar has to accept that Jesus has failed and is a false prophet or the New Testament is unreliable. Either possibility is curtains for Christianity.

The *"Not through all of Israel"* Prophecy

Jesus prophesied many things would happen between his death and when he returned. But one of the most definitive was when he predicted that the disciples would not have gone through all of Israel before his second coming. Listen to his own words.

But when they persecute you in this city, flee ye into another: for verily I say unto you, ***Ye shall not have gone over the cities of Israel, till the Son of man be come.*** *(Matthew 10:23)*

Jesus must have anticipated that he would return fairly quickly. He didn't think that the disciples would be able to preach the gospel to all of Israel before he came back, but Peter and the rest of the disciples had many years to accomplish the task. They actually had the rest of their lives. In their lifetimes, the gospel message reached the far reaches of the known world.

It is no doubt that all of the villages had heard about Jesus and his message, or at least the message that Paul had turned Jesus' words into by the time of the death of the disciples. In short, this is another failed prophecy.

The *"These Signs shall Follow"* Prophecy

Most Christians have heard about snake handling, but many don't know that Jesus actually prophesied that it would be a normal thing for the committed Christian to do.

And he said unto them, Go ye into all the world, and preach the gospel to every creature. He that believeth and is baptized shall be saved; but he that believeth not shall be damned. And these signs shall follow them that believe; In my name shall they cast out devils; they shall speak with new tongues; They shall take up serpents; and if they drink any deadly thing, it shall not hurt them; they shall lay hands on the sick, and they shall recover. (Mark 16:15-18)

I think that this passage is in the top ten New Testament passages that have created mass confusion in the Church.

Most people have heard of Benny Hinn or Ernest Angley and have seen their supposed miracles and their casting out of demons. The fact remains that most of these acts are unverifiable. People walk up on stage claiming to have cancer and an evangelist touches them. The *healer* claims that they are healed and, as a result, these people stop medical treatment. Later, they may die unnecessary horrible deaths. Others complain that they feel pain, then suddenly they are pain free and are able to walk although with noticeable difficulty across the stage. Then, there are the demon possession cases that are delivered.

Many a demon is blamed for just about every ailment or vice. There are demons of smoking and demons of deafness. These evangelists cast out the beast with one breath then ask for a tithe with the next. This is a deplorable show to see played out. It results in the deception of many people. Of course, most will admit they recognize these men are the fakes but does anyone know where the true healers or exorcists are? If true believers abound, then where are the ones that exhibit these characteristics described in Mark's gospel? Where are the true power Christians?

I have to admit that my father and I had witnessed what we believed to be actual miracles in his ministry. I erroneously thought that because we had seen miracles, God was showing approval for what we believed and practiced. God was shining his face on us because we were on the right track, so to speak. We were the true believers.

When I started looking at other religions, I was surprised to learn that atheists and people of other religions experience verifiable miracles and strange happenings. I think men in every belief system experience healing and miracles. This is because the One True God has pity on people that need help. A miracle or a healing is not a sign of approval of one's beliefs, it is only a sign of God's graciousness.

Many times, I have heard news reports of some backwoods assembly having one of their parishioners die during a worship service from a bite they received while handling a poisonous snake. Where are the true believers that are able to handle snakes and drink poison without being harmed?

This may disappoint you, but there aren't any. I have never seen or heard of any. I have never talked to anyone that has seen any either. Even a small percentage of Christians should be doing some of these acts that Jesus predicted. This is another false prophecy, but there is more to this story. Even Christian scholarship admits that there is a problem with the last chapter of Mark. Our oldest best manuscripts don't include this passage. As a matter of fact, these manuscripts don't include anything after verse 9. All these manuscripts end with verse 8 of chapter 16. Mark's Gospel is the oldest gospel. Sometime after it was put in circulation, someone altered it and added the 12 verses in question. The real question is, "Why don't these earliest manuscripts contain any sightings of Jesus after his supposed resurrection?"

The *"Greater Works than these Shall he Do"* Prophecy

Every Christian should know that Jesus performed miracles and healing. Most don't realize that although the Mark 16 passage may be questionable in its origin, there are other passages that predict a similar portrait of believers. This is another prophecy of Jesus.

Believest thou not that I am in the Father, and the Father in me? the words that I speak unto you I speak not of myself: but the Father that dwelleth in me, he doeth the works. Believe me that I am in the Father, and the Father in me: or else believe me for the very works' sake. Verily, verily, I say unto you, **He that believeth on me, the works that I do shall he do also; and greater works than these shall he do; because I go unto my Father.** *And whatsoever ye shall ask in my name, that will I do, that the Father may be glorified in the Son. If ye shall ask any thing in my name, I will do it. (John 14:10-14)*

Are we to believe that believers will perform greater miracles than Jesus? This is what the unambiguous meaning of these words indicate. Do you know any Christians that regularly raise the dead or restore sight to the blind? How about any Christians that have occasionally done miracles? How about one Christian that has ever restored even one withered arm? Have you ever read of any documented cases where a believer has calmed a stormy sea or even a small lake, for that matter? I don't want to sound contemptuous. I am being dead serious.

Jesus doesn't limit his statement here. He even says in his next statement that anything a believer asks in his name, he will do. How many Christians were disappointed when they have prayed for help in Jesus' name even in a simple matter after thinking they were required only to ask Jesus for help? Obviously, Christians have misunderstood the unambiguous words of Jesus here?

What we have here is another false prophecy. Pastors often try to make myriads of exceptions when they arrive at promises like this in the New Testament. Christians over-analyze the words of Jesus in an attempt to force them into a meaning never intended. This is done because these promises made by Jesus are not functioning for them. The problem, as I see it, is that these promises don't function for anyone especially for the most trusting people, the ones that truly believe with their whole heart in Jesus and live with disappointment every day because of hollow promises like these.

The Prophecy of "Daniel's Messiah(s)"

One of the things I hear repeated from Christian apologists like Lee Strobel is that the time frame of the end-time-king's arrival has been set in stone by the prophet Daniel. Their reasoning is that because, in their eyes, this supposed time frame corresponds to the life of Jesus, so he must be *The Messiah*.

The prophet Daniel did use the Hebrew word *mashiach* or *messiah* in his ninth chapter but there is a small problem. There are actually two *messiahs* mentioned in Daniel 9.

Here is the passage.

Know therefore and understand, that from the going forth of the commandment to restore and to build Jerusalem unto **the Messiah** *the Prince shall be seven weeks, and threescore and two weeks: the street shall be built again, and the wall, even in troublous times. And after threescore and two weeks shall* **Messiah** *be cut off, but not for himself: and the people of the prince that shall come shall destroy the city and the sanctuary; and the end thereof shall be with a flood, and unto the end of the war desolations are determined. And he shall confirm the covenant with many for one week: and in the midst of the week he shall cause the sacrifice and the oblation to cease, and for the overspreading of abominations he shall make it desolate, even until the consummation, and that determined shall be poured upon the desolate. (Daniel 9:25-27)*

Now let's discuss the problems with the way this passage is presented. First, Daniel uses the word *messiah* twice in this passage. Christians, of course, think there is only one messiah and of course they believe it's Jesus. Starting with that belief they insert Jesus into this passage. How do they accomplish this insertion? As I discussed in chapter 2 of this book, the Hebrew word *mashiach* is used 39 times in the Hebrew Bible. Only here in this passage the word is translated twice as *messiah*. All other occurrences of this word are translated *anointed*. In order to make the reader think that

Daniel is speaking of Jesus the translators make a decision to instead transliterate the Hebrew word into its English equivalent.

Next, the translators insert the definite article (which is not present in the Hebrew text) before the word messiah to create *The Messiah,* and then they capitalize the word *messiah* to make the reader believe that it is someone that the writer and the reader both know the identity of. Before I go any further, I must say that I owe credit for these observations to Rabbi Tovia Singer.

The next thing that the translators did was to combine two time periods into one. Remember this phrase from the passage we are examining?

Know therefore and understand, that from the going forth of the commandment to restore and to build Jerusalem unto the Messiah the Prince shall be **seven weeks, and threescore and two weeks***: the street shall be built again, and the wall, even in troublous times. And after threescore and two weeks shall Messiah be cut off, but not for himself.*

The words, *"seven weeks, and threescore and two weeks,"* sound as strange today as it did the first time I studied Daniel seriously when I was a Christian. There is a missing period or semi-colon in this phrase. If the translators had put a period after "seven weeks" the entire meaning would be changed. The ability to understand the presentation of the time line here is hampered because it is presented here erroneously as a single time period with a single messiah. This is wrong.

Why did the translators do this? They did this to establish a time period that corresponds to the lifetime of Jesus and to combine the two messiahs into a single person in an attempt to exclude any other single person from being the Christian Messiah. Christian translators are being dishonest when they do this.

If we were to look at an honest English translation of this passage, we would see an entirely different wording. Here is how it should be translated.

Know therefore and understand, that from the going forth of the word to restore and to build Jerusalem unto an anointed ruler shall be seven weeks. And for threescore and two weeks the street shall be built again, and the wall, even in troublous times. And after threescore and two weeks shall an anointed person be cut off, and have nothing.

Doesn't look or sound anything like the King James, does it? Notice that I have made a few other translation corrections. The word *commandment* has been changed to *word*. I have also corrected the obviously misleading phrase, "but not for himself" to read, "and have nothing". This phrase, "not for himself," is an attempt to make the "cutting off" or death of the anointed to be an atonement for someone else. I was very shocked to see that the translators tried to force their belief in the vicarious atonement of Jesus' death into this verse. How do you justify changing God's Word to push your agenda?

Now that we have an honest translation of the verse let's look at these anointed persons. Who are they?

The first one is a ruler. The Hebrew word used here is *nagid*. This could be a King or a Governor. Notice that Daniel did not use the Hebrew word *sar,* here instead he used *nagid. Sar* simply means *"a leader."* Here is the obvious question. Was Jesus ever a king or a governor or even a leader? No. He never ruled over any nation, large group of people, and I doubt having a small band of disciples would qualify him as an actual leader.

If this isn't Jesus, how could we possibly determine the identity of this ruler? The following are a few verses that shed light on this question.

That saith of Cyrus, He is my shepherd, and shall perform all my pleasure: even saying to Jerusalem, Thou shalt be built; and to the temple, Thy foundation shall be laid. (Isaiah 44:28)

Thus saith the LORD to his anointed, to Cyrus, whose right hand I have holden, to subdue nations before him; and I will loose the loins of kings, to open before him the two leaved gates; and the gates shall not be shut; (Isaiah 45:1)

Cyrus was used by God to give the order to rebuild the city of Jerusalem. This is the anointed person Daniel was speaking of. This is the first anointed *messiah* that came seven weeks or forty-nine years after Jerusalem fell. This demolishes the misuse of this passage and the combining the sixty-nine weeks to reveal one messiah instead of two that are actually presented here.

The second *anointed* mentioned in the passage is the high priest. How do we know this? History tells us that the Priesthood was ended when the Romans destroyed the Temple. Some time after the expiration of the sixty-two weeks the high priest was cut off. This term *Kah'-rat* or *cut off* is used to refer to how a wicked person is killed. A righteous person is simply *killed*. In the next verse in Daniel, we are given more details that also agree with history.

And he shall confirm the covenant with many for one week: and in the midst of the week he shall cause the sacrifice and the oblation to cease, and for the overspreading of abominations he shall make it desolate, even until the consummation, and that determined shall be poured upon the desolate. (Daniel 9:27)

The *he* that confirms *the covenant* is the Emperor Titus Vespasian. This is another passage where the translators play fast and loose with the text. The phrase, *"the covenant"* is actually not translated correctly. It should be translated simply as *covenant*. The translators wanted the reader to believe that this was *The Messiah* making the *New Covenant* with Israel. The fact is, Titus made an agreement that he would let sacrifices continue but after three and a half years he terminated that *covenant* and stopped the sacrifices. He then destroyed Jerusalem. Daniel's prophecy has nothing to do with Jesus.

Conclusion

Although, I haven't provided an exhaustive list of the *messianic* prophecies that the writers of the New Testament misused, misquoted or fabricated, I have given you a taste of the general abuse of Hebrew Scriptures the gospel writers employed to try to convince others to share their belief in Jesus. In chapter 11, I will outline the prophecies that point to the actual end-times-king and explain why Jesus isn't him.

I have also shown you that Jesus' prophecies, at least the ones I have examined, reveal him to be much less than perfect. This falls short of the 100% accuracy demanded by the Hebrew Scriptures. I will conclude this chapter with this Scripture passage.

I will raise them up a Prophet from among their brethren, like unto thee, and will put my words in his mouth; and he shall speak unto them all that I shall command him. And it shall come to pass, that whosoever will not hearken unto my words which he shall speak in my name, I will require it of him. But the prophet, which shall presume to speak a word in my name, which I have not commanded him to speak, or that shall speak in the name of other gods, even that prophet shall die. And if thou say in thine heart, How shall we know the word which the LORD hath not spoken? **When a prophet speaketh in the name of the LORD, if the thing follow not, nor come to pass, that is the thing which the LORD hath not spoken, but the prophet hath spoken it presumptuously: thou shalt not be afraid of him.** (Deuteronomy 18:18-22)

CHAPTER 6

Vain Genealogies

But avoid foolish questions, and genealogies, and contentions, and strivings about the law; for they are unprofitable and vain. (Titus 3:9)

The Apostle Paul warned Jesus' followers not to have anything to do with foolish genealogies but I had not considered Jesus' genealogies to be foolish until I realized he had two of them. Now, I realize that all men have both a father and mother, hence they have two genealogies. The situation with Jesus is a little unorthodox. Jesus actually has two genealogies through his one father.

Most Christians will say that the list of Jesus' ancestors in Matthew chapter 1 is through Joseph. The other genealogy found in Luke chapter 3 is through his mother Mary. This is not what you find if you ignore what Church tradition teaches and examine the actual text of the New Testament.

Matthew's genealogy is listed below. I have inserted numbers after each person's name to make it easier to identify each person.

The book of the generation of Jesus Christ, the son of David, the son of Abraham. Abraham (1) begat Isaac (2); and Isaac begat Jacob (3); and Jacob begat Judas (4) and his brethren; And Judas begat Phares (5) and Zara of Thamar; and Phares begat Esrom (6); and Esrom begat Aram (7); And Aram begat Aminadab (8); and Aminadab begat Naasson (9); and Naasson begat Salmon (10); And Salmon begat Booz (11) of Rachab; and Booz begat Obed (12) of Ruth; and Obed begat Jesse (13); And Jesse begat David (14) the king; and David the king begat Solomon (15) of her that had been the wife of Urias; And Solomon begat Roboam (16); and Roboam begat Abia (17); and Abia begat Asa (18); And Asa begat Josaphat (19); and Josaphat begat Joram (20); and Joram begat Ozias (21); And Ozias begat Joatham (22); and Joatham begat Achaz (23); and Achaz begat Ezekias (24); And Ezekias begat Manasses (25); and Manasses begat Amon (26); and Amon begat Josias (27); And Josias begat Jechonias (28) and his brethren, about the time they were carried away to Babylon: And after they were brought to Babylon, Jechonias begat Salathiel (29); and Salathiel begat Zorobabel (30); And Zorobabel begat Abiud (31); and Abiud begat Eliakim (32); and Eliakim begat Azor (33); And Azor begat Sadoc (34); and Sadoc begat Achim (35); and Achim begat Eliud (36); And Eliud begat Eleazar (37); and Eleazar begat Matthan (38); and Matthan begat Jacob (49); And Jacob begat Joseph (40) the husband of Mary, of whom was born Jesus (41), who is called Christ. **So all the generations from Abraham to David are fourteen generations; and from David until the carrying away into Babylon are fourteen generations; and from the carrying away into Babylon unto Christ are fourteen generations.** *(Matthew 1:1-17)*

CHAPTER 6

Let's deal with the obvious problems first. Christians believe that this is an integral part of their Holy Bible. Most Christians believe that it is inspired or God breathed and contains no contradictions or mistakes but there are problems with this passage regardless what they believe.

Matthew lists all of the names in his rendition of Jesus' family tree through Joseph all the way back to Abraham. After he is done, he makes a statement that there are three sets of fourteen generations that are said to be listed. He does this because the number *fourteen* is an important number. It is the number of David's name, the number of kingship. Although this sounds pretty good at first, there is an extremely big problem: there are only forty-one names. It appears that there is one name missing but the problem is worse than it seems.

There are actually four names that Matthew has omitted to make his accounting work. If you refer to the genealogy chart available on my website,[1] you will see Ahaziah, Jehoash, Amaziah and Jehoiakim are simply omitted. These men were all kings.

This was no arbitrary decision Matthew made. At least one name would present a problem for Jesus when it comes to kingly descendents. *Jechonias (28)* was a very wicked king but because Matthew doesn't read Hebrew very well, he leaves his name in. He mistakes his father Jehoiakim's name for his son and takes Jehoiakim's name out instead. *Jechonias (28)* was cursed by God and told that none of his children would sit on the throne in Israel again. Here is the passage.

Thus saith the LORD, Write ye this man childless, a man that shall not prosper in his days: for no man of his seed shall prosper, sitting upon the throne of David, and ruling any more in Judah. (Jeremiah 22:30)

God is saying that Jechonias *(28)* will have none of his children sit on the throne. Instead of his son, Salathiel *(29)* sitting on the throne, Jechonias' *(28)* brother Zedekiah takes his place.

Some Christian apologists have theorized that God lifted the curse and Jechonias' *(28)* descendants are now free to take the throne. This is not true because Zorobabel *(30)* was a righteous man but God only allows him to become a governor and **not** a king.

In the second year of Darius the king, in the sixth month, in the first day of the month, came the word of the LORD by Haggai the prophet unto Zerubbabel the son of Shealtiel, governor of Judah, and to Joshua the son of Josedech, the high priest, saying, Thus speaketh the LORD of hosts, saying, This people say, The time is not come, the time that the LORD'S house should be built. (Haggai 1:1,2)

And the LORD stirred up the spirit of Zerubbabel the son of Shealtiel, governor of Judah, and the spirit of Joshua the son of Josedech, the high priest, and the spirit of all the remnant of the people; and they came and did work in the house of the LORD of hosts, their God, In the four and twentieth day of the sixth month, in the second year of Darius the king. (Haggai 1:14,15)

In the seventh month, in the one and twentieth day of the month, came the word of the LORD by the prophet Haggai, saying, Speak now to Zerubbabel the son of Shealtiel, governor of Judah, and to Joshua the son of Josedech, the high priest, and to the residue of the people, saying, Who is left among you that saw this house in her first

---

1 http://www.leavingjesus.net/articles/JesusGenealogyChart-1.pdf

glory? and how do ye see it now? is it not in your eyes in comparison of it as nothing? Yet now be strong, O Zerubbabel, saith the LORD; and be strong, O Joshua, son of Josedech, the high priest; and be strong, all ye people of the land, saith the LORD, and work: for I am with you, saith the LORD of hosts: According to the word that I covenanted with you when ye came out of Egypt, so my spirit remaineth among you: fear ye not. (Haggai 2:1-5)

In that day, saith the LORD of hosts, will I take thee, O Zerubbabel, my servant, the son of Shealtiel, saith the LORD, and will make thee as a signet: for I have chosen thee, saith the LORD of hosts. (Haggai 2:23)

God reaffirms his love and approval for Zorobabel *(30)* but never makes him a king. This is probably where Matthew's virgin birth storyline came from. It stems from the need to solve the problem of the cursed lineage. The sad news for Christians is, if Matthew is correct and Jesus does come from this lineage then he cannot be eligible to be king. Conversely, if he is not of a human lineage he cannot be of David's line and he cannot be king because it can be seen in scripture that if your father is not a son of David, then you can't be either. The *Son of David* references in the New Testament are actually farcical. This is a paradox that Christians ignore.

Now that we know the problems in Matthew's lineage let's examine Luke's account to see what we have. This is the passage.

And Jesus (56) himself began to be about thirty years of age, being (as was supposed) the son of Joseph (55), which was the son of Heli (54), Which was the son of Matthat (53), which was the son of Levi (52), which was the son of Melchi (51), which was the son of Janna (50), which was the son of Joseph (49), Which was the son of Mattathias (48), which was the son of Amos (47), which was the son of Naum (46), which was the son of Esli (45), which was the son of Nagge (44), Which was the son of Maath (43), which was the son of Mattathias (42), which was the son of Semei (41), which was the son of Joseph (40), which was the son of Juda (39), Which was the son of Joanna (38), which was the son of Rhesa (37), which was the son of Zorobabel (36), which was the son of Salathiel (35), which was the son of Neri (34), Which was the son of Melchi (33), which was the son of Addi (32), which was the son of Cosam (31), which was the son of Elmodam (30), which was the son of Er (29), Which was the son of Jose (28), which was the son of Eliezer (27), which was the son of Jorim (26), which was the son of Matthat (25), which was the son of Levi (24), Which was the son of Simeon (23), which was the son of Juda (22), which was the son of Joseph (21), which was the son of Jonan (20), which was the son of Eliakim (19), Which was the son of Melea (18), which was the son of Menan (17), which was the son of Mattatha (16), which was the son of Nathan (15), which was the son of David (14), Which was the son of Jesse (13), which was the son of Obed (12), which was the son of Booz (11), which was the son of Salmon (10), which was the son of Naasson (9), Which was the son of Aminadab (8), which was the son of Aram (7), which was the son of Esrom (6), which was the son of Phares (5), which was the son of Juda (4), Which was the son of Jacob (3), which was the son of Isaac (2), which was the son of Abraham (1), which was the son of Thara, which was the son of Nachor. (Luke 3:23-34)

Luke reverses the order in his genealogy and starts with Jesus. I believe this is because he is not a Hebrew but a gentile convert. Although Mary is never mentioned, Church tradition teaches that this is her genealogy. If we look at Judah *(4)*, we realize that the line is through Judah but there is a serious showstopper when it comes to Nathan *(15)*. The Kingship of David flows from Solomon not Nathan. These are the words of God on this matter.

He shall build me an house, and I will stablish his throne for ever. I will be his father, and he shall be my son: and I will not take my mercy away from him, as I took it from him that was before thee: But I will settle him in mine house and in my kingdom for ever: and his throne shall be established for evermore. (1 Chronicles 17:12-14)

And David said to Solomon, My son, as for me, it was in my mind to build an house unto the name of the LORD my God: But the word of the LORD came to me, saying, Thou hast shed blood abundantly, and hast made great wars: thou shalt not build an house unto my name, because thou hast shed much blood upon the earth in my sight. Behold, a son shall be born to thee, who shall be a man of rest; and I will give him rest from all his enemies round about: for his name shall be Solomon, and I will give peace and quietness unto Israel in his days. He shall build an house for my name; and he shall be my son, and I will be his father; and I will establish the throne of his kingdom over Israel for ever. (1 Chronicles 22:7-10)

Although some Christian apologists would like to use complex theories and arguments this is actually a very simple problem with a very simple solution. Those who want to argue their point actually have set themselves against The Almighty in this matter and should repent of their rebellion toward Him and accept His Word on this issue.

God has plainly said that Solomon's throne will be forever. This means that God is able to make his presence known at any time to anoint a man that He knows is of Solomon's lineage and make him the end-times-king. This will be the messiah that will sit on the throne not Jesus who according to the simplicity of God's Hebrew Scriptures is simply ineligible to be a king over Israel.

CHAPTER 7

The Confident God vs. The Bashful God

There is no shortage of books that have been written to describe the nature of God, but I have to say, I see an extremely significant difference between the way the Hebrew Bible and The New Testament portray Him.

In the Hebrew Scriptures, God is bold and is always expressing himself as the God of creation. It seems as if he is continually saying that He is God and don't you forget it. The problem with the New Testament is that its subject isn't God. It's actually more concerned with *The Messiah*.

In the Hebrew Bible, the word *Elohim* (*God*) appears 2697 times and the word *messiah* or *anointed* 39 times. That is a 69:1 ratio, God being favored over the *Messiah*. In the New Testament the word *God* is used 1196 times, the word *Jesus* 942 times, *Christ* 532 times and *Messias* (*Messiah*) 2 times, *Messiah/Jesus/Christ* being favored 1.2 times to 1, resulting in a dramatic shift. Jesus or messiah is actually more prominent in the New Testament than God Himself. Are you beginning to see how the emphasis has shifted away from God to *the messiah*?

In the Hebrew Bible, God is continually reminding us who He is. It seems at every turn, he is reiterating to us that He is in charge.

And he said unto him, I am the LORD that brought thee out of Ur of the Chaldees, to give thee this land to inherit it. (Genesis 15:7)

And, behold, the LORD stood above it, and said, I am the LORD God of Abraham thy father, and the God of Isaac: the land whereon thou liest, to thee will I give it, and to thy seed; (Genesis 28:13)

And God spake unto Moses, and said unto him, I am the LORD:(Exodus 6:2)

Wherefore say unto the children of Israel, I am the LORD, and I will bring you out from under the burdens of the Egyptians, and I will rid you out of their bondage, and I will redeem you with a stretched out arm, and with great judgments: (Exodus 6:6)

And I will take you to me for a people, and I will be to you a God: and ye shall know that I am the LORD your God, which bringeth you out from under the burdens of the Egyptians. (Exodus 6:7)

And I will bring you in unto the land, concerning the which I did swear to give it to Abraham, to Isaac, and to Jacob; and I will give it you for an heritage: I am the LORD. (Exodus 6:8)

And I will sever in that day the land of Goshen, in which my people dwell, that no swarms of flies shall be there; to the end thou mayest know that I am the LORD in the midst of the earth. (Exodus 8:22)

And that thou mayest tell in the ears of thy son, and of thy son's son, what things I have wrought in Egypt, and my signs which I have done among them; that ye may know how that I am the LORD. (Exodus 10:2)

For I will pass through the land of Egypt this night, and will smite all the firstborn in the land of Egypt, both man and beast; and against all the gods of Egypt I will execute judgment: I am the LORD. (Exodus 12:12)

And I will harden Pharaoh's heart, that he shall follow after them; and I will be honoured upon Pharaoh, and upon all his host; that the Egyptians may know that I am the LORD. And they did so. (Exodus 14:14)

And the Egyptians shall know that I am the LORD, when I have gotten me honour upon Pharaoh, upon his chariots, and upon his horsemen. (Exodus 14:18)

And said, If thou wilt diligently hearken to the voice of the LORD thy God, and wilt do that which is right in his sight, and wilt give ear to his commandments, and keep all his statutes, I will put none of these diseases upon thee, which I have brought upon the Egyptians: for I am the LORD that healeth thee. (Exodus 15:26)

And I said unto you, I am the LORD your God; fear not the gods of the Amorites, in whose land ye dwell: but ye have not obeyed my voice. (Judges 6:10)

And, behold, there came a prophet unto Ahab king of Israel, saying, Thus saith the LORD, Hast thou seen all this great multitude? behold, I will deliver it into thine hand this day; and thou shalt know that I am the LORD. (1Kings 20:13)

And there came a man of God, and spake unto the king of Israel, and said, Thus saith the LORD, Because the Syrians have said, The LORD is God of the hills, but he is not God of the valleys, therefore will I deliver all this great multitude into thine hand, and ye shall know that I am the LORD. (1Kings 20:28)

I am the LORD: that is my name: and my glory will I not give to another, neither my praise to graven images. (Isaiah 42:8)

For I am the LORD thy God, the Holy One of Israel, thy Saviour: I gave Egypt for thy ransom, Ethiopia and Seba for thee. (Isaiah 43:3)

I, even I, am the LORD; and beside me there is no saviour. (Isaiah 43:11)

I am the LORD, your Holy One, the creator of Israel, your King. (Isaiah 43:15)

Thus saith the LORD, thy redeemer, and he that formed thee from the womb, I am the LORD that maketh all things; that stretcheth forth the heavens alone; that spreadeth abroad the earth by myself; (Isaiah 44:24)

I am the LORD, and there is none else, there is no God beside me: I girded thee, though thou hast not known me: (Isaiah 45:5)

These are only a few of the passages where God states who He is. This is God's signature approach. This is how He speaks. This God is confident. He never makes a secret of his identity as the God of Israel. He doesn't attempt to obscure his identity. It is not His nature to be fearful or bashful about who He is.

CHAPTER 7

While this is true, let's look at the New Testament God. Christians believe that Jesus is God in the flesh. If Jesus had the nature of God, then he would act like God.

The problem is that Jesus didn't act like God. Let's look at the New Testament, to verify this. Before we examine the words or actions of Jesus, we must ask a question.

"If Jesus is God and shares the true nature of the unchanging God of the Hebrew Bible, shouldn't we see Jesus use the same process and words to identify himself as the One True God did?"

These are some words from Jesus.

Then came the Jews round about him, and said unto him, How long dost thou make us to doubt? If thou be the Christ, tell us plainly. Jesus answered them, I told you, and ye believed not: the works that I do in my Father's name, they bear witness of me. But ye believe not, because ye are not of my sheep, as I said unto you. My sheep hear my voice, and I know them, and they follow me: And I give unto them eternal life; and they shall never perish, neither shall any man pluck them out of my hand. My Father, which gave them me, is greater than all; and no man is able to pluck them out of my Father's hand. I and my Father are one. Then the Jews took up stones again to stone him. Jesus answered them, Many good works have I shewed you from my Father; for which of those works do ye stone me? The Jews answered him, saying, For a good work we stone thee not; but for blasphemy; and because that thou, being a man, makest thyself God. Jesus answered them, Is it not written in your law, I said, Ye are gods? If he called them gods, unto whom the word of God came, and the scripture cannot be broken; Say ye of him, whom the Father hath sanctified, and sent into the world, Thou blasphemest; because I said, I am the Son of God? (John 10:24-36)

This was the perfect opportunity for Jesus to proclaim definitively that he was God, but he didn't. Instead, Jesus references a passage from the Hebrew Bible trying to defuse the anger of the *Jews*. Why doesn't Jesus plainly deny what *the Jews* accuse him of? Somehow Christians have come to believe that clouding the issues by using obfuscation is somehow godlike. Speaking circles around it is somehow spiritual. And all this time, I thought being honest and upfront was part of being godly. How silly was I?

After decades of trying to analyze Jesus' method of communicating with others, I would like to express my observations about Jesus and the way he speaks.

He is evasive. He is confusing. He uses *circumlocution* (or speaking around a subject) without actually speaking about it. He could have just answered the question at hand, *"Was he the messiah, or not?"* but he didn't. *The Jews* were asking the question out of necessity because Jesus was not showing them any evidence that he was *the messiah*. What was the evidence they were looking for? Was it dying on the cross? No, of course not. The leaders wanted to see *the Messiah* take the throne of David and deliver them from Rome. Jesus couldn't even prove he was the end-times-king, why would anyone think he was God? The question now to ask is, *"Is this how God would behave?"*

These are some other passages to consider.

Jesus answered and said unto them, Ye do err, not knowing the scriptures, nor the power of God. For in the resurrection they neither marry, nor are given in marriage, but are as the angels of God in heaven. But as touching the resurrection of the dead, have ye not read that which was spoken unto you by God, saying, I am the God of Abraham, and the God of Isaac, and the God of Jacob? God is not the God of the dead, but of the living. (Matthew 22:29-32)

And Jesus answering said unto them, Do ye not therefore err, because ye know not the scriptures, neither the power of God? For when they shall rise from the dead, they neither marry, nor are given in marriage; but are as the angels which are in heaven. And as touching the dead, that they rise: have ye not read in the book of Moses, how in the bush God spake unto him, saying, I am the God of Abraham, and the God of Isaac, and the God of Jacob? He is not the God of the dead, but the God of the living: ye therefore do greatly err. (Mark 12:24-27)

In these citations, Jesus is trying to make the point that God is the God of the living but Christians don't realize that he is making another point that most overlook. Jesus refers to a specific time when God spoke to Moses from the burning bush. Jesus states that God referred to himself as the God of Abraham, and the God of Isaac, and the God of Jacob. These words **he attributes to God not himself**. If Jesus is God, is it deceptive of him to attribute his words to another and not himself? He makes no mention or implication here that he is God, instead he steers far away from it. This is another missed opportunity for Jesus to declare his godhood. These are some other missed opportunities.

*And Jesus said unto them, **I am the bread of life**: he that cometh to me shall never hunger; and he that believeth on me shall never thirst. (John 6:35)*

***I am the living bread** which came down from heaven: if any man eat of this bread, he shall live for ever: and the bread that I will give is my flesh, which I will give for the life of the world. (John 6:51)*

*Then spake Jesus again unto them, saying, **I am the light of the world**: he that followeth me shall not walk in darkness, but shall have the light of life. (John 8:12)*

*As long as I am in the world, **I am the light of the world**. (John 9:5)*

*Then said Jesus unto them again, Verily, verily, I say unto you, **I am the door of the sheep**. (John 10:7)*

***I am the door**: by me if any man enter in, he shall be saved, and shall go in and out, and find pasture. (John 10:9)*

***I am the good shepherd**: the good shepherd giveth his life for the sheep. (John 10:11)*

***I am the good shepherd**, and know my sheep, and am known of mine. (John 10:14)*

*Jesus said unto her, **I am the resurrection, and the life**: he that believeth in me, though he were dead, yet shall he live: (John 11:25)*

*Jesus saith unto him, **I am the way, the truth, and the life**: no man cometh unto the Father, but by me. (John 14:6)*

***I am the true vine**, and my Father is the husbandman. (John 15:1)*

***I am the vine**, ye are the branches: He that abideth in me, and I in him, the same bringeth forth much fruit: for without me ye can do nothing. (John 15:5)*

This is Jesus' laundry list of things that he believes he is but, among them, he doesn't list being God. In John 14:6, he doesn't say he is God but he is the way to God.

Christians believe somehow that this is Jesus admitting to being God. This is like saying, "The highway that leads to Washington, D.C. is not the same thing as Washington, D.C.," and then coming to the conclusion that the city is the same thing as the road that leads to it.

Is Jesus only being bashful or modest? God was never modest. Could it be that he is afraid to tell anyone that he is God? Is Jesus afraid that if someone finds out that he is God then his plans will be derailed?

If this is God, I want to know why he is acting so strangely. What is wrong with him? If this is God, why is he mentioning another God that he is referring to as his father? Are you beginning to see how ridiculous the line of thinking that *Jesus is God* is? Christian pastors and apologists tell you that Jesus is actually using the name of God in these *I am* statements but this is not true. More on that later in the section of this chapter entitled, *"The Great I ain't"*.

There is something terribly puzzling about one particular passage above. Jesus says in John 9:5 that, "As long as I am in the world, I am the light of the world." Did God ever say anything that remotely resembles this? What would happen if Jesus leaves the world? He did leave the world. Did any of the gospel writers ever suggest that because Jesus had left, the light of the world has been extinguished? Consider these verses.

*I came forth from the Father, and am come into the world: again, **I leave the world**, and go to the Father. (John 16:28)*

*Ye have heard how I said unto you, I go away, and come again unto you. If ye loved me, ye would rejoice, because I said, **I go unto the Father: for my Father is greater than I**. (John 14:28)*

What is going on here? Now is the time to ask yourself a few questions. If God has a father, then who is his father? If Jesus is God and his Father was greater than him, then how can there be only one God? Remember there are other verses that also explain how the gospel writer saw Jesus' relationship with God. The following is probably the most quoted verse about their relationship.

In the beginning was the Word, and the Word was with God, and the Word was God. The same was in the beginning with God. All things were made by him; and without him was not any thing made that was made. (John 1:1-3)

So, we can easily see that this is a problematic passage. Most Christians read the words, "In the beginning," but they perceive the words, "Before anything existed." This is because they have been taught the error that Jesus is an eternal being. The way I see it, Christians don't read, "In the beginning was the word and the word was with God and the word was God," but instead they read, "In the beginning was the Son and the Son was with God and the Son was God," or "In the beginning was Jesus and Jesus was with God and Jesus was God."

Also, we have some impossibilities stated here. The *Word* was with God. This sounds like an acceptable thought until you consider the next phrase *"the Word was God"*. Can God be with himself? Christians must think so.

Let me be blunt. This is a ridiculous idea. Christians should question this whole passage, but they rarely do. It took me a long time to see the problems with this passage. There is an enormous problem with the thoughts of Jesus being with God in the beginning.

Of course, Christians continually spout that it is impossible to understand who God is and if He is one or three. I would disagree when it comes to the God of the Hebrew Scriptures. Wouldn't it make sense to think God would want us to understand him? If He thought that it was possible to understand who He was and how many persons were in His being, wouldn't He have told us? Well, He actually does in the following passage.

Ye are my witnesses, saith the LORD, and my servant whom I have chosen: that ye may know and believe me, and understand that I am he: before me there was no God formed, neither shall there be after me. (Isaiah 43:10)

This verse contains many pronouns but God only uses singular ones like my, I and me to refer to Himself. He also says that His desire is to have us understand Him and know that there are no other Gods than Him. Simple isn't it? Understandable isn't it? These are the Words of God but they are discounted by Christians every day.

Compare this verse to the mystery and confusion created by the New Testament. Let's look at another verse containing Jesus' words.

And now, O Father, glorify thou me with thine own self with the glory which I had with thee before the world was. (John 17:5)

Jesus is saying that he shares glory with God but this is a problem. Jesus uses the word *"with"* to describe how he shares God's glory. God had already spoken about this possibility. These are the words of God from the Hebrew Bible.

*I am the LORD: that is my name: and **my glory will I not give to another**, neither my praise to graven images. (Isaiah 42:8)*

*For mine own sake, even for mine own sake, will I do it: for how should my name be polluted? and **I will not give my glory unto another**. (Isaiah 48:11)*

*I, even I, am the LORD; and **beside me there is no saviour**. (Isaiah 43:11)*

*Thus saith the LORD the King of Israel, and his redeemer the LORD of hosts; I **am the first, and I am the last**; and **beside me there is no God**. (Isaiah 44:6)*

*Fear ye not, neither be afraid: have not I told thee from that time, and have declared it? ye are even my witnesses. **Is there a God beside me?** yea, **there is no God; I know not any**. (Isaiah 44:8)*

*I am the LORD, and there is **none else, there is no God beside me**: I girded thee, though thou hast not known me: (Isaiah 45:5)*

*That they may know from the rising of the sun, and from the west, that **there is none beside me**. I am the LORD, and **there is none else**. (Isaiah 45:6)*

*Tell ye, and bring them near; yea, let them take counsel together: who hath declared this from ancient time? who hath told it from that time? have not I the LORD? **and there is no God else beside me; a just God and a Saviour; there is none beside me**. (Isaiah 45:21)*

Let's break this down logically. This is the way things stand as of now.

- Jesus' father is God
- Jesus is God
- Jesus is not his father and always refers to him as another person
- Jesus' father is greater than him
- God says there are no Gods beside Him
- God says he won't share His Glory with another
- Jesus says that he shares God's Glory
- God says that He is the only God and savior
- Jesus is the light of the world as long as he is in the world so if he leaves the world there is no light of the world

If you weigh all of these statements, you would have to come to the logical conclusion that someone is not telling the truth. Christians refuse to accept that these statements of Jesus contradict the clear words of the *Eternal God*. They start with Jesus' statements and work backwards explaining away God's own Words. Shame on them.

Man was created in God's image with a mind. The mind is a tool that can be used to investigate the facts and come to a logical conclusion. The problem when people have a belief system that they think is beyond scrutiny is that they are unable or unwilling to process the examination normally. This almost always ends in this person living a life in gross error.

It is said that Christianity is based on the Hebrew Bible. If this is true, then Christians would have to admit that the Hebrew Bible must be the Word of God. Rabbi Tovia Singer stated the rule that, *"Although the Old Testament can be true and the New Testament false, it is impossible for the New Testament to be true and the Old Testament false."*

In a popular Christian apologetic book entitled, *"Evidence That Demands a Verdict,"* the author, Josh McDowell, postulates that concerning Jesus' identity there exists three and only three possibilities. Either *Jesus is a liar, a lunatic or he is Lord.* If the New Testament is untrue and disagrees with the Hebrew Bible then it is because of a fourth possibility.

The first time I heard of this fourth possibility was in a lecture by Tovia Singer. The fourth possibility being that, *"someone wrote statements about Jesus that simply weren't true."* This was unaddressed by Josh McDowell. Like most Christians, Josh starts with the assumption that the New Testament and every word it says came out of Jesus' mouth must be true, even if they disagree with God's Words that came first. Most Christians don't give God a fair hearing. They assume He's wrong by believing Jesus' and the New Testament's words above His.

Most Christians live their entire life and never consider what they might not be aware of. As soon as someone is converted to Christianity, they are told to read the New Testament. Most evangelists have their converts read their Bible starting with the Gospel of John. With the first words they read, they are deeply immersed into the doctrine of the *divinity of Jesus*. The average Christian will store this away as fact and weigh everything else they learn against it. Often, if they hear or read an opposing thought they will discount it against their primary belief that Jesus is God. If you are a Christian you should honestly ask yourself, *"Do I do that?"*

It isn't surprising that Christians are unaware of the passages that would prove that there is only one God and that the end-times-king *Messiah* is only a man. This is because there is no emphasis on the Hebrew Bible being the standard that beliefs are to be tested against. Most Christians take the New Testament as the final word in what is Biblical and don't consider that God had defined what the true test of truth was before the New Testament was penned. In the book of Deuteronomy, God gave us the test of a prophet or anyone that speaks out in the name of The Almighty. This standard would apply to Peter, James, John, Paul and even Jesus.

When the LORD thy God shall cut off the nations from before thee, whither thou goest to possess them, and thou succeedest them, and dwellest in their land; Take heed to thyself that thou be not snared by following them, after that they be destroyed from before thee; and that thou enquire not after their gods, saying, How did these nations serve their gods? even so will I do likewise. Thou shalt not do so unto the LORD thy God: for every abomination to the LORD, which he hateth, have they done unto their gods; for even their sons and their daughters they have burnt in the fire to their gods. What thing soever I command you, observe to do it: thou shalt not add thereto, nor diminish from it. If there arise among you a prophet, or a dreamer of dreams, and giveth thee a sign or a wonder, And the sign or the wonder come to pass, whereof he spake unto thee, saying, Let us go after other gods, which thou hast not known, and let us serve them; Thou shalt not hearken unto the words of that prophet, or that dreamer of dreams: for the LORD your God proveth you, to know whether ye love the LORD your God with all your heart and with all your soul. Ye shall walk after the LORD your God, and fear him, and keep his commandments, and obey his voice, and ye shall serve him, and cleave unto him. And that prophet, or that dreamer of dreams, shall be put to death; because he hath spoken to turn you away from the LORD your God, which brought you out of the land of Egypt, and redeemed you out of the house of bondage, to thrust thee out of the way which the LORD thy God commanded thee to walk in. So shalt thou put the evil away from the midst of thee. If thy brother, the son of thy mother, or thy son, or thy daughter, or the wife of thy bosom, or thy friend, which is as thine own soul, entice thee secretly, saying, Let us go and serve other gods, which thou hast not known, thou, nor thy fathers; Namely, of the gods of the people which are round about you, nigh unto thee, or far off from thee, from the one end of the earth even unto the other end of the earth; Thou shalt not consent unto him, nor hearken unto him; neither shall thine eye pity him, neither shalt thou spare, neither shalt thou conceal him: But thou shalt surely kill him; thine hand shall be first upon him to put him to death, and afterwards the hand of all the people. And thou shalt stone him with stones, that he die; because he hath sought to thrust thee away from the LORD thy God, which brought thee out of the land of Egypt, from the house of bondage. And all Israel shall hear, and fear, and shall do no more any such wickedness as this is among you. (Deuteronomy 12:29-13:11)

It should shock the average Christian to read this and consider the consequences if Jesus were a false prophet. It was a sobering thought for me. God says that a prophet may come to you and perform a miracle or give you a sign of a future event that comes to pass but if that prophet entices you to follow another way that God has not told you to go or to follow another God who you have not known[1] then you are not to listen to him.

For a long while, I pondered the verse, "other gods, which thou hast not known," and the thought occurred to me that Israel did not know of any concept of God coming as a man to die for their sins. They understood God as an invisible deity that wasn't ashamed of stating who He was. A God that didn't mince words about being the *greatest* being with no possibility of anyone being like him. This is one example found in Deuteronomy 4.

Now therefore hearken, O Israel, unto the statutes and unto the judgments, which I teach you, for to do them, that ye may live, and go in and possess the land which the LORD God of your fathers giveth you. Ye shall not add unto the word which I command you, neither shall ye diminish ought from it, that ye may keep the commandments of the LORD your God which I command you. Your eyes have seen what the LORD did because of Baalpeor: for all the men that followed Baalpeor, the LORD thy God hath destroyed them from among you. But ye that did cleave unto the LORD your God are alive every one of you this day. Behold, I have taught you statutes and judgments, even as the LORD my God commanded me, that ye should do so in the land whither ye go to possess it. Keep therefore and do them; for this is your wisdom and your understanding in the sight of the nations, which shall hear all these statutes, and say, Surely this great nation is a wise and understanding people. For what nation is there so great, who hath God so nigh unto them, as the LORD our God is in all things that we call upon him for? And what nation is there so great, that hath statutes and judgments so righteous as all this law, which I set before you this day? **Only take heed to thyself, and keep thy soul diligently, lest thou forget the things which thine eyes have seen, and lest they depart from thy heart all the days of thy life: but teach them thy sons, and thy sons' sons; Specially the day that thou stoodest before the LORD thy God in Horeb, when the LORD said unto me, Gather me the people together, and I will make them hear my words, that they may learn to fear me all the days that they shall live upon the earth, and that they may teach their children. And ye came near and stood under the mountain; and the mountain burned with fire unto the midst of heaven, with darkness, clouds, and thick darkness. And the LORD spake unto you out of the midst of the fire: ye heard the voice of the words, but saw no similitude; only ye heard a voice. And he declared unto you his covenant, which he commanded you to perform, even ten commandments; and he wrote them upon two tables of stone. And the LORD commanded me at that time to teach you statutes and judgments, that ye might do them in the land whither ye go over to possess it. Take ye therefore good heed unto yourselves; for ye saw no manner of similitude on the day that the LORD spake unto you in Horeb out of the midst of the fire: Lest ye corrupt yourselves, and make you a graven image, the similitude of any figure, the likeness of male or female, The likeness of any beast that is on the earth, the likeness of any winged fowl that flieth in the air, The likeness of any thing that creepeth on the ground, the likeness of any fish that is in the waters beneath the earth: And lest thou lift up thine eyes unto heaven, and when thou seest the sun, and the moon, and the stars, even all the host of heaven, shouldest be driven to worship them, and serve**

---

1 This commandment of not following a God that you have not know was given in the Torah. The God that Israel knew up to that time was an invisible God that lived in and spoke from the sky. He taught them that obedience to His Laws was supreme. This may seem simplistic and archaic but this is the way God presented himself.

them, which the LORD thy God hath divided unto all nations under the whole heaven. (Deuteronomy 4:1-19)

I can't emphasize the following thoughts strongly enough. God is unchanging. He constantly reminds Israel about his creating the world and the things he has done in the past. In this particular passage, He reminds Israel how he destroyed the men that followed a false God. He then tells them to be extremely careful, not only once, but twice, not forget how they knew and understood Him in the desert. He is being extremely specific in this passage about one single occasion when he revealed himself in the fire on Mount Horeb.[2] He makes sure to teach them that they heard his voice, but they did not see Him. God goes on to forbid them from making an image of Him, so they will not follow the nations and worship the image. He even goes on to repeat the warning a second time. This is how Israel's God represented himself.

Contrast this with the New Testament's presentation of Jesus. The New Testament presents a confusing, conflicted, fuzzy picture of what is going on. Jesus never once announces himself as the Creator although the author of John's gospel does. Jesus never makes a habit of saying anything about what he had done for Israel in the past as God did. Jesus never builds himself up as the greatest being of all time as God constantly did. As a matter of fact, unbelievably, he says that there is no one greater than John the Baptist[3]. He also tells people that his father is greater than him. Can God be greater than God?

Where does that leave Jesus? Again, I ask, "Has God become bashful?"

The "Great I ain't"

Some Christians teach that Jesus declared himself to be God by using God's name. This is not true. Jesus does use a Greek phrase in the following passage that is believed to be used in the Greek translation of the Torah. Let's examine it.

Jesus said unto them, Verily, verily, I say unto you, Before Abraham was, **I am.**

(John 8:58)

Here, Jesus uses the Greek words, *"ego eimi"* in what Christians believe is Jesus uttering the Sacred Name of The Almighty. They believe that he is saying that He is God Almighty. They believe this, because in the Septuagint, this is how the Greek translators translated a name God used to refer to Himself in Exodus chapter 3. This is the verse.

And God said unto Moses, I AM THAT I AM: and he said, Thus shalt thou say unto the children of Israel, I AM hath sent me unto you. (Exodus 3:14)

Most Christians don't read or study Greek. Most that do are only concerned with the New Testament and have never had a Septuagint (a Greek translation of the Hebrew Bible) in their hands.

As a serious student of the Bible, I own a Zondervan edition Septuagint. Keep in mind, this is a Christian Translation. When I first looked at Exodus 3:14, I was surprised to

---

2 Mount Horeb is the same as Mount Sinai.
3 Luke 7:28 has Jesus saying, "For I say unto you, Among those that are born of women there is not a greater prophet than John the Baptist: but he that is least in the kingdom of God is greater than he."

learn that the sacred name, which actually is expressed as *yud-heh-vav-heh* in Hebrew Letters, or *YHVH* in English, does not appear in this verse. The second oddity is that the translators rendered the Hebrew expression, *ehyeh asher ehyeh* or *"I AM THAT I AM"* as *"ego eimi ho On"* not simply *"ego eimi."* The Septuagint Greek in Exodus 3:14 translates to *I am the Being* not simply *I am*. This Greek rendering does not fully disclose what God said to Moses in Hebrew.

This *ego eimi ho On* or *I am The Being* is not to be found in Jesus' words anywhere in the New Testament. As a matter of fact, *ego eimi* is used 48 times in the New Testament and not always by Jesus. Judas Iscariot uses the phrase when he asks if he is the traitor in Matthew 26:25. Likewise, Peter uses the same phrase in Acts 10:21. I seriously doubt that any christian would think Judas or Peter were trying to say that they were the *Great I Am*.

Christians believe that Jesus used this phrase, *"ego eimi,"* in an attempt to indicate that he was God. Most don't realize that Jesus did not speak Greek. The New Testament writers who wrote in Greek failed to communicate how they understood Jesus' words. It is clear to me that they didn't understand the Hebrew in the Exodus passage either. To put it simply, the author of this New Testament Gospel has made a mess of this entire situation.

Please understand that it is *only John that attempts to address the issue of Jesus declaring that he is God*, the other gospel writers simply don't.

Let's get down and dirty about the subject of Jesus saying that he was the Eternal Being, The God of Abraham, The God of Isaac and The God of Jacob. He did not say he was God. If he had, he would have said something entirely different in Greek.

When we revisit the moment when Moses stood before the burning bush, we read about God saying particular specific words to Moses[4]. Although, the writers of the Greek Septuagint record that God said, *"ego eimi ho On"* or *"I am The Being"* to Moses, that is not what he actually said if his words had been properly translated to Greek. This is either another attempt at the *"reverse engineering"* of the Hebrew Scriptures, or perhaps the Christians that penned the Septuagint could not properly read the Hebrew of Exodus chapter 3.

Let me explain. What the Almighty said to Moses was in the Hebrew language and also used a different verb tense. He said to Moses in Hebrew, *Ehyeh Asher Ehyeh,* which cannot possibly be translated, *I am that I am* or *I am who I am*. This phrase must be (and I repeat must be) translated, *I will be who I will Be*. Jesus did not say, "before Abraham was, I will be." Jesus mistakenly used the first person present tense, but God, when speaking to Moses, used the first person future tense. Even, what the King James Version records that God told Moses, *"Thus shalt thou say unto the children of Israel, I AM has sent me unto you,"* is incorrect. When God told Moses to tell them who had sent him, He repeated the same word, *"Ehyeh"* or *"I WILL BE."*

The translators of the King James and the Christian Septuagint are forced to use the present tense, not because the Hebrew Bible does but because either Jesus misspoke or the writer of the gospel of John made a mistake. Either Jesus or John did not know how to read the Hebrew of Exodus chapter 3. If they had been able to read the Hebrew, they

---

4 There is another fact to consider about the words of Jesus recorded in John. The author of John never states that he is an eyewitness, while Moses was.

would have rendered the verb correctly but they did not. This resulted in the confusing mishmash of statements. If Jesus were the *Eternal Being* then he would have been at the burning bush and would have known what was said there.

When your pastor preaches on the *"I AM"* statements of Jesus and tries to steer you into the belief that Jesus was saying that he was God, remember the clear translation of Exodus three's Hebrew Text, "*I WILL BE WHO I WILL BE.*"

In reality, Jesus was not trying to say that he was the Almighty here or anywhere else in the New Testament. These attempts are probably the invention of the authors. If he was the Almighty, and he was trying to announce who he was, then he would have done so in a way to remove all doubt. That is not what we see in the New Testament. The only thing we see is innuendo, circumlocution and confusion from Jesus.

The God of Abraham, Isaac and Jacob, was not afraid to assert that He was the Creator. He was not shy and openly admitted that there was none greater than Him. He was not inhibited. His character doesn't change. God appeared to the entire Nation of Israel at one time. I surmise that Jesus, on the other hand, did not succeed, if he ever actually made an effort, to convince anyone that he was God. Jesus warns his disciples not to tell others that he is *the Messiah*. If he were God, why would he care? No one could possibly defeat his plan, could they?

The final word is that if Jesus were on trial being accused of being God there wouldn't be enough evidence for a conviction.

CHAPTER 8

Paul: Apostle or Pretender Prophet

Christians should know that the New Testament supposedly is based on the Hebrew Bible. Very few Christians have studied their Bible well enough to discover that many ideas in the New Testament don't actually agree with or originate in the Hebrew Bible.

Among the writers of the New Testament, no one contributed more material than the man known as the Apostle Paul. Of the twenty-seven books of the New Testament, Paul authored thirteen of them. Christians even at times refer to their religion as Pauline Christianity. As a matter of fact, Paul penned much of his material before the Gospels were written. Paul is introduced to the Apostles in the fifteenth chapter in the Book of Acts as one of the partners of a miracle working team.

Ignorance of the Torah allowed Paul to deceive the Apostles

Then all the multitude kept silence, and gave audience to Barnabas and Paul, declaring what miracles and wonders God had wrought among the Gentiles by them. (Acts 15:12)

Isn't it strange that instead of being introduced as great teachers of the law, their credibility is based on the miracles and wonders that were being accomplished through them? Per our discussion earlier in this book as to the qualifications of a prophet we learned not only that a prophet was a man that did miraculous signs or foretelling of future events but he also had to be a stickler when it came to agreeing with and teaching others to follow the way to walk in the Torah or instructions of God. Were the Apostles unaware of these rules in the Torah? Was the Council of Acts 15 comprised of unlearned men?

Now when they saw the boldness of Peter and John, and perceived that they were unlearned and ignorant men, they marvelled; and they took knowledge of them, that they had been with Jesus. (Acts 4:13)

There is other evidence of ignorance in the early church. When Stephen was chosen as one of the first deacons, it is said that he was a man full of faith and of the Holy Ghost in Acts 6:5 but it says nothing of his education. How versed in the Hebrew Bible were these men in the early church? When Stephen was being questioned by the Jewish Elders as to defend his being accused of blasphemy he makes the following statement during a very long sermon that he gives in their presence.

Then sent Joseph, and called his father Jacob to him, and all his kindred, threescore and fifteen souls. So Jacob went down into Egypt, and died, he, and our fathers, And were carried over into Sychem (Shechem), and laid in the sepulchre that Abraham bought for a sum of money of the sons of Emmor the father of Sychem (Shechem). (Acts

CHAPTER 8

7:14-16)

There are two major problems here with what Stephen says. The first thing is that there were seventy-five (threescore and fifteen) souls that came from Canaan to Egypt. This is incorrect. The number recorded in the Hebrew Bible is seventy not seventy-five.

And the sons of Joseph, which were born him in Egypt, were two souls: all the souls of the house of Jacob, which came into Egypt, were threescore and ten. (Genesis 46:27)

It was a shock to me when I found out about this glaring error in the recounting of history. The second thing wrong with the statement of Stephen is that he indicates that Joseph was buried in a field that Abraham bought from Shechem but that is incorrect. It was Jacob that purchased the sepulcher not Abraham as we see in this passage.

And the bones of Joseph, which the children of Israel brought up out of Egypt, buried they in Shechem, in a parcel of ground which Jacob bought of the sons of Hamor the father of Shechem for an hundred pieces of silver: and it became the inheritance of the children of Joseph. (Joshua 24:32)

This passage tells us the details of the field and cave that Abraham bought.

*And Ephron dwelt among the children of Heth: and **Ephron the Hittite** answered Abraham in the audience of the children of Heth, even of all that went in at the gate of his city, saying, Nay, my lord, hear me: the field give I thee, and the cave that is therein, I give it thee; in the presence of the sons of my people give I it thee: bury thy dead. And Abraham bowed down himself before the people of the land. And he spake unto Ephron in the audience of the people of the land, saying, But if thou wilt give it, I pray thee, hear me: I will give thee money for the field; take it of me, and I will bury my dead there. And Ephron answered Abraham, saying unto him, My lord, hearken unto me: the land is worth four hundred shekels of silver; what is that betwixt me and thee? bury therefore thy dead. And Abraham hearkened unto Ephron; and Abraham weighed to Ephron the silver, which he had named in the audience of the sons of Heth, four hundred shekels of silver, current money with the merchant. And the field of Ephron, which was in Machpelah, which was before Mamre, the field, and the cave which was therein, and all the trees that were in the field, that were in all the borders round about, were made sure Unto Abraham for a possession in the presence of the children of Heth, before all that went in at the gate of his city. And after this, Abraham buried Sarah his wife in the cave of the field of Machpelah before Mamre: the same is **Hebron** in the land of Canaan. And the field, and the cave that is therein, were made sure unto Abraham for a possession of a buryingplace by the sons of Heth. (Genesis 23:10-20)*

I can understand Stephen making this mistake but there is more going on in this passage than meets the eye. Immediately, before Stephen launches into his sermon there are several strange statements made about Stephen.

And Stephen, full of faith and power, did great wonders and miracles among the people.*[1]** *Then there arose certain of the synagogue, which is called the synagogue of the Libertines, and Cyrenians, and Alexandrians, and of them of Cilicia and of Asia, disputing with Stephen.* ***And they were not able to resist the wisdom and the spirit by which he spake. *Then they suborned men, which said, We have heard him speak*

---

[1] Although this statement is made about Stephen performing great wonders and miracles, there are no details given. It seems strange to me that a better record would have been written here because he is heralded as the first *martyr*.

blasphemous words against Moses, and against God. And they stirred up the people, and the elders, and the scribes, and came upon him, and caught him, and brought him to the council, And set up false witnesses, which said, This man ceaseth not to speak blasphemous words against this holy place, and the law: For we have heard him say, that this Jesus of Nazareth shall destroy this place, and shall change the customs which Moses delivered us. **And all that sat in the council, looking stedfastly on him, saw his face as it had been the face of an angel.** *(Acts 6:8-15)*

The words recorded here lead us to see that Stephen not only spoke under the power of the Holy Spirit but also the Elders "*saw his face as it had been the face of an angel.*" If this man was speaking under the power of the Holy Spirit and received words directly from God then how did he make such serious mistakes in his sermon? If you are wondering why I would ask this question, let me remind you of the words of Jesus himself when he said to his disciples:

And when they bring you unto the synagogues, and unto magistrates, and powers, take ye no thought how or what thing ye shall answer, or what ye shall say: For the Holy Ghost shall teach you in the same hour what ye ought to say. (Luke 12:11,12)

Did the Holy Spirit make mistakes when the words were given to Stephen or was he uneducated and simply did not know for sure what the details of the history of Israel were when he recounted it to the Elders? Take note that Jesus didn't say that one should learn about the words of the Torah, so the Holy Spirit could bring them to your remembrance. He said the Holy Spirit would teach you what to say when you need the words. This didn't happen, although this was a man full of *power.*

This may seem like a small point to make but if these men were uneducated then they were vulnerable to Paul's advanced knowledge and sly ways. They could have easily been misled by him. This is not the best example to be found in the New Testament regarding our sometimes ignorant cast of characters. Before I finish the story of Stephen let's take a short trip down a rabbit trail to examine the confused erroneous statements of Jesus. Jesus makes a historical blunder in the gospels. The passage is found in Mark, the second chapter.

And he said unto them, Have ye never read what David did, when he had need, and was an hungred, he, and they that were with him? How he went into the house of God in the days of Abiathar the high priest, and did eat the shewbread, which is not lawful to eat but for the priests, and gave also to them which were with him? And he said unto them, The sabbath was made for man, and not man for the sabbath: (Mark 2:25-27)

One sabbath, the Disciples and Jesus are walking through a field. The Disciples take heads of grain in their hands and rubbing them together to remove the husks, performing what the Pharisees consider to be work. The Pharisees object so Jesus defends them. During a short speech about David and the eating of the showbread, Jesus makes a huge historical mistake. This is the story of David as presented in the Hebrew Bible.

Then came David to Nob to Ahimelech the priest: and Ahimelech was afraid at the meeting of David, and said unto him, Why art thou alone, and no man with thee? And David said unto Ahimelech the priest, The king hath commanded me a business, and hath said unto me, Let no man know any thing of the business whereabout I send thee, and what I have commanded thee: and I have appointed my servants to such and such a place. Now therefore what is under thine hand? give me five loaves of bread in mine hand, or what there is present. And the priest answered David, and said, There is no common bread under mine hand, but there is hallowed bread; if the young men have kept themselves at least from women. And David answered the priest, and said unto him, Of a truth women have been kept from us about these three days, since I came out, and the vessels of the young men are holy, and the bread is in a manner common, yea, though it were sanctified this day in the vessel. So the priest gave him hallowed bread: for there was no bread there but the shewbread, that was taken from before the LORD, to put hot bread in the day when it was taken away. (1 Samuel 21:1-6)*

Jesus tells this story to illustrate that there are times when the commandments are to be broken. When this event occurred, Abiathar was not High Priest. Many Christian apologists have defended Jesus but the facts remain. During the event the only priest mentioned was Ahimelech. His son Abiathar is not mentioned until much later after Saul kills Ahimelech.

Even in the broader context, Abiathar only has a small role and isn't involved in the least in the story that Jesus is referring to. Never once in the Hebrew Scriptures is it recorded in exact words that Abiathar was High Priest. I cannot help but conclude that Jesus was wrong. One apologist indicates that if Jesus had made a blunder of this magnitude the Pharisees would have immediately called him on the misstatement. This assumes that this incident actually occurred in the first place. If Mark, the first one to pen his gospel, had concocted this story and he himself believed that Abiathar was the High Priest then it is easy to understand why the Pharisees didn't react to the mistake then it is easy to understand why he would not write down any reaction from the Pharisees. Besides, are we to believe that instead of being at the Temple or a synagogue on the sabbath the *Pharisees* have little to do but follow Jesus around and harass him?

Mark is the only one of the synoptic gospels that mentions Abiathar in his text. Perhaps the other authors omitted the offending mistake and solved the problem for their readers. Even if this is not the case, this misstatement of Jesus is not helpful when Christians try to prove their doctrine of inerrancy. Let's, now, continue with the story of Stephen.

Paul involved in a Stephen's Death

*When they heard these things, they were cut to the heart, and they gnashed on him with their teeth. But he, being full of the Holy Ghost, looked up stedfastly into heaven, and saw the glory of God, and Jesus standing on the right hand of God, And said, Behold, I see the heavens opened, and the Son of man standing on the right hand of God. Then they cried out with a loud voice, and stopped their ears, and ran upon him with one accord, And cast him out of the city, and stoned him: and the witnesses laid down their clothes at a young man's feet, **whose name was Saul**. And they stoned Stephen, calling upon God, and saying, Lord Jesus, receive my spirit. And he kneeled down, and cried with a loud voice, Lord, lay not this sin to their charge. And when he had said this, he fell asleep. **And Saul was consenting unto his death**. And at that time there was a great persecution against the church which was at Jerusalem; and they were all scattered abroad throughout the regions of Judaea and Samaria, except the apostles. And devout men carried Stephen to his burial, and made great lamentation over him. **As for Saul, he made havock of the church, entering into every house, and haling men and women committed them to prison.** (Acts 7:54-8:3)*

When Stephen was finished with his history lesson and condemnation of the Elders, he is attacked by them. It seems that he was physically assaulted and the Elders may have actually bit him with their teeth.

This strikes me as a unbelievable surreal event. Is the author trying to paint a picture that the Jewish Elders are like a pack of wild dogs? Finally, he is driven out of the city where he is stoned to death.

This is worth noting. All this occurs in and around Jerusalem which is still under siege and the control of the Romans. Are we to believe that when Jesus is tried, the Sanhedrin is powerless to put Jesus to death because the Roman Government has taken away their right to execute criminals but suddenly only a short time later they could stone to death a man for insulting them? This is not the only unbelievable thing going on here.

Paul, being employed by the Elders (most likely the Sadducees), is on a manhunt going door to door, *making havoc*, and throwing anyone associated with *the church* in prison. It stretches reality for me to believe that the Romans, who wanted to maintain peace and control in order to collect taxes for the Emperor, would allow this young renegade Pharisaical Rabbi Saul to roam around Jerusalem with a band of soldiers making trouble by *entering into every house*, as the passage says. I doubt that this was allowed to happen.

Was Paul Important in his Time?

The problem in determining Paul's importance is that we have no idea if any of these things or things similar to these actually happened. No other historian that lived in the time of Paul wrote about him. Much like in Jesus' case we have no external sources that we could rely on to validate any of these claims that are made in the New Testament about Paul. We also can't verify anything that Paul claims in his writing about himself or his conversion story. The New Testament contains three different accounts of Paul's conversion that do not agree with one another. Originally, I was going to spend some time on Paul's conversion but after much thought I decided it was outside the scope of this book which was to be about the contrasts between the Hebrew and Christian concepts of the Messiah.

Paul's Outlandish Thoughts on the Role of Messiah

Paul said many strange things in his writings but I want to point out one of the most egregious things Paul says regarding the concept of the role of messiah. Here is a passage from Paul's letter to the Galatians.

Knowing that a man is not justified by the works of the law, but by the faith of Jesus Christ, even we have believed in Jesus Christ, that we might be justified by the faith of Christ, and not by the works of the law: for by the works of the law shall no flesh be justified. But if, while we seek to be justified by Christ, we ourselves also are found sinners, is therefore Christ the minister of sin? God forbid. For if I build again the things which I destroyed, I make myself a transgressor. For I through the law am dead to the law, that I might live unto God. I am crucified with Christ: nevertheless I live; yet not I, but Christ liveth in me: and the life which I now live in the flesh I live by the faith of the Son of God, who loved me, and gave himself for me. I do not frustrate the grace of God: for if righteousness come by the law, then Christ is dead in vain. (Galatians

2:16-21)

Paul is saying here that literally obeying the law or behaving righteously doesn't make one righteous. Righteousness can actually come from a couple of reasons. Paul says that Christ's faith, as in the actual faith that Jesus possesses, and his death make men righteous not their keeping of the law. Also he says that if you are righteous (or justified and made righteous) you better not get caught sinning because you are making Christ the minister of sin. Remember Paul believed that the New Covenant had been instituted by Christ which took away man's sin nature. Paul believes that men should be able to walk daily without sinning because they have died to the law, and without the law, sin's power is broken. Paul also goes head first into the pool of perversion of God's Word and writes,

For if I build again the things which I destroyed, I make myself a transgressor. For I through the law am dead to the law, that I might live unto God. I am crucified with Christ: nevertheless I live; yet not I, but Christ liveth in me."

He has torn down the law (he is dead to it) and if he actually builds up (exalts and obeys) the law he becomes a transgressor (sinner) again. Paul distances Christ (*Messiah*) from the law and he stands against the entirety of the Hebrew Scriptures and God Himself by doing so. Paul is saying that it makes one a sinner to obey the letter of the law. When the end-times-king that Christians refer to as *The Messiah* is shown to us, and he sits on the throne of God in Jerusalem, he will teach the entire world the Torah or the teachings of God. Paul will be so disappointed but I doubt anyone will notice.

Paul is Hard to Understand

I have met many Christians that have expressed their frustration and disagreement with Paul. Their disagreements range from how he treats the law to his tendency to appear confusing to the point of becoming incomprehensible. Paul embodies the idea of being too smart for one's own good. A few have even expressed that they believe he condones the telling of lies to spread the good news of Jesus. Others express that they can't understand Paul and don't think they ever will.

Personally, I can almost ignore all the previous reasons for disliking Paul. My biggest problem with Paul is that he won't accurately quote the Hebrew Bible. I believe Paul shows disdain for God's word by continually doing surgery on it, often tossing out functioning parts and replacing them with cancerous masses.

While I will discuss some of the numerous times when Paul misuses the Hebrew Scriptures, first I would like to bring out a point that few if any have addressed about his writings.

In the Torah, we see patterns. The Torah specifically emphasizes choosing life. We see this on many levels. We see that the commandments are geared to prolong one's life. Many times, the commandments tell us what to do in order to protect us and nurture our relationship with God and our fellow man. This is one passage most Christians have heard read that is used in the fight against abortion.

I call heaven and earth to record this day against you, that I have set before you life and death, blessing and cursing: therefore choose life, that both thou and thy seed may live: (Deuteronomy 30:19)

This verse is actually found inside a much larger passage that most Christians have not examined. This is the passage that provides context to the previous verse.

The secret things belong unto the LORD our God: but those things which are revealed belong unto us and to our children for ever, that we may do all the words of this law. And it shall come to pass, when all these things are come upon thee, the blessing and the curse, which I have set before thee, and thou shalt call them to mind among all the nations, whither the LORD thy God hath driven thee, And shalt return unto the LORD thy God, and shalt obey his voice according to all that I command thee this day, thou and thy children, with all thine heart, and with all thy soul; That then the LORD thy God will turn thy captivity, and have compassion upon thee, and will return and gather thee from all the nations, whither the LORD thy God hath scattered thee. If any of thine be driven out unto the outmost parts of heaven, from thence will the LORD thy God gather thee, and from thence will he fetch thee: And the LORD thy God will bring thee into the land which thy fathers possessed, and thou shalt possess it; and he will do thee good, and multiply thee above thy fathers. And the LORD thy God will circumcise thine heart, and the heart of thy seed, to love the LORD thy God with all thine heart, and with all thy soul, that thou mayest live. And the LORD thy God will put all these curses upon thine enemies, and on them that hate thee, which persecuted thee. And thou shalt return and obey the voice of the LORD, and do all his commandments which I command thee this day. And the LORD thy God will make thee plenteous in every work of thine hand, in the fruit of thy body, and in the fruit of thy cattle, and in the fruit of thy land, for good: for the LORD will again rejoice over thee for good, as he rejoiced over thy fathers: If thou shalt hearken unto the voice of the LORD thy God, to keep his commandments and his statutes which are written in this book of the law, and if thou turn unto the LORD thy God with all thine heart, and with all thy soul. For this commandment which I command thee this day, it is not hidden from thee, neither is it far off. It is not in heaven, that thou shouldest say, Who shall go up for us to heaven, and bring it unto us, that we may hear it, and do it? Neither is it beyond the sea, that thou shouldest say, Who shall go over the sea for us, and bring it unto us, that we may hear it, and do it? But the word is very nigh unto thee, in thy mouth, and in thy heart, that thou mayest do it. See, I have set before thee this day life and good, and death and evil; In that I command thee this day to love the LORD thy God, to walk in his ways, and to keep his commandments and his statutes and his judgments, that thou mayest live and multiply: and the LORD thy God shall bless thee in the land whither thou goest to possess it. But if thine heart turn away, so that thou wilt not hear, but shalt be drawn away, and worship other gods, and serve them; I denounce unto you this day, that ye shall surely perish, and that ye shall not prolong your days upon the land, whither thou passest over Jordan to go to possess it. I call heaven and earth to record this day against you, that I have set before you life and death, blessing and cursing: therefore choose life, that both thou and thy seed may live: That thou mayest love the LORD thy God, and that thou mayest obey his voice, and that thou mayest cleave unto him: for he is thy life, and the length of thy days: that thou mayest dwell in the land which the LORD sware unto thy fathers, to Abraham, to Isaac, and to Jacob, to give them. (Deuteronomy 29:29 -30:20)

In this passage, we see that Moses associates obedience not belief with choosing life. We can also see in the passage that disobedience will lead to curses and obedience leads to blessings. Therefore, obedience leads to life and disobedience leads to death. When we choose obedience we are choosing life but by choosing disobedience we are choosing death.

There is no mention in this passage of belief in any messiah or any similar concept. If God had this plan of belief in the messiah in the works, why did he deceive Israel and drill into them the thought to obey his teaching? Remember, Israel is supposed to be a light to the world. Did God instruct Israel to teach the entire world an erroneous concept? Even the words of Jesus point to salvation coming from the Jews and in other places he places great importance on keeping the commandments.

And, behold, one came and said unto him, Good Master, what good thing shall I do, that I may have eternal life? And he said unto him, Why callest thou me good? there is none good but one, that is, God: but if thou wilt enter into life, keep the commandments. (Matthew 19:16,17)

Jesus himself ties obedience of the commands of God to obtaining eternal life. Why didn't Paul know this? Wasn't he speaking for God? We also see in the Deuteronomy passage above that the word (God's Torah or instruction) is near us and we do not need anyone to go to heaven and return with special understanding in order to obey the instructions of God. In other words, we do not need an angel or God's son to bring us an explanation of the commandments so we could obey. This is because unlike the words of Jesus and/or Paul which are almost impossible to understand, the words of the Torah are simple enough for children to comprehend. The Torah is very easily followed, where Paul's writings in particular are as difficult to decipher as messages from Germany's Enigma Machine.

These are some examples of Paul's hard to understand writings.

I am crucified with Christ: nevertheless I live; yet not I, but Christ liveth in me: and the life which I now live in the flesh I live by the faith of the Son of God, who loved me, and gave himself for me. (Galatians 2:20)

And...

Know ye not, brethren, (for I speak to them that know the law,) how that the law hath dominion over a man as long as he liveth? For the woman which hath an husband is bound by the law to her husband so long as he liveth; but if the husband be dead, she is loosed from the law of her husband. So then if, while her husband liveth, she be married to another man, she shall be called an adulteress: but if her husband be dead, she is free from that law; so that she is no adulteress, though she be married to another man. Wherefore, my brethren, ye also are become dead to the law by the body of Christ; that ye should be married to another, even to him who is raised from the dead, that we should bring forth fruit unto God. For when we were in the flesh, the motions of sins, which were by the law, did work in our members to bring forth fruit unto death. But now we are delivered from the law, that being dead wherein we were held; that we should serve in newness of spirit, and not in the oldness of the letter. What shall we say then? Is the law sin? God forbid. Nay, I had not known sin, but by the law: for I had not known lust, except the law had said, Thou shalt not covet. But sin, taking occasion by the commandment, wrought in me all manner of concupiscence. For without the law sin was dead. For I was alive without the law once: but when the commandment came, sin revived, and I died. And the commandment, which was ordained to life, I found to be unto death. For sin, taking occasion by the commandment, deceived me, and by it slew me. Wherefore the law is holy, and the commandment holy, and just, and good.

(Romans 7:1-12)

What person can really comprehend these passages? Paul is saying that as long as a man is alive to the Torah or God's Teachings he is sinning because he is not relying on Jesus, but if a man *dies to the law* he can live and bear fruit. Did I miss something? What is meant by the allegory of the two husbands? Is Paul saying that God our first husband died but Christians are married to Jesus now? Is Paul saying that God and Jesus are playing *Good God, Bad God?*

Paul is saying that Christians are adulterers if we try to obey the law when you are relying on Jesus. This idea is ludicrous. I can no longer consider this line of reasoning without at least a chuckle welling up in me. Sometimes when I read things like this that Paul wrote, I almost roll on the floor!

If we boil this thinking down to its basic elements, to put it simply, Paul is teaching that it is unrighteousness to obey the letter of the law but to believe in Jesus is pure righteousness.

This is completely contrary to the plain and simple words of God but Christians rely on Paul's words for their doctrine, even if they can't understand them.

What is to be made of his statement, *"For without the law sin was dead"?* Does Paul mean that when Cain killed Abel it wasn't a sin because the Law had not been given yet? After Paul spews out his pathetic and illogical discourse against the Law, he concludes with the statement, *"Wherefore the law is holy, and the commandment holy, and just, and good."* Is Paul being double-tongued?

It is unimaginable to think that Moses could have even spoke once in any manner similar to this. This is a radical departure from the way God had instructed to walk in, a way that they were told not to veer off of, either to the right or the left. They were to be careful and follow the *letter of the law* but you would never know it from the way Paul teaches. This is how Israel was instructed to obey the Law.

Ye shall observe to do therefore as the LORD your God hath commanded you: ye shall not turn aside to the right hand or to the left. Ye shall walk in all the ways which the LORD your God hath commanded you, that ye may live, and that it may be well with you, and that ye may prolong your days in the land which ye shall possess. Now these are the commandments, the statutes, and the judgments, which the LORD your God commanded to teach you, that ye might do them in the land whither ye go to possess it: That thou mightest fear the LORD thy God, to keep all his statutes and his commandments, which I command thee, thou, and thy son, and thy son's son, all the days of thy life; and that thy days may be prolonged. Hear therefore, O Israel, and observe to do it; that it may be well with thee, and that ye may increase mightily, as the LORD God of thy fathers hath promised thee, in the land that floweth with milk and honey. Hear, O Israel: The LORD our God is one LORD: And thou shalt love the LORD thy God with all thine heart, and with all thy soul, and with all thy might. And these words, which I command thee this day, shall be in thine heart: And thou shalt teach them diligently unto thy children, and shalt talk of them when thou sittest in thine house, and when thou walkest by the way, and when thou liest down, and when thou risest up. And thou shalt bind them for a sign upon thine hand, and they shall be as frontlets between thine eyes. And thou shalt write them upon the posts of thy house, and on thy gates. And it shall be, when the LORD thy God shall have brought thee into the land which he sware unto thy fathers, to Abraham, to Isaac, and to Jacob, to give thee great and goodly cities, which thou buildedst not, And houses full of all good things, which thou filledst not, and wells digged, which thou diggedst not, vineyards and olive trees, which thou plantedst not; when thou shalt have eaten and be full; Then beware lest thou forget the LORD, which brought thee forth out of the land of Egypt, from the house of bondage. Thou shalt fear the LORD thy God, and serve him, and shalt swear by his name. Ye shall not go after other gods, of the gods of the people which are round about you; (For the LORD thy God is a jealous God among you) lest the anger of the LORD thy God be kindled against thee, and destroy thee from off the face of the earth. Ye shall not tempt the LORD your God, as ye tempted him in Massah. Ye shall diligently keep the commandments of the LORD your God, and his testimonies, and his statutes, which he hath commanded thee. And thou shalt do that which is right and good in the sight of the LORD: that it may be well with thee, and that thou mayest go in and possess the good land which the LORD sware unto thy fathers. (Deuteronomy 5:32-6:18)

Nowhere in the Hebrew Bible is the Torah or God's Instructions ever spoken about in a bad light. Paul can't seem to make up his mind how he thinks he should regard the Torah.

There is something else going on here in this passage that one cannot see if one doesn't study Greek. It is the New Testament's use of the Greek word *Nomos* for *Law*. In Hebrew, the word translated as *Law* is *Torah*. It actually means *instruction* or *teaching* not *Law* as represented in the New Testament. Paul and Jesus did not approach the concept of *Torah* from a Hebrew perspective. They present a skewed view of it. To present *Torah* from proper perspective they would have used a form of the Greek word *didache*. The word *didache* means *teaching* and is used throughout the New Testament. The King James Translators rendered it as *doctrine*. What's amazing is that Paul being a *supposed Torah observant Rabbi* only uses the word *Torah (didache)* six times in the entirety of his writings. These are the verses where Paul uses this Greek word.

But God be thanked, that ye were the servants of sin, but ye have obeyed from the heart that form of doctrine (didache) which was delivered you. (Romans 6:17)

Now I beseech you, brethren, mark them which cause divisions and offences contrary to the doctrine (didache) which ye have learned; and avoid them. (Romans 16:17)

Now, brethren, if I come unto you speaking with tongues, what shall I profit you, except I shall speak to you either by revelation, or by knowledge, or by prophesying, or by doctrine (didache)? (1 Corinthians 14:6)

How is it then, brethren? when ye come together, every one of you hath a psalm, hath a doctrine (didache), hath a tongue, hath a revelation, hath an interpretation. Let all things be done unto edifying. (1 Corinthians 14:26)

Preach the word; be instant in season, out of season; reprove, rebuke, exhort with all longsuffering and doctrine (didache). (2 Timothy 4:2)

Holding fast the faithful word as he hath been taught (didache), that he may be able by sound doctrine (didaskalia) both to exhort and to convince the gainsayers. (Titus 1:9)

We can only guess what was going on in Paul's thought processes. Had Paul rejected the *Torah (Instructions)* that God had delivered to Moses and substituted what he believed to be a new set of teachings, specifically believing in the death and resurrection of Jesus? What was the *didache* that Paul had delivered to the *Gentile* believers? Maybe this verse will give us a taste of what Paul taught.

For all have sinned, and come short of the glory of God; Being justified by his grace through the redemption that is in Christ Jesus: Whom God hath set forth to be a propitiation through faith in his blood, to declare his righteousness for the remission of sins that are past, through the forbearance of God; To declare, I say, at this time his righteousness: that he might be just, and the justifier of him which believeth in Jesus. Where is boasting then? It is excluded. By what law? of works? Nay: but by the law of faith. Therefore we conclude that a man is justified by faith without the deeds of the law. (Romans 3:23-28)

While Paul is writing to Gentiles, he reduces God's Instructions to a set of ordinances that have been annulled replacing them with this *law of faith* in Christ Jesus. This is also the first use of the concept of blood that Paul uses in Romans. While we never see the *law of faith* explained in any concrete terms, we see Paul remove the emphasis on covenant, obedience and faithfulness, and he replaces them all with the blood of Jesus. As Paul sees it, the Gentiles have no use for the covenant. They don't need circumcision or the *Torah (instructions of God)*. These things presented by Paul are new teachings and are foreign to the Hebrew Bible. So, are we to believe that Paul is justified in bringing a new set of teachings that informs Gentiles how to have a relationship with the Almighty?

It is difficult for me to accept that Paul believed that until now God had not addressed a way for Gentiles to come to God so that they also could become God's children. Did God address the possibility in the Hebrew Scriptures? Did God foretell of a messiah that would come in order for the Gentiles to believe in and receive *salvation* through him?

God actually did address this through the prophet Isaiah. God probably doesn't think very highly of Paul's thoughts on the relationship between Gentiles and the Covenant and Torah. This is a passage from Isaiah.

Thus saith the LORD, Keep ye judgment, and do justice: for my salvation is near to come, and my righteousness to be revealed. Blessed is the man that doeth this, and the son of man that layeth hold on it; that keepeth the sabbath from polluting it, and keepeth his hand from doing any evil. Neither let the son of the stranger, that hath joined himself to the LORD, speak, saying, The LORD hath utterly separated me from his people: neither let the eunuch say, Behold, I am a dry tree. For thus saith the LORD unto the eunuchs that keep my sabbaths, and choose the things that please me, and take hold of my covenant; Even unto them will I give in mine house and within my walls a place and a name better than of sons and of daughters: I will give them an everlasting name, that shall not be cut off. Also the sons of the stranger, that join themselves to the LORD, to serve him, and to love the name of the LORD, to be his servants, every one that keepeth the sabbath from polluting it, and taketh hold of my covenant; Even them will I bring to my holy mountain, and make them joyful in my house of prayer: their burnt offerings and their sacrifices shall be accepted upon mine altar; for mine house shall be called an house of prayer for all people. The Lord GOD which gathereth the outcasts of Israel saith, Yet will I gather others to him, beside those that are gathered unto him. (Isaiah 56:1-8)

How many Christians have read this? Doesn't Paul think that the Words of God are true and sufficient? If this Jesus was such a great prophet where are his writings? Why did a man that wrote such highly confusing language have to give us Jesus' theology? Why couldn't have this new theology been delivered by a man that wrote in such simple understandable language like Moses? Paul is always qualifying every thought with high-minded words, hardly ever writing short easily digestible sentences. Even Peter, the disciple that Jesus left the keys to the Kingdom to, had difficulty following Paul's writings.

And account that the longsuffering of our Lord is salvation; even as our beloved brother Paul also according to the wisdom given unto him hath written unto you; As also in all his epistles, speaking in them of these things; **in which are some things hard to be understood,** *which they that are unlearned and unstable wrest, as they do also the other scriptures, unto their own destruction. (2 Peter 3:15,16)*

I don't remember Peter saying, anywhere, that Moses' writings were hard to understand, and that's coming from an unlearned fisherman (Acts 4:13)! I, myself, got tired of fellow church teachers always adding to Paul's words, "What I think Paul meant to say here was..."

Consider this! If God wanted to make sure you understood the way to have abundant life and have a relationship with him would he send someone like Paul to give you His words? Personally, I can understand Moses but Paul, well, I digress.

Believe me, every pastor will tell you that Paul is misunderstood but, of course, they understand what he really means. The problem is you would be hard pressed to find any two pastors that agree on what he did mean by his words. Paul did not transmit his meaning through successive generations through an unbroken chain, so those who try to guess what he meant are actually speculating, using interpretation methods of their own choice, which makes understanding of his words **very** subjective. This brings to mind a couple of strange New Testament verses.

Howbeit when he, the Spirit of truth, is come, he will guide you into all truth: for he shall not speak of himself; but whatsoever he shall hear, that shall he speak: and he will shew you things to come. (John 16:13)

But the anointing which ye have received of him abideth in you, and ye need not that any man teach you: but as the same anointing teacheth you of all things, and is truth, and is no lie, and even as it hath taught you, ye shall abide in him. (1 John 2:27)

According to these verses, we should all know what the truth is because the Holy Spirit should teach each of us all of the truth. Being that all truth is universal, we should all agree. To make double sure, the last verse says that not only will this *anointing* teach you all things, these teachings will not be lies. This, unfortunately, is not the case, as we all know, or we would all be able to understand Paul's writings, and, of course, they would agree with the former sayings of God in his Hebrew Bible.

Strangely enough, there is more evidence of Paul's true attitude toward the Instructions of God. Paul uses the Greek *nomos* eighty-nine times in his writing. This doesn't include instances in the letter to the Hebrews which I don't believe Paul could have written. Paul doesn't look at the Torah as a set of teachings. He looks at them as if they were street signs that can be taken down or modified as he sees fit. But this is a far cry from the words of Jesus as we read in one of the gospels.

Think not that I am come to destroy the law, or the prophets: I am not come to destroy, but to fulfil. For verily I say unto you, Till heaven and earth pass, one jot or one tittle shall in no wise pass from the law, till all be fulfilled. Whosoever therefore shall break one of these least commandments, and shall teach men so, he shall be called the least in the kingdom of heaven: but whosoever shall do and teach them, the same shall be called great in the kingdom of heaven. For I say unto you, That except your righteousness shall exceed the righteousness of the scribes and Pharisees, ye shall in no case enter into the kingdom of heaven. (Matthew 5:17-20)

Jesus certainly disagrees with Paul in this passage. Not only is Jesus saying that the *Law* will continue until all is fulfilled but he is also saying that its proper interpretation is essential. This is indicated in the phrase *"but to fulfil,"* as this is an idiom that means to interpret correctly. We can know this because Jesus launches immediately into a session of explaining what he believes to be a proper interpretation of the commandment of *not to kill*.

Paul Twists the Scriptures and Creates Theology out of Thin Air

While it is not my intention to bring to light every misuse or misquote of the Hebrew Bible that Paul wrote, I will show what I think can be considered the most egregious. Almost stealthily, Paul makes the error of misquoting scripture and magically creates theology out of thin air. Paul creates many new concepts that he indicates are in the Hebrew Bible. He must do this to justify the need for Jesus' sacrifice. It is worth noting that Paul's "quotes" from the Hebrew Bible agree at times with the Christian Septuagint. But other times, he just goes his own way, not even accurately reflecting the Hebrew Bible. His methodology with actually quoting scripture is similar to his interpretation of it: he will use or twist any scripture any way he chooses to prove his point! Remember that Paul's letters were supposedly written before the Gospels.

The following is a great example of how Paul wields the Hebrew Scriptures not as a scalpel but as a machete.

And so all Israel shall be saved: as it is written, There shall come out of Sion the Deliverer, and shall turn away ungodliness from Jacob: (Romans 11:26)

vs.

And the Redeemer shall come to Zion, and unto them that turn from transgression in Jacob, saith the LORD. (Isaiah 59:20)

By changing a word here and there, Paul does a disservice to God and His Word. Paul makes the deliverer turn away ungodliness instead of coming to those who themselves turned from transgression. Such simple changes could fool the Gentiles that Paul was so devoted to saving. Instead of Paul becoming a contemporary Jonah[2] and instructing the sinners to repent, Paul offers deceit and lies. Maybe this explains this verse that came from Paul's pen.

For if the truth of God hath more abounded through my lie unto his glory; why yet am I also judged as a sinner? (Romans 3:7)

---

2 It is also worth noting that the main teaching in the book of Jonah is repentance. There is no mention of any blood sacrifices being preached to the people of Nineveh.

CHAPTER 8

Perhaps Paul had been accused of lying and misusing Scripture and he is attempting to defend himself in this passage. Of course, when you read the statements of Paul, like this one, you find that you think you are beginning to understand what he is saying then suddenly he takes a left turn leaving the reader in the aftermath to wonder, *"What just happened?"*

Paul would get along very well with the Democratic Party because Paul was actually very liberal. Paul says that he spoke Hebrew but read and quoted the Greek Septuagint instead of the Hebrew Scriptures. His habit of trading simple understandable words for difficult philosophical arguments makes the situation almost unbearable, making the reader wonder if they or the writer is more intelligent. His use of high-minded language is almost condescending at times.

Paul stands in sharp contrast to Moses. Moses spoke in easy to understand concrete physical terms and concepts while Paul didn't. It is no wonder that philosophy reigns supreme in the modern church because Paul himself was the first to introduce philosophy to it.

Paul at times shows complete contempt for the Torah. At times he twists the simple meaning of important passages in an attempt to make a point and the result is the revelation of how dishonest he will be to promote Jesus.

In a letter to the Galatians, Paul tries to make a point that has continued to astound me. This passage is hard to stomach especially since a supposed intellectually superior rabbi penned it. This one takes the cake.

Now to Abraham and his seed were the promises made. He saith not, And to seeds, as of many; but as of one, And to thy seed, which is Christ. And this I say, that the covenant, that was confirmed before of God in Christ, the law, which was four hundred and thirty years after, cannot disannul, that it should make the promise of none effect. For if the inheritance be of the law, it is no more of promise: but God gave it to Abraham by promise. Wherefore then serveth the law? It was added because of transgressions, till the seed should come to whom the promise was made; and it was ordained by angels in the hand of a mediator. (Galatians 3:16-19)

Paul discusses the seed of Abraham in his passage but he does a little wordplay. Paul performs some magic on the word *seed* which is a collective noun referring to all of Abraham's children and transforms it to a singular reference applying to Jesus only. Do you think he ever read the following verses?

And he said unto Abram, Know of a surety that thy seed shall be a stranger in a land that is not theirs, and shall serve them; and they shall afflict them four hundred years; (Genesis 15:13)

That in blessing I will bless thee, and in multiplying I will multiply thy seed as the stars of the heaven, and as the sand which is upon the sea shore; and thy seed shall possess the gate of his enemies; (Genesis 22:17)

And in thy seed shall all the nations of the earth be blessed; because thou hast obeyed my voice. (Genesis 22:18)

And I will make thy seed to multiply as the stars of heaven, and will give unto thy seed all these countries; and in thy seed shall all the nations of the earth be blessed;

(Genesis 26:4)

And thy seed shall be as the dust of the earth, and thou shalt spread abroad to the west, and to the east, and to the north, and to the south: and in thee and in thy seed shall all the families of the earth be blessed. (Genesis 28:1)

Surely these verses cannot be construed as meaning a singular person. Paul throws away the inheritance of the entire nation of Israel and gives it to Jesus. Now, the inheritance of Israel can only be accessed through belief in Jesus. Could Paul have not been well read in the Torah? The poor Galatians probably didn't realize that they had been duped. I wonder what the Jews would have said about this. This is clearly adding to God's Torah and forbidden by God Himself. But this isn't the end of the perversion. This is developed into the concept of *being in Christ*.

Therefore if any man be in Christ, he is a new creature: old things are passed away; behold, all things are become new. (2 Corinthians 5:17)

Paul introduces another new concept to the church in this passage. This is in odds with everything that the Hebrew Scriptures teach. This phrase *in Christ* or anything similar is foreign to the Torah or the Hebrew Scriptures. Remember that there can be no legitimate prophet that can bring a new way to have a relationship with God. It is forbidden to teach another way to follow, other than what was already revealed in the Torah. Even if Paul had displayed miracles, he would still be only a false prophet because he disregards the Torah or Instructions of God.

What follows are more verses that contain more of the same by Paul concerning this false teaching of being *in Christ*.

Being justified freely by his grace through the redemption that is in Christ Jesus: (Romans 3:24)

For though ye have ten thousand instructors in Christ, yet have ye not many fathers: for in Christ Jesus I have begotten you through the gospel. (1 Corinthians 4:15)

For this cause have I sent unto you Timotheus, who is my beloved son, and faithful in the Lord, who shall bring you into remembrance of my ways which be in Christ, as I teach every where in every church. (1 Corinthians 4:17)

Then they also which are fallen asleep in Christ are perished. (1 Corinthians 15:18)

If in this life only we have hope in Christ, we are of all men most miserable.(1 Corinthians 15:19)

For as in Adam all die, even so in Christ shall all be made alive. (1 Corinthians 15:22)

But I fear, lest by any means, as the serpent beguiled Eve through his subtilty, so your minds should be corrupted from the simplicity that is in Christ.(2 Corinthians 11:3)

Simplicity in Christ? What simplicity? Paul offers no simplicity when it comes to providing instructions to the Church. He only offers confusing, complex and conflicting teachings. Below is more Scripture twisting courtesy of Paul.

What shall we say then? That the Gentiles, which followed not after righteousness, have attained to righteousness, even the righteousness which is of faith. But Israel, which followed after the law of righteousness, hath not attained to the law of righteousness. Wherefore? Because they sought it not by faith, but as it were by the works of the law. For they stumbled at that stumblingstone; As it is written, Behold, I lay in Sion a stumblingstone and rock of offence: and whosoever believeth on him shall not be ashamed. (Romans 9:30-33)

Paul makes a stumblingstone out of the foundation stone which disagrees with the passage in Isaiah. Whatever the context is, Paul doesn't seem to mind if he rips it out and twists it into an almost unrecognizable mass that says something totally unrelated.

Therefore thus saith the Lord GOD, Behold, I lay in Zion for a foundation a stone, a tried stone, a precious corner [stone], a sure foundation: he that believeth shall not make haste. (Isaiah 28:16)

Again Paul misquotes God's Words recorded by Isaiah and makes this stone into a metaphor for Jesus without justification. The following is another example.

For Christ is the end of the law for righteousness to every one that believeth. For Moses describeth the righteousness which is of the law, That the man which doeth those things shall live by them. But the righteousness which is of faith speaketh on this wise, Say not in thine heart, Who shall ascend into heaven? (that is, to bring Christ down from above:) Or, Who shall descend into the deep? (that is, to bring up Christ again from the dead.) But what saith it? The word is nigh thee, even in thy mouth, and in thy heart: that is, the word of faith, which we preach; That if thou shalt confess with thy mouth the Lord Jesus, and shalt believe in thine heart that God hath raised him from the dead, thou shalt be saved. For with the heart man believeth unto righteousness; and with the mouth confession is made unto salvation. For the scripture saith, Whosoever believeth on him shall not be ashamed. (Romans 10:4-11)

It seems that we have discussed part of this passage before but not actually. Paul makes a complete mess out of this text. Paul introduces his misquote with the phrase, *"For Christ is the end of the law for righteousness to every one that believeth."* Contrary to what many Christians teach, Paul is not saying that Christ results in doing away with the Law. He is saying, the goal or end result of the Law is Christ. He goes on to say that Moses taught that there was a righteousness that resulted from following God's Law or Teachings and his statement is correct. Then Paul really departs from the logic and truth of the Hebrew Scriptures and starts going off into left field. He butchers the Hebrew Scripture text that he is supposedly quoting and weaves Jesus into the cloth he is trying to make. This is the way that he performs his bait and switch. This is Paul admitting he is not teaching what Moses taught. He is admitting to changing the Torah. This is a fatal mistake and is enough to make me throw out every word that Paul wrote. So should you!

Let's examine the two scriptures side by side and see the differences. By doing a side-by-side reading we will reveal the violence against God's Word that Paul has committed.

This is the passage Paul bases his Romans 10:6-11 on:

For this commandment which I command thee this day, it is not hidden from thee, neither is it far off. It is not in heaven, that thou shouldest say, Who shall go up for us to heaven, and bring it unto us, that we may hear it, and do it? Neither is it beyond the sea, that thou shouldest say, Who shall go over the sea for us, and bring it unto us, that we may hear it, and do it? **But the word is very nigh unto thee, in thy mouth, and in** *thy heart, that thou mayest do it. (Deuteronomy 30:11-14)*

This is Paul's construction of Romans 10:6-11:

But the righteousness which is of faith speaketh on this wise, Say not in thine heart, Who shall ascend into heaven? (that is, to bring Christ down from above:) Or, Who shall descend into the deep? (that is, to bring up Christ again from the dead.) But what saith it? **The word is nigh thee, even in thy mouth, and in thy heart: that is, the word of faith, which we preach; That if thou shalt confess with thy mouth the Lord Jesus, and shalt believe in thine heart that God hath raised him from the dead, thou shalt be saved. For with the heart man believeth unto righteousness; and with the mouth confession is made unto salvation.** *For the scripture saith, Whosoever believeth on him shall not be ashamed. (Romans 10:6-11)*

We can plainly see what Paul has done. Paul removes the phrase in Deuteronomy that states plainly that the *Law* can be obeyed and replaces it with *believing in Jesus*. What possible justification could he have for doing this? He has none.

Remember, Paul is writing to Gentiles and they don't have the advantage of having a good translation of the Hebrew Scriptures that contain these warnings that are found in Deuteronomy.

Now therefore hearken, O Israel, unto the statutes and unto the judgments, which I teach you, for to do them, that ye may live, and go in and possess the land which the LORD God of your fathers giveth you. Ye shall not add unto the word which I command you, neither shall ye diminish ought from it, that ye may keep the commandments of the LORD your God which I command you. (Deuteronomy 4:1,2)

What thing soever I command you, observe to do it: thou shalt not add thereto, nor diminish from it. (Deuteronomy 12:32)

I could continue further with this discourse on Paul's misuse of Scripture and fill many more pages of this book but I have already accomplished my goal of proving my point. Paul is not trustworthy when it comes to handling God's Word and everything he wrote should be rejected.

Paul Turns Others Off

Not only do we find that Paul will misuse the Hebrew Scriptures but also he will disagree with other New Testament authors. Before he gets far into writing his letter to the Romans he makes a statement that would rub two of the gospel writers the wrong way.

Concerning his Son Jesus Christ our Lord, which was made of the seed of David according to the flesh; (Romans 1:3)

Remember, Paul actually wrote these epistles before the gospels were penned. Paul writes that Jesus *"was made the seed of David according to the flesh."* Paul never once in his letters records anything about Jesus' birth other than that he was *"born of a woman."* Matthew and Luke both state that Jesus was born of a virgin.

There are other times when Paul is at odds with Church leadership. During the Council of Jerusalem, the Apostles and James had come up with a formula of basic concessions that the gentile believers would have to make in order to come into the Church. James and the leadership wrote a letter to the Gentiles to explain what was necessary for them to join. This is the passage that contains that letter.

And they wrote letters by them after this manner; The apostles and elders and brethren send greeting unto the brethren which are of the Gentiles in Antioch and Syria and Cilicia:

> *Forasmuch as we have heard, that certain which went out from us have troubled you with words, subverting your souls, saying, Ye must be circumcised, and keep the law: to whom we gave no such commandment: It seemed good unto us, being assembled with one accord, to send chosen men unto you with our beloved Barnabas and Paul, Men that have hazarded their lives for the name of our Lord Jesus Christ. We have sent therefore Judas and Silas, who shall also tell you the same things by mouth. For it seemed good to the Holy Ghost, and to us, to lay upon you no greater burden than these necessary things; That ye abstain from meats offered to idols, and from blood, and from things strangled, and from fornication: from which if ye keep yourselves, ye shall do well. Fare ye well.*

So when they were dismissed, they came to Antioch: and when they had gathered the multitude together, they delivered the epistle: Which when they had read, they rejoiced for the consolation. And Judas and Silas, being prophets also themselves, exhorted the brethren with many words, and confirmed them. (Acts 15:23-32)

There are many problems with this passage. As to the content of the letter, I find it strange that there is no mentioning of what are supposed to be the very basic beliefs of Christianity, such as: repentance from sin; belief in Jesus, or his blood; confession of Jesus' name; confession of Jesus' deity or the commitment to learning Torah (or instructions of God). Why was there no reference to Isaiah's passage about the requirements for Gentiles? If Isaiah 56 required Gentiles to keep the Sabbath and the Covenant, which would have required circumcision for males, why was not one of these requirements listed? This was probably because they didn't think that Gentiles would appreciate those requirements.

The letter did omit the comment James made earlier in Acts chapter 15 when the requirements were assembled as to the fact that Moses is taught in the synagogues each Sabbath. James' hope was probably that the Gentiles would naturally want to learn the Torah if they were sincere in their beliefs. Although this is true, the point I want to make is that Paul agreed with these requirements. Later, Paul would go against the council and drop the requirement of the gentiles not eating meats sacrificed to idols. He leaves the choice up to the Gentile converts in the following passage. He does so under the premise of: if they do it in front of a weaker brother they might offend them and cause them to sin.

As concerning therefore the eating of those things that are offered in sacrifice unto idols, we know that an idol is nothing in the world, and that there is none other God but one. For though there be that are called gods, whether in heaven or in earth, (as there be gods many, and lords many,) But to us there is but one God, the Father, of whom are all things, and we in him; and one Lord Jesus Christ, by whom are all things, and we by him. Howbeit there is not in every man that knowledge: for some with conscience of the idol unto this hour eat it as a thing offered unto an idol; and their conscience being weak is defiled. But meat commendeth us not to God: for neither, if we eat, are we the better; neither, if we eat not, are we the worse. But take heed lest by any means this liberty of yours become a stumbling block to them that are weak. For if any man see thee which hast knowledge sit at meat in the idol's temple, shall not the conscience of him which is weak be emboldened to eat those things which are offered to idols; And through thy knowledge shall the weak brother perish, for whom Christ died? But when ye sin so against the brethren, and wound their weak conscience, ye sin against Christ. Wherefore, if meat make my brother to offend, I will eat no flesh while the world standeth, lest I make my brother to offend. (1 Corinthians 8:4-13)

Paul gives us a lesson in this passage on how we shouldn't reason. He starts out by saying that an idol is nothing and there is only one God and one Christ. He then tries to make a connection between possessing the proper knowledge about God and having the strength of conscience to eat food offered to idols. This is a ridiculous argument. He then instructs one with a strong conscience to not make a brother of lesser conscience stumble. This is nothing short of moral relativism and yet the Church accepts this and at the same time repeats their mantra, *"Truth is the same for everyone!"*

Another question here is what this vague requirement of *"blood"* is. Most Christians want to believe it only prohibits the eating of blood but there are also other commandments in the Torah that pertain to *"blood"*. There is the requirement for a man to refrain from being with their wife during her menstrual cycle. There are requirements for the handling of blood during slaughter of animals. Which of these requirements were they referring to? We may never know. The lack of details in the New Testament is in sharp contrast to the details that exist in the Torah that God gave Moses to deliver to his children.

I have had Christians tell me that the Gentiles only had to follow these requirements. My response was to ask if they were free to lie, disrespect their parents, or use unequal weights and measures with impunity? Christians would, of course, after considering the result, say "No." After all, doesn't God want people to behave properly?

The question as to how Gentiles relate to God and his Torah was already answered in the Hebrew Bible itself. Whether you are an Israelite or not, everyone has their responsibility before God or obligations to keep. The fact that other nations are culpable for their sins before and apart from Israel, as shown in the numerous judgments he has against all the other peoples, like the Caananites, Sodom, Egypt, Assyria, Tyre, makes it clear that the Gentiles have their responsibility. The Hebrew Bible also makes it clear that there is also the opportunity for a Gentile to even become an Israelite through a full conversion. But regardless of what anyone does, Jew or Gentile,

The end of the matter is, let us hear the whole: Fear God, and keep his commandments; for this is the whole [duty] of man. (Ecclesiastes 12:13)

The essence of every person, whether Jew or Gentile, is to identify with Israel and its God. The Gentile should seek to know the one true God, the God of Israel, through whom he learns his obligations to that God, not through individuals like Paul. Problems set in for anyone, Israelite or not, if they have the wrong starting point. If their starting point is not the God of Israel and the Torah as it applies to everyone, but rather their starting point is Jesus or, even worse, Paul, then they miss Ecclesiastes 12:13, their whole purpose and duty. Instead, they take a different route. To use the distorted message of Isaiah in the mouth of Jesus:

This people draweth nigh unto me with their mouth, and honoureth me with their lips; but their heart is far from me. But in vain they do worship me, teaching for doctrines the commandments of men. (Matthew 15:8,9)

The Passover Circumcision Flip-Flop

Basically, according to God's own Words, if one is to eat the Passover meal one must be circumcised if you are male.

And the LORD said unto Moses and Aaron, This is the ordinance of the passover: There shall no stranger eat thereof: But every man's servant that is bought for money, when thou hast circumcised him, then shall he eat thereof. A foreigner and an hired servant shall not eat thereof. In one house shall it be eaten; thou shalt not carry forth ought of the flesh abroad out of the house; neither shall ye break a bone thereof. All the congregation of Israel shall keep it. And when a stranger shall sojourn with thee, and will keep the passover to the LORD, let all his males be circumcised, and then let him come near and keep it; and he shall be as one that is born in the land: for no uncircumcised person shall eat thereof. One law shall be to him that is home born, and unto the stranger that sojourneth among you. (Exodus 12:43-49)

Christians are quick to admit they believe that the last meal that Jesus ate was a Passover and that he said, *"Do this, in remembrance of me."* With that said, let's refresh our memory of how Paul treated the subject of the Passover.

For I have received of the Lord that which also I delivered unto you, That the Lord Jesus the same night in which he was betrayed took bread: And when he had given thanks, he brake it, and said, Take, eat: this is my body, which is broken for you: this do in remembrance of me. After the same manner also he took the cup, when he had supped, saying, This cup is the new testament in my blood: this do ye, as oft as ye drink it, in remembrance of me. For as often as ye eat this bread, and drink this cup, ye do shew the Lord's death till he come. Wherefore whosoever shall eat this bread, and drink this cup of the Lord, unworthily, shall be guilty of the body and blood of the Lord. But let a man examine himself, and so let him eat of that bread, and drink of that cup. (1 Corinthians 11:23-28)

Paul indicates that this information came directly from the Lord. He lays out the basics of the meal removing any resemblance to the Passover, which is a celebration of The Almighty taking Israel out of Egypt. Paul instead associates it only with Jesus' death and the New Covenant. Here is the problem. This meal when it was eaten by Jesus and the disciples was called *Passover*. Paul renames it the *Lord's supper*. He doesn't mention any requirement for the males eating it to be circumcised, instead he creates a subjective standard of "inner worthiness" in order to eat it. He goes as far to say this.

For he that eateth and drinketh unworthily, eateth and drinketh damnation to himself, not discerning the Lord's body. For this cause many are weak and sickly among you, and many sleep. For if we would judge ourselves, we should not be judged. (1 Corinthians 11:29-31)

Do you realize what Paul is saying to these gentiles? He is saying, although the requirement of *inner worthiness* was never given to them before, some are sick and some are dead because they were *not worthy* in some manner when they drank the cup or ate the bread. Remember, Paul has thrown out the requirement for circumcision and he never mentions it to these Gentiles. This is one example of the twisted mind of this false prophet that has lead many people down another path that God never commanded them to go down. Paul gives the Gentiles some sort of substitute for passover yet he keeps the feast and encourages Gentiles to also. The message we get from Paul about passover is confusing.

Paul also presents strange thoughts in other writings concerning circumcision. It would seem to me from his statements, that he doesn't care much for circumcision. What are we to make of statements like these made by Paul.

Is any man called being circumcised? let him not become uncircumcised. Is any called in uncircumcision? let him not be circumcised. Circumcision is nothing, and uncircumcision is nothing, but the keeping of the commandments of God. Let every man abide in the same calling wherein he was called. Art thou called being a servant? care not for it: but if thou mayest be made free, use it rather. (1 Corinthians 7:18-21)

Have you ever read anything so confusing? Paul is acting as if he is being neutral in this passage but he is actually discouraging circumcision. Why would Paul discourage men from being circumcised that are joining themselves to Israel? The Torah and the Prophets contain passages that I have shown that clearly present the fact that a relationship is available to gentiles. Paul steers clear of these passages and presents a totally different way for Gentiles to come to God, that way being Jesus.

Paul's End

I find it hilarious that the New Testament has Paul trying to defend himself from the Jews accusing him of trying to turn God's people from the Torah. This accusation, of course, is true and the Jews are the ones to realize it because they are looking at their Hebrew Scriptures and what Paul is teaching isn't lining up so well.

Regardless, Paul always seems to slither out of being convicted of the crime but several times he narrowly escapes meeting his maker. On one occasion, he manages to be stoned but doesn't actually die from the affair. This is probably why he decided to spend his time reaching out to the Gentiles because they didn't have the pesky copies of the Hebrew Scriptures around to compare to his teaching. The following passage shows Paul not wanting to be judged by the Jews in his defense of teaching against the Law but he appeals to what he believes to be an higher authority.

Now when Festus was come into the province, after three days he ascended from Caesarea to Jerusalem. Then the high priest and the chief of the Jews informed him against Paul, and besought him, And desired favour against him, that he would send for him to Jerusalem, laying wait in the way to kill him. But Festus answered, that Paul should be kept at Caesarea, and that he himself would depart shortly thither. Let them therefore, said he, which among you are able, go down with me, and accuse this man, if there be any wickedness in him. And when he had tarried among them more than ten days, he went down unto Caesarea; and the next day sitting on the judgment seat commanded Paul to be brought. And when he was come, the Jews which came down from Jerusalem stood round about, and laid many and grievous complaints against

Paul, which they could not prove. While he answered for himself, Neither against the law of the Jews, neither against the temple, nor yet against Caesar, have I offended any thing at all. But Festus, willing to do the Jews a pleasure, answered Paul, and said, Wilt thou go up to Jerusalem, and there be judged of these things before me? Then said Paul, I stand at Caesar's judgment seat, where I ought to be judged: to the Jews have I done no wrong, as thou very well knowest. For if I be an offender, or have committed any thing worthy of death, I refuse not to die: but if there be none of these things whereof these accuse me, no man may deliver me unto them. I appeal unto Caesar. Then Festus, when he had conferred with the council, answered, Hast thou appealed unto Caesar? unto Caesar shalt thou go. (Acts 25:1-12)

Paul actually appeals his case to Caesar. What does Paul possibly think that being tried by Caesar can do to clear his name? Is Caesar an observant religious Jew that is an expert on the Torah? Are we to believe that Paul is so important that Caesar has time to try him personally? We may never know what actually happened but Church historians indicate that he was tried and was eventually beheaded as a martyr.

Last Words on Paul

As I see it, Paul started another religion. He rejects Judaism and much of what Jesus taught. As a matter of fact, Paul does little to pass any of the words of Jesus to believers. It has been my experience that the first step in a Christian leaving Christianity is to start questioning the validity of Paul's ramblings. I realize that Christians will probably belittle me and will say that I must be simple-minded and unable to understand what Paul wrote. But when challenged, most serious New Testament scholars will tell you they can't understand Paul either.

Paul is accused in the New Testament of telling people to not get circumcised. This passage is only more evidence of the confusion that Paul is peddling.

Stand fast therefore in the liberty wherewith Christ hath made us free, and be not entangled again with the yoke of bondage. Behold, I Paul say unto you, that if ye be circumcised, Christ shall profit you nothing. For I testify again to every man that is circumcised, that he is a debtor to do the whole law. Christ is become of no effect unto you, whosoever of you are justified by the law; ye are fallen from grace. For we through the Spirit wait for the hope of righteousness by faith. For in Jesus Christ neither circumcision availeth any thing, nor uncircumcision; but faith which worketh by love. Ye did run well; who did hinder you that ye should not obey the truth? This persuasion cometh not of him that calleth you. A little leaven leaveneth the whole lump. I have confidence in you through the Lord, that ye will be none otherwise minded: but he that troubleth you shall bear his judgment, whosoever he be. And I, brethren, if I yet preach circumcision, why do I yet suffer persecution? then is the offense of the cross ceased. I would they were even cut off which trouble you. For, brethren, ye have been called unto liberty; only use not liberty for an occasion to the flesh, but by love serve one another. For all the law is fulfilled in one word, even in this; Thou shalt love thy neighbour as thyself. But if ye bite and devour one another, take heed that ye be not consumed one of another. This I say then, Walk in the Spirit, and ye shall not fulfil the lust of the flesh. For the flesh lusteth against the Spirit, and the Spirit against the flesh: and these are contrary the one to the other: so that ye cannot do the things that ye would. But if ye be led of the Spirit, ye are not under the law. (Galatians 5:1-18)

Paul is writing that he doesn't want the believers in Galatia to be "*entangled again with*

CHAPTER 8

the yoke of bondage." Notice that Paul uses the word *"again"* to indicate that they at one time had began to either have an interest in obeying or actually had obeyed the Torah. Paul reduces the Torah to a *yoke of bondage.* He also uses the phrase *led by the spirit* which he indicates is the opposite of being *under the law.* How could he show disdain for God's Instructions like this and continue to present himself as if he was chosen as *another Moses.* Despite having all these things against him, how does Paul manage to pull the wool over the Gentiles' eyes?

Paul calls himself the *"Apostle to the Gentiles"* and he proves to be wildly successful in his mission. Why is he successful with the Gentiles after being such a dismal failure with the Jews? Paul couldn't have any success with the Jews because the Jews know what God's Torah actually says about what he is teaching. The Jews could not be fooled by his shenanigans because, unlike the gentiles, the Jews have knowledge of the Hebrew Scriptures. The Gentiles didn't have the basis of the Hebrew Scriptures in order to properly analyze Paul's claims. The Gentiles were fooled into believing what he said about their having no need for circumcision or the covenants of the Jews. Paul presents the gentiles with a *New Covenant*. Paul's view of the *New Covenant* is echoed by the author of the book of Hebrews. This type of elementary misunderstanding is hugely problematic to Christianity.

Paul presents many ideas that seem to be at odds with the Torah. If my interpretation of Paul's writings is wrong and I am only misunderstanding them then please consider that most Christians aren't able to understand them either. If you were to assemble ten pastors in a room and poll them on the meanings of Paul's writing, you would probably find most would not agree very often. Why would God lead a man through his Holy Spirit to write using such confusing language and be so different than the authors of the Hebrew Bible? It is not as if we are addressing prophetic passages. These are passages that were written to instruct believers on matters that are essential to everyday living. This is at odds with how God used authors in the Hebrew Bible to instruct his children. The question one needs to ask is, *"Why would God change his method of instruction from clear and precise to clearly confusing?*

This is what we are to believe:

Moses wrote with such easily understandable language and was misunderstood but in order to correct the misunderstanding of the Jews, God enlists someone that can't be understood clearly in his writings.

Does that make sense to you? Does that sound like a loving God? One might decide to try to live out this *New Covenant* by using only the words of Jesus. I have seen some try to do this but as you have read earlier in this book even the words of Jesus contain confusing, contradictory statements. I have not even addressed the fact that if you remove the writings of Paul from the New Testament, there isn't much left. Even using what is left over, Jesus doesn't offer enough information to assemble a systematic theology to live by.

Many have tried to assemble one but all have failed because you are still stuck with many internal and external contradictions that are obviously opposed to the Hebrew Bible.

While most Christians believe that Paul's writings are inspired and directly from God, I disagree totally. Paul sets himself against almost every author in the Hebrew Scriptures and therefore God Himself, and his writings should be considered heresy when weighed against the Hebrew Bible.

Look what happened when Paul addressed circumcision and importance of obedience to the Torah. These are the two most important issues that could be stumbling-blocks that would hinder Gentiles from joining the Jews on what would be a side-by-side adventure and relationship with The Almighty. Paul disregards what the Torah teaches and throws it under the proverbial bus. Any serious Hebrew Bible scholar must realize that Paul's writings must be rejected. That would, of course, be devastating to Christianity, because it would do irreparable damage to the entire New Testament and render it irrelevant.

CHAPTER 9

Satan: God's Servant, Nemesis or...

No good thriller would be complete without the hero of the story having an archenemy. The hero of our story must have an opposing force to constantly do battle with. This struggle will lead to a overwhelming victory by our hero in the end of our story. In the Christian Bible or the New Testament, Satan is seen as a fallen angel, the author of sin and the real cause of man's fall. He is God's enemy. This chapter will answer the question,

"Is Satan God's Servant, Nemesis or...?"

Although the concept of a Satan is very important in Judaism, it has taken on a even higher importance in the New Testament.

A Christian Origin of Satan

Although the idea of a fallen angel named Satan is not mentioned anywhere in the Hebrew Bible or the Old Testament, it is pervasive in the Christian Bible. The word *satan* is used fifteen times in the Hebrew Scriptures, eleven of those times are found in the book of Job alone. In contrast, in the New Testament *Satan* is used thirty four times. The Hebrew word *sah'-tawn* means *adversary.* This does not include any instances where New Testament authors use other names for Satan like *the dragon,* twelve times and *the devil,* thirty six times.

In the Genesis story of man's fall, Christians believe that the serpent in the story is Satan. Christians would quickly tell you that they would bet their life on it. Although there is no reference to Satan and the word never appears in the story, they seem convinced otherwise. For many years, I believed this also but began to see problems with the serpent being Satan. Was the story of a walking talking serpent to be taken literally or was it an allegory? Let's assume, for the sake of argument, that it is a literal story and take a quick look at the serpent to see if there is any reason to believe he is a fallen angel?

Here is the scripture passage.

Now the serpent was more subtil than any beast of the field which the LORD God had made. And he said unto the woman, Yea, hath God said, Ye shall not eat of every tree of the garden? And the woman said unto the serpent, We may eat of the fruit of the trees of the garden: But of the fruit of the tree which is in the midst of the garden, God hath said, Ye shall not eat of it, neither shall ye touch it, lest ye die. And the serpent said unto the woman, Ye shall not surely die: For God doth know that in the day ye eat thereof, then your eyes shall be opened, and ye shall be as gods, knowing good and evil. And when the woman saw that the tree was good for food, and that it was pleasant to the eyes, and a tree to be desired to make one wise, she took of the fruit thereof, and did eat, and gave also unto her husband with her; and he did eat. And the eyes of them both were opened, and they knew that they were naked; and they sewed fig leaves together, and made themselves aprons. And they heard the voice of the LORD God walking in the garden in the cool of the day: and Adam and his wife hid themselves from the presence of the LORD God amongst the trees of the garden. And the LORD God called unto Adam, and said unto him, Where art thou? And he said, I heard thy voice in the garden, and I was afraid, because I was naked; and I hid myself. And he said, Who told thee that thou wast naked? Hast thou eaten of the tree, whereof I commanded thee that thou shouldest not eat? And the man said, The woman whom thou gavest to be with me, she gave me of the tree, and I did eat. And the LORD God said unto the woman, What is this that thou hast done? And the woman said, The serpent beguiled me, and I did eat. And the LORD God said unto the serpent, Because thou hast done this, thou art cursed above all cattle, and above every beast of the field; upon thy belly shalt thou go, and dust shalt thou eat all the days of thy life: And I will put enmity between thee and the woman, and between thy seed and her seed; it shall bruise thy head, and thou shalt bruise his heel. Unto the woman he said, I will greatly multiply thy sorrow and thy conception; in sorrow thou shalt bring forth children; and thy desire shall be to thy husband, and he shall rule over thee. And unto Adam he said, Because thou hast hearkened unto the voice of thy wife, and hast eaten of the tree, of which I commanded thee, saying, Thou shalt not eat of it: cursed is the ground for thy sake; in sorrow shalt thou eat of it all the days of thy life; Thorns also and thistles shall it bring forth to thee; and thou shalt eat the herb of the field; In the sweat of thy face shalt thou eat bread, till thou return unto the ground; for out of it wast thou taken: for dust thou art, and unto dust shalt thou return. And Adam called his wife's name Eve; because she was the mother of all living. Unto Adam also and to his wife did the LORD God make coats of skins, and clothed them. And the LORD God said, Behold, the man is become as one of us, to know good and evil: and now, lest he put forth his hand, and take also of the tree of life, and eat, and live for ever: Therefore the LORD God sent him forth from the garden of Eden, to till the ground from whence he was taken. So he drove out the man; and he placed at the east of the garden of Eden Cherubims, and a flaming sword which turned every way, to keep the way of the tree of life. (Genesis 3:1-24)

This scripture says nothing about Satan but Christians believe there is a reference to him here. The serpent or *nah'-cosh* in Hebrew is introduced here as a beast of the field. The word *beast* is *chai'* in Hebrew and it means *living thing*. The word field is *saw-deh'* and it simply means *land* as in a field or pasture. There seems to be nothing mysterious going on here, if we are considering this to be a literal narrative. According to Rabbi David Fohrman, as well as Rabbi Tovia Singer, what we are seeing here is a walking talking snake, a simple creation of God. Is this so difficult to believe? We don't have any direct evidence presented here to make us believe anything else at this point. So, why must Christians believe this is Satan?

Christians must have tunnel vision to see Satan in this passage. They must ignore some important things revealed in this passage to believe that God's arch-enemy is to be found here or anywhere else in the Hebrew Scriptures. These are a few of the items that they ignore.

- The word *satan* is not to be found in this passage.

- The Serpent is presented as a beast of the field not as an angel or other divine being.

- The Serpent has offspring[1] while angels do not.[2] The concept of angels leaving their proper place and taking wives is inserted into Christianity when Paul found a need to marry *Dualism*[3] to his perverted brand of Judaism.

- There is no implication of this being an angel in another form here or anywhere else in the Hebrew Scriptures.

- The Serpent is punished by having to crawl on its belly and eat dirt for the rest of its life. How could this have any possible correlation to any angel? Does this in any way fit the picture of Satan that is painted in the New Testament?

Christian apologists make a lot of noise when they say it takes more faith to believe that evolution created this world than to simply accept that God created everything. They say the reason it is easy to believe God had his hand in creation is that it is written in his Word. Because of this, I find it puzzling they cannot accept that God says what we have here is simply a beast.

Christians have a hard time, in my experience, even considering the possibility that the Serpent is not the fallen angel that is talked about in the New Testament and referred to as *Satan*. If it is not true that Satan had fallen from heaven with a third of the angels, where did this false doctrine originate? We will answer this question later but now we want to see exactly what the Hebrew Scriptures say about satan.

Everything I needed to know about Satan I didn't learn in Church

Once before in the chapter entitled, *"Is "Who is the Messiah?" the Right Question?"*, I showed each and every scripture in the Hebrew Bible that contained the Hebrew word *Mashiach*. This time I will give to you each occurrence of the Hebrew word *satan*. When I do this, you will see that there aren't actually that many to examine. With each time that the Hebrew word is used I will also display the full form of the word. In other words, if the word is found by itself it will appear as *(satan)* but if the word is preceded by a definite article it will be shown as *(the satan)*.

*And **Satan** (satan) stood up against Israel, and provoked David to number Israel. (1 Chronicles 21:1)*

---

1 Many times God states that beasts reproduce "after their kind." See Genesis 1:21,25; 6:20; 7:14. Christians say they rely on God's Word but when they ignore this primary concept they shoot themselves in the foot and show their real disrespect for the Holiness of the Torah.
2 Although this is true, many unscrupulous people have taught that angels came down and took wives resulting in children hybrids being born. This is an attempt to make this Serpent into an angelic being. It is not in the scope of this book to address this false doctrine. If one searches one will find many articles that address this subject and successfully refute it.
3 Paul was from Tarsus and must have been deeply influenced by Persian Dualism that was taught in his homeland.

CHAPTER 9   *132*

*Set thou a wicked man over him: and let **Satan** (satan) stand at his right hand. (Psalm 109:6)*

There are three other sets of Scriptures that are not listed above. One group contains the same Hebrew word but the translators dared not translate it as Satan because it would interfere with popular Christian theology of the day in 1611.

*And God's anger was kindled because he went: and the angel of the LORD stood in the way for an adversary (**satan**) against him. Now he was riding upon his ass, and his two servants were with him. (Numbers 22:22)*

*And the angel of the LORD said unto him, Wherefore hast thou smitten thine ass these three times? behold, I went out to withstand (**satan**) thee, because thy way is perverse before me: (Numbers 22:32)*

*And the princes of the Philistines were wroth with him; and the princes of the Philistines said unto him, Make this fellow return, that he may go again to his place which thou hast appointed him, and let him not go down with us to battle, lest in the battle he be an adversary (**satan**) to us: for wherewith should he reconcile himself unto his master? should it not be with the heads of these men? (1 Samuel 29:4)*

*And David said, What have I to do with you, ye sons of Zeruiah, that ye should this day be adversaries (**satan**) unto me? shall there any man be put to death this day in Israel? for do not I know that I am this day king over Israel? (2 Samuel 19:22)*

*But now the LORD my God hath given me rest on every side, so that there is neither adversary (**satan**) nor evil occurrent. (1 Kings 5:4)*

*And the LORD stirred up an adversary (**satan**) unto Solomon, Hadad the Edomite: he was of the king's seed in Edom. (1 Kings 11:14)*

*And God stirred him up another adversary (**satan**), Rezon the son of Eliadah, which fled from his lord Hadadezer king of Zobah: (1 Kings 11:23)*

*And he was an adversary (**satan**) to Israel all the days of Solomon, beside the mischief that Hadad did: and he abhorred Israel, and reigned over Syria.. (1 Kings 11:25)*

The other set are the passages found in the Book of Job. They are listed in the section entitled *"The book of Job and "The Satan""* found later in this chapter.

O Lucifer, where art thou?

In the King James Version, in Isaiah 14, there is a passage that contains a name used only once in the Hebrew Bible. The name, of course, is *"Lucifer."* Most Christians haven't heard their pastor read the complete passage from the pulpit. This instead is what most Christians hear read.

*How art thou fallen from heaven, **O Lucifer**, son of the morning! how art thou cut down to the ground, which didst weaken the nations! For thou hast said in thine heart, I will ascend into heaven, I will exalt my throne above the stars of God: I will sit also upon the mount of the congregation, in the sides of the north: I will ascend above the heights of the clouds; I will be like the most High. (Isaiah 14:12-14)*

Christians will quickly point to this passage, that at first glance seems to fit the bill, but after we examine it you may change your mind. These words are from Isaiah in their full context.

*That thou shalt take up this proverb **against the king of Babylon**, and say, **How hath the oppressor ceased! the golden city ceased!** The LORD hath broken the staff of the wicked, and the sceptre of the rulers. He who smote the people in wrath with a continual stroke, he that ruled the nations in anger, is persecuted, and none hindereth. The whole earth is at rest, and is quiet: they break forth into singing. Yea, the fir trees rejoice at thee, and the cedars of Lebanon, saying, Since thou art laid down, no feller is come up against us. Hell from beneath is moved for thee to meet thee at thy coming: it stirreth up the dead for thee, even all the chief ones of the earth; it hath raised up from their thrones all the kings of the nations. All they shall speak and say unto thee, Art thou also become weak as we? art thou become like unto us? Thy pomp is brought down to the grave, and the noise of thy viols: the worm is spread under thee, and the worms cover thee. How art thou fallen from heaven, O Lucifer, son of the morning! how art thou cut down to the ground, which didst weaken the nations! For thou hast said in thine heart, I will ascend into heaven, I will exalt my throne above the stars of God: I will sit also upon the mount of the congregation, in the sides of the north: I will ascend above the heights of the clouds; I will be like the most High. Yet thou shalt be brought down to hell, to the sides of the pit. **They that see thee shall narrowly look upon thee, and consider thee, saying, Is this the <u>man</u> that made the earth to tremble, that did shake kingdoms;** That made the world as a wilderness, and destroyed the cities thereof; that opened not the house of his prisoners? All the kings of the nations, even all of them, lie in glory, every one in his own house. But thou art cast out of thy grave like an abominable branch, and as the raiment of those that are slain, thrust through with a sword, that go down to the stones of the pit; as a carcase trodden under feet. Thou shalt not be joined with them in burial, because thou hast destroyed thy land, and slain thy people: the seed of evildoers shall never be renowned. (Isaiah 14:4-20)*

If I have learned anything it is that context makes or breaks the truth. Sure, you can say that the shortened passage of Isaiah 14:12-14 above is truth, but outside the greater context the truth can become a powerful weapon in the hands of unscrupulous people. Let me make some simple observations. The first thing you should notice is that this was a parable addressed against the King of Babylon, who we know was Nebuchadnezzar. This is Hebrew *hyperbolic prose* [4] to illustrate how God views the situation with the wicked king.

To provide a second witness we also point to the question presented in the passage, **"They that see thee shall narrowly look upon thee, and consider thee, saying, Is this the <u>man</u> that made the earth to tremble, that did shake kingdoms?"** This is consistent with the picture of the conquering King Nebuchadnezzar that we see in the Hebrew Bible narratives. Ask yourself, *"Is Satan a man or an angel? Did Satan ever make the earth tremble?"* This is a poetic picture of Nebuchadnezzar being brought low and the nations seeing it. Did the nations ever see Satan brought low?[5] Remember, Christians

---

4 Hyperbolic Prose is a poetic form that uses hyperbole or exaggeration to make a point hit the mark. Even in the New Testament John uses it in the book of Revelation. Passages such as Revelation 14:20 where we see blood flowing for 1,600 furlongs. This is an example of Hebrew Hyperbole. It is pervasive in the Hebrew Bible and this includes the story prose of Nebuchadnezzar's fall in Isaiah 14.

5 Even in the New Testament when it is supposed that God made an example of Satan and he was defeated on the cross, we see no real difference in Satan's reign or power. He must later be cast into the pit for a thousand years only to be released to bring destruction again upon

teach that the fall of Satan occurred before man ever existed, so how could anyone have observed him falling?

It would be ridiculous to think that Satan is a man. There is nothing in the Hebrew Scriptures to suggest that he is. For those who would think that this had a parallel application to Satan then you should ask yourself where you got this information from! Did you get it from Paul, the twister of the Hebrew Scriptures? Did you get it from your pastor? Did you get it from a televangelist or perhaps your seminary professor?

Christians invent all sorts of *mechanisms* to explain how things that aren't found in the Hebrew Scriptures actually exist there. This is the hidden liberalism of Christianity. Their favorite mechanism, *foreshadowing*, used by New Testament authors as well as theologians, is used to show the relationship between a Hebrew Scripture and some aspect of Jesus' life. This is stretched to the breaking point as we have already seen in chapter 5, *"Examining the "Messianic" Prophecies."* Christian apologists wield this weapon like a machete to cut all bonds to reasoning and use it to explain everything that Jesus did during his lifetime. They invent connections to prophecies that even the writers of the New Testament couldn't have dreamed of.

It's not surprising that Jesus and others in the New Testament use elements of the Hebrew Scriptures to point to Satan in what they saw as prophecies related to him.

Let's return to the immediate subject at hand. Let's revisit the short passage that most Christian pastors use. I want to point out a few things about the passage. The phrase "O Lucifer" is actually best translated as *morning star*. It was a reference to the planet Venus. It was the first light seen in the evening and the last point of light seen in the morning. Nebuchadnezzar saw himself as a divine being and must have associated himself with the planet Venus as we see in this passage. Jesus is also called the *"Morning Star"* in the New Testament in this passage.

I Jesus have sent mine angel to testify unto you these things in the churches. I am the root and the offspring of David, and the bright and morning star. (Revelation 22:16)

Is he somehow related to Satan? You will have to be the judge.

Daniel tells us about Nebuchadnezzar's fall in this passage in Daniel 4.

This is the interpretation, O king, and this is the decree of the most High, which is come upon my lord the king: That they shall drive thee from men, and thy dwelling shall be with the beasts of the field, and they shall make thee to eat grass as oxen, and they shall wet thee with the dew of heaven, and seven times shall pass over thee, till thou know that the most High ruleth in the kingdom of men, and giveth it to whomsoever he will. And whereas they commanded to leave the stump of the tree roots; thy kingdom shall be sure unto thee, after that thou shalt have known that the heavens do rule. Wherefore, O king, let my counsel be acceptable unto thee, and break off thy sins by righteousness, and thine iniquities by shewing mercy to the poor; if it may be a lengthening of thy tranquillity. All this came upon the king Nebuchadnezzar. At the end of twelve months he walked in the palace of the kingdom of Babylon. The king spake, and said, Is not this great Babylon, that I have built for the house of the kingdom by the might of my power, and for the honour of my majesty? While the word was in the king's mouth, there fell a voice from heaven, saying, O king Nebuchadnezzar, to thee it is

---

the Earth and its inhabitants.

spoken; The kingdom is departed from thee. And they shall drive thee from men, and thy dwelling shall be with the beasts of the field: they shall make thee to eat grass as oxen, and seven times shall pass over thee, until thou know that the most High ruleth in the kingdom of men, and giveth it to whomsoever he will. The same hour was the thing fulfilled upon Nebuchadnezzar: and he was driven from men, and did eat grass as oxen, and his body was wet with the dew of heaven, till his hairs were grown like eagles' feathers, and his nails like birds' claws. (Daniel 4:24-32)

Nebuchadnezzar was brought down by the Almighty. He lived like a beast of the field. God did this to him because he thought of himself so highly. There are other passages that tell us that he demanded worship from his subjects. If they didn't worship his image they were thrown in a fiery furnace.

Nebuchadnezzar the king made an image of gold, whose height was threescore cubits, and the breadth thereof six cubits: he set it up in the plain of Dura, in the province of Babylon. Then Nebuchadnezzar the king sent to gather together the princes, the governors, and the captains, the judges, the treasurers, the counsellors, the sheriffs, and all the rulers of the provinces, to come to the dedication of the image which Nebuchadnezzar the king had set up. Then the princes, the governors, and captains, the judges, the treasurers, the counsellors, the sheriffs, and all the rulers of the provinces, were gathered together unto the dedication of the image that Nebuchadnezzar the king had set up; and they stood before the image that Nebuchadnezzar had set up. Then an herald cried aloud, To you it is commanded, O people, nations, and languages, That at what time ye hear the sound of the cornet, flute, harp, sackbut, psaltery, dulcimer, and all kinds of musick, ye fall down and worship the golden image that Nebuchadnezzar the king hath set up: And whoso falleth not down and worshippeth shall the same hour be cast into the midst of a burning fiery furnace. Therefore at that time, when all the people heard the sound of the cornet, flute, harp, sackbut, psaltery, and all kinds of musick, all the people, the nations, and the languages, fell down and worshipped the golden image that Nebuchadnezzar the king had set up. (Daniel 3:1-6)

Nebuchadnezzar was a tyrannical conqueror. God put him in his place after he had come against Israel and taken them into captivity. This man, not *Satan*, is the subject of this passage in Isaiah 14. Let me say that, in Jewish thought Nebuchadnezzar can be seen as **a satan** or **an adversary** to Israel because he actually was their enemy and treated them horribly but the Isaiah passage does not point to any angel that fell from God's abode. Christians will have to look elsewhere to find the evil angel, Satan.

The Anointed Cherub

More often than not, Christians have tunnel vision. I speak from experience. They find a passage and cannot imagine there is anything before or after it that they need to examine to discern the truth. Such is the case with the next passage we will be examining. This passage is presented to Christians as another place where they can find that fallen angel, Satan. This is from the prophet Ezekiel.

The word of the LORD came again unto me, saying, Son of man, say unto the prince of Tyrus, Thus saith the Lord GOD; Because thine heart is lifted up, and thou hast said, I am a God, I sit in the seat of God, in the midst of the seas; yet thou art a man, and not God, though thou set thine heart as the heart of God: Behold, thou art wiser than Daniel; there is no secret that they can hide from thee: With thy wisdom and with thine understanding thou hast gotten thee riches, and hast gotten gold and silver into thy *treasures: By thy great wisdom and by thy traffick hast thou increased thy riches, and thine heart is lifted up because of thy riches: Therefore thus saith the Lord GOD; Because thou hast set thine heart as the heart of God; Behold, therefore I will bring strangers upon thee, the terrible of the nations: and they shall draw their swords against the beauty of thy wisdom, and they shall defile thy brightness. They shall bring thee down to the pit, and thou shalt die the deaths of them that are slain in the midst of the seas. Wilt thou yet say before him that slayeth thee, I am God? but thou **shalt** [6] be a man, and no God, in the hand of him that slayeth thee. Thou shalt die the deaths of the uncircumcised by the hand of strangers: for I have spoken it, saith the Lord GOD. Moreover the word of the LORD came unto me, saying, Son of man, take up a lamentation upon the king of Tyrus, and say unto him, Thus saith the Lord GOD; Thou sealest up the sum, full of wisdom, and perfect in beauty. Thou hast been in Eden the garden of God; every precious stone was thy covering, the sardius, topaz, and the diamond, the beryl, the onyx, and the jasper, the sapphire, the emerald, and the carbuncle, and gold: the workmanship of thy tabrets and of thy pipes was prepared in thee in the day that thou wast created. Thou art the anointed cherub that covereth; and I have set thee so: thou wast upon the holy mountain of God; thou hast walked up and down in the midst of the stones of fire. Thou wast perfect in thy ways from the day that thou wast created, till iniquity was found in thee. By the multitude of thy merchandise they have filled the midst of thee with violence, and thou hast sinned: therefore I will cast thee as profane out of the mountain of God: and I will destroy thee, O covering cherub, from the midst of the stones of fire. Thine heart was lifted up because of thy beauty, thou hast corrupted thy wisdom by reason of thy brightness: I will cast thee to the ground, I will lay thee before kings, that they may behold thee. Thou hast defiled thy sanctuaries by the multitude of thine iniquities, by the iniquity of thy traffick; therefore will I bring forth a fire from the midst of thee, it shall devour thee, and I will bring thee to ashes upon the earth in the sight of all them that behold thee. All they that know thee among the people shall be astonished at thee: thou shalt be a terror, and never shalt thou be any more. (Ezekiel 28:1-19)*

Let me say that there are definitely some very interesting elements in this passage but there are some phrases that must be considered before the big picture is visible. Christians must learn to consider the entire passage and not only the parts that interest them or they will fall prey to false doctrine such as the one currently under investigation. Before we dive into this passage, let's back up a little ways so maybe we won't see only one tree but maybe an entire forest. Immediately before and after this set of verses, the greater context reveals something that most Christians and their pastors miss.

In chapter 25, Ezekiel begins with other prophecies against other lands and peoples starting with Ammon progressing through Moab then Edom and finally ending with the Philistines. In chapter 26 we see the actual start of the prophecies against Tyre. We can see that Tyre was a real place here on Earth, not a celestial kingdom of some evil angel. The prophecies we see in chapter 28 were not written in a vacuum. They are book-ended by other passages that create a context that contains much more information than the supposed verses that Christians believe that are about Satan. The right hand book-end is found immediately after our passage in question. It contains prophecies again Sidon. Then what follows is a prophecy about Israel's ingathering. Then there is a set of

---

6 The word "shalt" is not found in the Hebrew. It has been added to make this future and not present tense in attempt to mislead the reader.

prophecies about Egypt that extend to chapter 32. Then we have a lament or dirge against Pharoah (another leader like the King of Tyre) similar to what we see in chapter 28 against Tyre. If you have never read any of these other chapters you should stop and do so now.

This prophecy which Christians think is about Satan, is sandwiched between others that tell of what God will do to other nations. Let's examine it carefully to see first which elements do not sound like they apply to Satan. There are a myriad of issues here in this passage of hyperbolic prose. Because it is outside of the scope of this book to discuss all of them here, I will only touch on the salient points which negate the possibility of the subject of this dirge being about the Satan we find in the New Testament. The main point of this book is to reveal the truth about what Christianity teaches about Jesus and if he is the end-times-king. Any information and conclusions I present only bolsters arguments that I present in the rest of the book. Here is a list of passage elements that show that this passage is about an actual mortal man not a fallen angel.

- Again, in this dirge we are talking about a mortal man. *"Thus saith the Lord GOD; Because thine heart is lifted up, and thou hast said, I am a God, I sit in the seat of God, in the midst of the seas;* **yet thou art a man**, *and not God, though thou set thine heart as the heart of God:"*

- God announces how the prince of Tyrus will be punished, *"Behold, therefore I will bring strangers upon thee, the terrible of the nations: and* **they shall draw their swords** *against the beauty of thy wisdom, and they shall defile thy brightness. They shall bring thee down to the pit, and thou shalt die the deaths of them that are slain in the midst of the seas. Wilt thou yet say before him that slayeth thee, I am God? but thou shalt be a man, and no God, in the hand of him that slayeth thee."* Can men attack Satan with swords and slay him?

- The king of Tyrus will die in this manner, *"Thou shalt die the deaths of the uncircumcised* **by the hand of strangers**.*"* Does this agree with the New Testament that has God throwing Satan in the Lake of fire?[7] It certainly does not. Can Christians ignore this and say they believe God's Word?

- There is a second person this dirge is said over. This person is called *"the king of Tyrus."* Is this the same person as the prince? If not then, are there two fallen angels named Satan? If it is the same person, then this only adds to the fact that this is a man that will die a death like any other man. Either way this is only a mortal man destined for destruction.

- The phrase, *"Thou hast been in Eden the garden of God; every precious stone was thy covering, the sardius, topaz, and the diamond, the beryl, the onyx, and the jasper, the sapphire, the emerald, and the carbuncle, and gold: the workmanship of thy tabrets and of thy pipes*

---

7 *(Revelation 20:10) And the devil that deceived them was cast into the lake of fire and brimstone, where the beast and the false prophet are, and shall be tormented day and night for ever and ever.*

was prepared in thee in the day that thou wast created," is believed to not be referring to Satan by Jesus following Christians in many articles I have read. One of the best dissertations I have found is at www.biblepages.web.surftown.se/ed05e.htm

In this article, the author states,

The phrase "the day when you were made" (some translations have, "the day you were created") will be considered a bit later. Let us first consider the phrase "garden of God" or "garden of the mighty ones" in that verse. Was that man, the ruler of the trading city of Tyre, in Paradise, the true garden of Eden? In the earthly one, or perhaps in the heavenly one? Obviously, the answer is no, to both questions. As the context shows, these words were a part of a mocking song. In such songs, hyperbole is used, even in the Bible. In a similar way, the phrase "garden of God" appears even in Ezekiel 31 where "the Assyrian" was described as "a beautiful cedar tree".

The author says much more in his words of explanation about this subject and I suggest that you read the entire article in order to understand the concepts touched on here. Another possible explanation to the question here is that in this attempt (and success) to mock the king. It could be that the phrase about the garden is presented as a rhetorical question that sounds similar to this, *"Where you in the garden of Eden ... when you were created?"*

- The same article addresses the phrase,

    "Thou art the anointed cherub that covereth; and I have set thee so: thou wast upon the holy mountain of God; thou hast walked up and down in the midst of the stones of fire. Thou wast perfect in thy ways from the day that thou wast created, till iniquity was found in thee."

    It is an interesting read and his explanation is too long to give full reference here. When reading this article, keep in mind that this is a Christian writing this article and not a unbeliever or atheist.

- The following phrase should confuse any Christian if they think it is about Satan.

    By the multitude of thy merchandise they have filled the midst of thee with violence, and thou hast sinned: therefore I will cast thee as profane out of the mountain of God: and I will destroy thee, O covering cherub, from the midst of the stones of fire.

    This part of the passage is certainly interesting as it sounds nothing like Satan. That would be because the entire passage has nothing to do with him. Tyre was a city on the water that traded much merchandise. Did Satan ever trade in merchandise that caused him to sin? Christians believe instead that Satan was jealous of God and wanted to murder Him in order to place himself above God. Any rational person would have to say that this is totally unrelated to anything to do with an angel.

I have to wonder if most Christians can logically process any of this because even I didn't until a handful of years ago. It takes many years of study and prayer to come to an understanding of the truth. I pray that if you are a Christian at the time you are reading this that you ignore your first reaction to discount the things I have discussed with you in this book. Don't fall back on your teachings about Jesus and fail to examine these passages logically.

When I was in the Messianic Movement, a good friend approached me about the problems that he saw when he had started looking at the *Messianic* prophecies in the Hebrew Scriptures. He, of course, was starting to see that *prophecies* like the passages we have discussed in this chapter were being taken out of context. My response was, *"Don't worry about it. Jesus is the context."* How wrong I was.

I always regrettably think back to what I said but then I am immediately comforted by the fact that my friend has followed the path I did and has left Christianity also. There are those who are reading this book that will carefully consider this book and change the course they are on. Are you one of these, or are you a person that will lay this book down, right now, and never give it another thought?

What else do the Hebrew Scriptures have to say about Satan? To be honest, there isn't much more that it actually does say. We are almost finished going down this rabbit hole and will soon get back to the more primary subject.

The Book of Job and "The Satan"

Christians believe two things: Satan is the embodiment of sin and that sin cannot enter in God's presence. That is not what we see in the book of Job. We observe what appears to be an **obedient** Satan or adversary enter into God's presence in the book of Job. The real problem is that there is no angel named *Satan* found anywhere in the entire book. Below are all of the verses found in Job that contain the occurrences of the word, *Satan.*

*Now there was a day when the sons of God came to present themselves before the LORD, and **Satan (the satan)** came also among them. (Job 1:6)*

*And the LORD said unto **Satan (the satan)**, Whence comest thou? Then Satan **(the satan)** answered the LORD, and said, From going to and fro in the earth, and from walking up and down in it. (Job 1:7)*

*And the LORD said unto **Satan (the satan)**, Hast thou considered my servant Job, that there is none like him in the earth, a perfect and an upright man, one that feareth God, and escheweth evil? (Job 1:8)*

*Then **Satan (the satan)** answered the LORD, and said, Doth Job fear God for nought? (Job 1:9)*

*And the LORD said unto **Satan (the satan)**, Behold, all that he hath is in thy power; only upon himself put not forth thine hand. So **Satan (the satan)** went forth from the presence of the LORD. (Job 1:12)*

Again there was a day when the sons of God came to present themselves before the LORD, and **Satan** *(**the satan**) came also among them to present himself before the LORD. (Job 2:1)*

And the LORD said unto **Satan (the satan)**, *From whence comest thou? And Satan answered the LORD, and said, From going to and fro in the earth, and from walking up and down in it. (Job 2:2)*

And the LORD said unto **Satan (the satan)**, *Hast thou considered my servant Job, that there is none like him in the earth, a perfect and an upright man, one that feareth God, and escheweth evil? and still he holdeth fast his integrity, although thou movedst me against him, to destroy him without cause. (Job 2:3)*

And **Satan (the satan)** *answered the LORD, and said, Skin for skin, yea, all that a man hath will he give for his life. (Job 2:4)*

And the LORD said unto **Satan (the satan)**, *Behold, he is in thine hand; but save his life. (Job 2:6)*

So went **Satan (the satan)** *forth from the presence of the LORD, and smote Job with sore boils from the sole of his foot unto his crown. (Job 2:7)*

Although you won't notice it in most any Christian Bible, every occurrence of the Hebrew word *satan* in Job is attached to the definite article *the*.[8] Every time one reads the word *Satan* in Job, one must realize that it was purposely mistranslated and should have been rendered *the satan* or the *adversary*. The word *satan* is not being used here as a personal name.

Could it be that the conversations between God and this adversary is an allegorical view of what the author of Job thought must have occurred in Heaven before Job was tested? One major rabbinical opinion does see Job as an allegorical representation of every man and his situation illustrates how God tests each of us. No one can be sure if it is purely allegorical or not but this is not the question to be answered in this section. The question to be answered would have to be, *"Is this a fallen angel with the proper name Satan?"*

Based on the evidence I see here, there is no doubt to me that this certainly is not Satan as the New Testament presents him. The burden of proof is on Christianity including the New Testament writers in this case. They are the ones making the ridiculous assertion and they have no supporting evidence. It seems to me that what we have, in this case and many other places where an adversary is portrayed in the Hebrew Scriptures, is a misunderstanding carried to an extreme that culminates in the creation of a heretical doctrine.

The Lord rebuke thee, the satan!

We have come to the third set of special *satan* Scriptures. At times, one must get beyond the pompous King James language to see what's really going on behind the scenes. Sometimes you must wade through the muck, reach down deep and then pull hard to find the pearls.

And he shewed me Joshua the high priest standing before the angel of the LORD, and

---

8 In Hebrew a definite article is shown by placing a the Hebrew Letter *Hay* before the word.

Satan *(the satan) standing at his right hand to* **resist him (satan)**. *(Zechariah 3:1)*

And the LORD said unto **Satan** *(the satan), The LORD rebuke thee, O* **Satan** *(the satan); even the LORD that hath chosen Jerusalem rebuke thee: is not this a brand plucked out of the fire? (Zechariah 3:2)*

The two Scriptures follow in context.

And he shewed me Joshua the high priest standing before the angel of the LORD, and Satan standing at his right hand to resist him. And the LORD said unto Satan, The LORD rebuke thee, O Satan; even the LORD that hath chosen Jerusalem rebuke thee: is not this a brand plucked out of the fire? Now Joshua was clothed with filthy garments, and stood before the angel. And he answered and spake unto those that stood before him, saying, Take away the filthy garments from him. And unto him he said, Behold, I have caused thine iniquity to pass from thee, and I will clothe thee with change of raiment. And I said, Let them set a fair mitre upon his head. So they set a fair mitre upon his head, and clothed him with garments. And the angel of the LORD stood by. And the angel of the LORD protested unto Joshua, saying, Thus saith the LORD of hosts; If thou wilt walk in my ways, and if thou wilt keep my charge, then thou shalt also judge my house, and shalt also keep my courts, and I will give thee places to walk among these that stand by. Hear now, O Joshua the high priest, thou, and thy fellows that sit before thee: for they are men wondered at: for, behold, I will bring forth my servant the BRANCH. For behold the stone that I have laid before Joshua; upon one stone shall be seven eyes: behold, I will engrave the graving thereof, saith the LORD of hosts, and I will remove the iniquity of that land in one day. In that day, saith the LORD of hosts, shall ye call every man his neighbour under the vine and under the fig tree. And the angel that talked with me came again, and waked me, as a man that is wakened out of his sleep,   *(Zechariah 3:1-4:1)*

I am almost tempted to say "Step back folks! Nothing to see here," but I think this passage does deserve a little ink to be spilled over it.

The situation addressed in this passage is that a man named Joshua is being opposed as high priest, because there is a *stain* in his family. First, when we read this passage, we must realize this is a vision that the prophet Zechariah experiences and not an actual historical event. The "stain" on Joshua's family was that his sons had married non-Jewish wives. This is where we learn this:

And among the sons of the priests there were found that had taken strange wives: namely, of the sons of Jeshua (Joshua) the son of Jozadak, and his brethren; Maaseiah, and Eliezer, and Jarib, and Gedaliah. (Ezra 10:18)

The angel says in poetic language to remove the *stain* on Joshua's sons they must put away their strange wives. It is no doubt that these women did not behave as other women from other nations had done as in the story of Ruth. Ruth was a Moabite but she had embraced the God of Israel even before she married Boaz. The women in question in this passage must have still been worshiping their foreign gods.

This passage is about the ones, whomever he/they are, that are opposing Joshua's priesthood and not about any fallen angel. It again is Hebrew hyperbolic prose and not a historical account. This satan or adversary is a symbol of those opposing Joshua, the high priest and not a fallen angel.

CHAPTER 9

The Best for Last

As we can see from the evidence that I have presented in this chapter there is no evidence in the Hebrew Scriptures that there is any fallen angel named *Satan* as we see in the New Testament.

Most Christians become angry when they read anything like this. I know that I did. I thought that it would have exhibited great stupidity to even propose the thoughts I have laid out here to you.

I am sure that this must be frustrating to some Christians reading this but nevertheless it must be dealt with. You will either examine it and weigh all of the details against what you currently believe or ignore it as most do.

Before I close this chapter, I want to point out one more passage. Early in this chapter I presented a single scripture that showed Satan influencing a king of Israel to perform a census or numbering of Israel. If you don't recall it and don't want to look back in this chapter to locate it, this is it.

*And **Satan** (satan) stood up against Israel, and provoked David to number Israel. (1 Chronicles 21:1)*

If you noticed that there is no definite article attached to the Hebrew word *satan* then you are very observant. Now for the shocker that I have saved for the finale of this chapter. Committed Christians, please pay close attention. If you really want to believe that Satan is a fallen angel that is in total rebellion against God then read this next verse very carefully and let it sink in.

And again the anger of the LORD was kindled against Israel, and he moved David against them to say, Go, number Israel and Judah. (2 Samuel 24:1)

Did God move this satan to influence David to do something that David was not to do or is God being called an adversary? In all honesty, I do not think for one moment that because of these two scriptures we can say that God is *Satan* (as defined in the New Testament) but it is possible for Him to become our adversary or *a satan* if we act in opposition to him.

I believe that we all have our own adversary. The Jewish sages call it the *yetzer hara* or the evil inclination. Some have called it the *evil creative desire.*

All men have a desire to create or dominate others and things. When men give into these *drives* or *desires* and let them control them disregarding the instructions of God then evil is born in our will and sin is committed. This is actually shown to us very early in the Torah. The following set of verses show us God teaching an individual an important truth. A truth so important that it is presented to us in the early chapters of Genesis. This particular person, who we can see as a representative of every human being that has ever lived, failed to learn from this Torah or instruction and became a chilling reminder of the serious consequences of not directing our desires in the right direction.

And in process of time it came to pass, that Cain brought of the fruit of the ground an offering unto the LORD. And Abel, he also brought of the firstlings of his flock and of the fat thereof. And the LORD had respect unto Abel and to his offering: But unto Cain and to his offering he had not respect. And Cain was very wroth, and his countenance fell. And the LORD said unto Cain, Why art thou wroth? and why is thy countenance fallen? If thou doest well, shalt thou not be accepted? and if thou doest not well, sin lieth at the door. And unto thee shall be his desire, and thou shalt rule over him. (Genesis 4:3-7)

What God is saying to Cain in modern language is not too much different than what I have said to my children many times.

"What are you upset about? Stop and think! You know that you are letting the desires you have inside control you. If you don't learn to direct your desires instead of letting them direct you, you will end up continually sinning. Regardless of what has happened in the past, it's not as bad as you think! If you stop going the way you are and turn around, I will forgive you! Never forget, you have the power to rule over your desires."

The desires inside us aren't a bad thing. It's when they become the driver and we let them take us where they will that the problem begins. That is what leads to sin being conceived and eventually it will be born. This is our personal *satan or adversary*.

God gave us our desires in order to test us. He also gave us the free will to allow us to overcome them. That's when true righteousness is realized, when we have chosen to do what is in agreement with God's instructions. True righteousness isn't poured on our exterior or imputed to us as Christianity has come to teach. Without our free will and our ability to allow or disallow our desires to control us, there could be no real righteousness or wickedness. The reward or punishment for our actions would all become absurd.

Without free will, we would simply be like any other animal, like the serpent in the garden, only able to choose to do according to our instincts or desires that drive us. I believe this is the point of the story of the snake in the garden. The snake could hear only one voice, his instincts tied together with stimuli from his environment but we as children of Adam have our instincts and an additional voice that we can hear, God's *Torah* or *Instructions*.[9] We are blessed greatly because of this difference between us and the animals.

We see a seamless teaching in God's *Torah*, which I have adopted as the guide for my life. From the story of Adam and Eve in the garden to the final statements of Moses we see that a gracious God has given each of us the power to overcome and defeat our own real worst *adversary* or *satan*, our inner desires ... if we are willing.

The real test in life is to make one desire the strongest and most prominent: the desire to obey God. That desire must be nurtured and carefully developed as it does not come naturally. Then and only then can we easily defeat our personal *satan*.

---

9 I credit Rabbi David Fohrman for this conclusion.

CHAPTER 10

Crucifying the Resurrection

Before I actually get into this chapter, I want to reiterate a very important thought. Christians believe that the New Testament is the word of God. It is the only source of the details and description of events we are studying in this chapter. Although Christians believe the New Testament is true when viewed as a single document they also hold that each book stands by itself as truth. What if one gospel presentation portrays one event in opposition to another? I am not speaking of minor complementary detail differences but major themes, such as on which day the crucifixion occurred. This one major principle difference will be discussed shortly.

How did we arrive at the contents of the New Testament? Specifically, who decided which of the many gospels in circulation would be included in the New Testament? It is commonly known that the Tanach or Hebrew Bible was canonized by the Jewish People but they had nothing to do with the canonization of the New Testament. Men that Christians refer to as the Church Fathers used reasons like there being only four winds or four directions for having only four gospels. Also such archaic reasoning as this: there were only four elements so there would be no need for more than four gospels. The real reason was because the four gospels chosen were already the most popular in circulation. If you analyze the gospels in a parallel fashion, one can only come to the conclusion that none of these Church Fathers had actually studied them for logical contradictions especially in the subject matter we now address.

God indicates more than once, as we have discussed earlier in this book, that the gentile nations will come to the Jews to learn the truth, not the other way around. I always found it strange that the Jewish people were not involved in the formation of the New Testament. If God indicates that his chosen people would be the guardians of the truth, why have they no interest in the story of the Christian Jesus? Instead, men, that were at best antisemitic and at worst outright hateful enemies of the Jews and their Hebrew Scriptures, tried to replace or suppress the Hebrew Scriptures that the Jews had given their lives at times to protect, preserve and pass down to their posterity. The need to critically examine the subject matter found in the New Testament is important. The apostles thought what we are looking at now, the resurrection of Jesus, is the most important subject... **in time and space!**

Paul not only thought that the resurrection was important but to him it was the zenith of the Christian religion. Paul put this forward to illustrate his thought.

And if Christ be not raised, your faith is vain; ye are yet in your sins. (1 Corinthians 15:17)

I remember once, while I sat in my father's living room on a particular Easter morning, our family was reading through the accounts of the crucifixion and resurrection in the different gospels. We were trying to reconcile the different accounts when I realized either there must have been a problem with the New Testament or a problem with me. I decided there must have been a fault in my ability to think clearly because surely the New Testament was true and perfect. I justified this by reasoning that because this is God's Word, there could be no mistakes in it so the error had to be in my thinking.

The major theme of the New Testament is forgiveness of sins through the death of *the Messiah*. Although, it never says anywhere in the Hebrew Scriptures that any *messiah* is required to die for a guarantee for forgiveness, Paul indicates that the resurrection is necessary for forgiveness. Although Jesus mentioned it, he never said that his resurrection was an integral part of the guarantee.

Here is one question that we must consider, *"Did anyone receive forgiveness for sins before Jesus was supposedly crucified and raised from the dead?"* The answer is, *"Yes."*

This is how Christians present the scenario. Starting with Adam, men performed sacrifices for their sins. All these sacrifices were performed in anticipation of *the Messiah* coming and sacrificing himself once and for all. This foreshadowing of *Messiah's* arrival, crucifixion and resurrection is the cornerstone of the Christian faith. Christians use verses, that contain what I would consider to be, at best, veiled references to predict this future savior that will come and accomplish these things. This is probably the most common passage that Christians use to show this future event.

And Isaac spake unto Abraham his father, and said, My father: and he said, Here am I, my son. And he said, Behold the fire and the wood: but where is the lamb for a burnt offering? And Abraham said, My son, God will provide himself a lamb for a burnt offering: so they went both of them together. And they came to the place which God had told him of; and Abraham built an altar there, and laid the wood in order, and bound Isaac his son, and laid him on the altar upon the wood. (Genesis 22:7-9)

The way Christians read this passage is different than you would think at first glance. Christians read the phrase *"God will provide himself a lamb for a burnt offering,"* as if it says, *"God will provide himself **as** a lamb for a burnt offering."* Christians think it reads as if God will be the lamb. This is because later after this passage Abraham observes a *"ram,"* and not a literal *"lamb,"* caught by its horns in the thicket. Christians also believe this is a reference to the Passover Lamb sacrifice that prefigures Jesus dying on Passover. I disagree. I think, in order to understand what is actually going on in this passage, the reader needs to look beyond the English and look at the Hebrew behind the passage.

When Isaac asked where the lamb he used the Hebrew *Seh* which is translated also as *cattle* in the King James Version Bible in ten places. It can also mean *goat*. It is a generic term that can also mean *flock in the collective sense*. Isaac isn't asking where the *lamb* is: he is asking where *the animal* is for the sacrifice. The plain fact is that *seh* can be used for a generic reference to a *domesticated flockling*. When God gave instructions to Israel for the first Passover sacrifice He told them to take a *seh* or *domesticated animal* from the *sheep* or the *goats*. The following passage from Exodus proves this.

Your lamb (seh) shall be without blemish, a male of the first year: ye shall take it out from the sheep (keb-eshim), or from the goats (ah-zehim): (Exodus 12:5)

What God is saying here is that the one year old passover animal that must be a flockling or *seh* (generic) can be either of the *sheep* or *kebeshim* (a specific variety) or the *goats* or *ahzehim* (specific variety). A sheep is a *seh*. A goat is a *seh*. Another animal that is a *seh* is the ram that was caught in the thickets in Genesis 22. Isaac and Abraham both use the term *seh* in reference to the animal that is to be sacrificed and in the end the ram is also a *seh*. It is a generic term for an animal that could be sacrificed. The thing to realize is that there is no actual *lamb* being discussed by either of the two people in the story.

Christians like this passage because they believe that Isaac and Abraham both are looking for an actual little white *lamb*. The reason is, they see this can be nothing less than a foreshadowing of the Passover lamb. In this passage, Isaac is *saved*[1] because God provided another to die in his place, the ram.

Because Abraham and his son are speaking generically about the type of animal that is normally sacrificed there is no hidden message here. The real issue is that Abraham is being taught a specific lesson in this story. Up to this point in history it was the common practice to sacrifice children to pagan gods in other societies. God wanted to draw a distinction between the pagans and his family that He was calling out of the world. He wanted Abraham to follow his commands and at the same time set a precedent that teaches that human sacrifice is forbidden. We see later in the Torah that Israel would still struggle with this abhorrent behavior. Israel was not to sacrifice children to Molech, a foreign deity.

This was so important that God made a special command regarding the practice. For those Christians that would fault God for using this method of testing Abraham to teach us how revolting human sacrifice was to Him, let me warn you. You are in dangerous territory. God often uses what man would call *unorthodox ways* to reveal his nature to us. If there is any adjustment to be made to anyone's thinking, it would have to be done in our own minds, not God's.

And thou shalt not let any of thy seed pass through the fire to Molech, neither shalt thou profane the name of thy God: I am the LORD. (Leviticus 18:21)

This verse not only contains the command not to sacrifice children but it also teaches that doing this profanes the name of the Almighty instead of glorifying it. This fact will be important later. Store it in the back of your mind. The following are two verses that also address the sacrifice of children in order to appease a god.

They have built also the high places of Baal, to burn their sons with fire for burnt offerings unto Baal, which I commanded not, nor spake it, neither came it into my mind: (Jeremiah 19:5)

And they built the high places of Baal, which are in the valley of the son of Hinnom, to cause their sons and their daughters to pass through the fire unto Molech; which I commanded them not, neither came it into my mind, that they should do this abomination, to cause Judah to sin. (Jeremiah 32:35)

These two verses present an interesting comment made by God himself. In the condemnation of the practice of sacrificing children, God actually says that he had

---

1 In the *Christian prophetic sense*.

never thought in his own mind that his family could fall so far as to sacrifice their own children. He actually says this twice. Now fast forward to a statement that John makes later in the New Testament.

And all that dwell upon the earth shall worship him, whose names are not written in the book of life of the Lamb slain from the foundation of the world. (Revelations 13:8)

Let's put this together. Is this what we are to believe? God indicated early on in the Hebrew Bible that He hates the sacrifice of children. He says in Jeremiah that He had never once thought that His own people would do this to their own children, but before time began He knew that He would send His own son to die on a cross to appease Himself. Maybe you haven't fully grasped what I am saying yet, so let me rephrase it a different way.

In Genesis 22, God teaches Abraham that human sacrifice is an abomination. He later backs this up with the command for Israel not to sacrifice their children to Molech. Later in Jeremiah, He reiterates again that it is a terrible abomination when He recaps the history of His people. He goes on to state that this thing is so terrible that he couldn't even have conceived of this horrendous thing in His own mind. Amazingly, later He does it to His own child to glorify Himself. Remember the reference in Leviticus 18:21 to profaning God's name? This God of the New Testament is acting differently than the God of the Hebrew Bible would.

Prophecies of the Crucifixion and Resurrection

Let's try, for only a few minutes, to ignore the previous thought and examine the crucifixion and resurrection, as we find them in the New Testament. First, let's look at a couple of references to prophecies that are supposedly found in the Hebrew Bible that characters in the New Testament tell us about. The first is from the mouth of Jesus himself. After the resurrection, he appeared to the disciples and said these words.

And he said unto them, These are the words which I spake unto you, while I was yet with you, that all things must be fulfilled, which were written in the law of Moses, and in the prophets, and in the psalms, concerning me. Then opened he their understanding, that they might understand the scriptures, And said unto them, Thus it is written, and thus it behoved Christ to suffer, and to rise from the dead the third day: (Luke 24:44-46)

For a long time I looked for this prophecy. The following passage is the closest thing to what Jesus says that I can find.

Come, and let us return unto the LORD: for he hath torn, and he will heal us; he hath smitten, and he will bind us up. After two days will he revive us: in the third day he will raise us up, and we shall live in his sight. Then shall we know, if we follow on to know the LORD: his going forth is prepared as the morning; and he shall come unto us as the rain, as the latter and former rain unto the earth. (Hosea 6:1-3)

Sometimes prophecy is difficult to understand but this one has nothing to do with the Messiah being raised from the dead. This prophecy says nothing about it being beneficial (behoved) for Christ to suffer. Even if you want to split this up and say that part of this is referring to the suffering servant of Isaiah then you would have to ignore all that I have shown you in the previous chapter on Isaiah 53. This is another case of someone, namely the author of Luke, inventing a prophecy.

We all know by now, if someone is going to chime in on the resurrection it is going to be Paul. He shoots his mouth off also and alludes to prophecy also.

Moreover, brethren, I declare unto you the gospel which I preached unto you, which also ye have received, and wherein ye stand; By which also ye are saved, if ye keep in memory what I preached unto you, unless ye have believed in vain. For I delivered unto you first of all that which I also received, how that Christ died for our sins according to the scriptures; And that he was buried, and that he rose again the third day according to the scriptures:(1 Corinthians 15:1-4)

Paul makes the same mistake by saying, *"For I delivered unto you first of all that which I also received, how that Christ died for our sins according to the scriptures."* He also indicates that he gave this information to the Corinthians after he received it from someone else. Who gave him this information? Could it have been the author of Luke? Why don't Jesus, Luke or Paul tell us which prophet wrote this prophecy? They couldn't because it's a fraudulent reference. This is just another case of the gentiles not being able to check out the facts because they didn't have the ability to read the Hebrew Scriptures.

The important question here is, "Why don't Christians question passages like this?" It is because they start with Jesus and the New Testament and work backwards. By the time they get through reading Paul, they have no interest in the Hebrew Scriptures.

It's like a man that walks into a bookstore and picks up a four hundred page novel. He flips to the last fifty pages and reads to the end. He closes the book, walks out of the store and convinces himself he's read the whole story. Would you consider that man wise?

Crucifixion and Resurrection: Allusions and Confusions

There are many times that the crucifixion and resurrection are alluded to by Jesus. When Christians think of Jesus talking about his death and resurrection they often recall Jesus speaking about tearing down the Temple and building it again in three days. What I find really strange is that he is accused in three gospels of saying this but he actually speaks about doing this only in John's gospel. Luke mentions nothing about the whole matter. The accusation and the mockery in Matthew goes like this.

And said, This fellow said, I am able to destroy the temple of God, and to build it in three days.(Matthew 26:61)

And saying, Thou that destroyest the temple, and buildest it in three days, save thyself. If thou be the Son of God, come down from the cross. (Matthew 27:40)

The accusation and the mockery in Mark are similar.

We heard him say, I will destroy this temple that is made with hands, and within three days I will build another made without hands. (Mark 14:58)

And they that passed by railed on him, wagging their heads, and saying, Ah, thou that destroyest the temple, and buildest it in three days, Save thyself, and come down from the cross. (Mark 15:29,30)

In Mark 14:58, the author has Jesus being accused but the retelling is not what we see in the other gospels. Mark has Jesus speaking as if he is going to destroy the actual

Temple building because the phrase, *"made with hands"* is used, as opposed to the second phrase, *"made without hands."* Generally, buildings are made by hands and people are not. This, I think, presents this story as it probably occurred although I find it puzzling that there is no account of Jesus saying what is reported at his trial.

It is more probable that this gospel presents what actually happened because Mark was the first to record his gospel. This retelling actually portrays more truthfully what Jesus probably thought. This is how I see it.

Jesus believed that he was the end-times-king. He calculated that in order to cleanse the Temple it would first be destroyed then God would miraculously rebuild it in three days upon his resurrection. One must still realize that Jesus for some reason concocted this three day scenario even though there were no Hebrew Scriptures that portrayed it the way Jesus presented it. Let's proceed through the rest of the gospels.

Luke, of course, is silent on what Christians consider to be a very important analogy of the resurrection. This is John's account. It contains no accusation at the trial but the conversation between Jesus and the Jews contains a strange element.

Jesus answered and said unto them, Destroy this temple, and in three days I will raise it up. Then said the Jews, Forty and six years was this temple in building, and wilt thou rear it up in three days? But he spake of the temple of his body. When therefore he was risen from the dead, his disciples remembered that he had said this unto them; ***and they believed the scripture****, and the word which Jesus had said. (John 2:19-22)*

Did you catch the strange statement, *"and they believed the scripture"*? It is a mystery. We are not told which scripture the author has in mind because it is all an invention of Jesus or the writer of this gospel. But the sad part is the disciples fell for this deception.

Perhaps he is referring to the scripture Luke *invented* earlier in Luke 24:46. John also seems to refute the claim that Jesus was speaking about the actual Temple building because he adds a short comment that reads, *"But he spake of the temple of his body"* and not the physical Temple. Perhaps this is in response to Mark's gospel presentation of this material. None of the gospel accounts agree and some are missing important information that is only realized when the accounts are scrutinized side by side.

A Resurrection Mishmash

Do the New Testament accounts of the resurrection stand up to close examination? When a Christian reads about the resurrection they usually read from one gospel at a time. A few years ago, I read a book by Bart D. Erhman entitled *"Jesus, Interrupted."* Bart proposes the idea that if someone wants to realize the contradictions in the New Testament accounts of the crucifixion and resurrection, the gospels have to be read in a parallel manner. Before we get into the parallel reading, there are some surprising facts about the general subject of the crucifixion and resurrection.

- In the synoptic gospels, which are comprised of Matthew, Mark, and Luke, Jesus is crucified during the daylight hours following the Passover meal the night before.

    As we will see later, in John, he is crucified the day before the passover meal so he can be "sacrificed" at the same time as the actual passover lambs are being slaughtered. It is essential to John for Jesus to be as close to a lamb as possible. This is also attested to by the statement that the night before Jesus was crucified (after Jesus had eaten his Passover meal as shown in the synoptic gospels), the elders did not want to defile themselves so they could eat the passover.

- Mark's gospel was the first gospel written. Its best earliest manuscripts known to exist, abruptly end at verse 8 of the 16th chapter. This is the last verse found in those manuscripts.

    And they went out quickly, and fled from the sepulchre; for they trembled and were amazed: neither said they any thing to any man; for they were afraid. (Mark 16:8)

    This fact is not debated by translators or scholars and notes about this appear in the footnotes of many translations. Why would Mark not mention the resurrection... if it occurred? Did he simply forget?

The following is a parallel reading of the major points of the crucifixion and resurrection. Because Mark was the first gospel written I list his passages first.

The Trial before Caiaphas and the Sanhedrin

Mark

And they led Jesus away to the high priest: and with him were assembled all the chief priests and the elders and the scribes. And Peter followed him afar off, even into the palace of the high priest: and he sat with the servants, and warmed himself at the fire. And the chief priests and all the council sought for witness against Jesus to put him to death; and found none. For many bare false witness against him, but their witness agreed not together. And there arose certain, and bare false witness against him, saying, We heard him say, I will destroy this temple that is made with hands, and within three days I will build another made without hands. But neither so did their witness agree together. And the high priest stood up in the midst, and asked Jesus, saying, Answerest thou nothing? what is it which these witness against thee? But he held his peace, and answered nothing. Again the high priest asked him, and said unto him, Art thou the Christ, the Son of the Blessed? And Jesus said, I am: and ye shall see the Son of man sitting on the right hand of power, and coming in the clouds of heaven. Then the high priest rent his clothes, and saith, What need we any further witnesses? Ye have heard the blasphemy: what think ye? And they all condemned him to be guilty of death. And some began to spit on him, and to cover his face, and to buffet him, and to say unto him, Prophesy: and the servants did strike him with the palms of their hands... And straightway in the morning the chief priests held a consultation with the elders and scribes and the whole council, and bound Jesus, and carried him away, and delivered him to Pilate. (Mark 14:53-65;15:1)

Matthew

And they that had laid hold on Jesus led him away to Caiaphas the high priest, where the scribes and the elders were assembled. But Peter followed him afar off unto the high priest's palace, and went in, and sat with the servants, to see the end. Now the chief priests, and elders, and all the council, sought false witness against Jesus, to put him to death; But found none: yea, though many false witnesses came, yet found they none. At the last came two false witnesses, And said, This fellow said, I am able to destroy the temple of God, and to build it in three days. And the high priest arose, and said unto him, Answerest thou nothing? what is it which these witness against thee? But Jesus held his peace. And the high priest answered and said unto him, I adjure thee by the living God, that thou tell us whether thou be the Christ, the Son of God. Jesus saith unto him, Thou hast said: nevertheless I say unto you, Hereafter shall ye see the Son of man sitting on the right hand of power, and coming in the clouds of heaven. Then the high priest rent his clothes, saying, He hath spoken blasphemy; what further need have we of witnesses? behold, now ye have heard his blasphemy. What think ye? They answered and said, He is guilty of death. Then did they spit in his face, and buffeted him; and others smote him with the palms of their hands, Saying, Prophesy unto us, thou Christ, Who is he that smote thee?...When the morning was come, all the chief priests and elders of the people took counsel against Jesus to put him to death: And when they had bound him, they led him away, and delivered him to Pontius Pilate the governor. (Matthew 26:57-68;27:1,2)*

Luke

Then took they him, and led him, and brought him into the high priest's house. And Peter followed afar off... And the men that held Jesus mocked him, and smote him. And when they had blindfolded him, they struck him on the face, and asked him, saying, Prophesy, who is it that smote thee? And many other things blasphemously spake they against him. And as soon as it was day, the elders of the people and the chief priests and the scribes came together, and led him into their council, saying, Art thou the Christ? tell us. And he said unto them, If I tell you, ye will not believe: And if I also ask you, ye will not answer me, nor let me go. Hereafter shall the Son of man sit on the right hand of the power of God. Then said they all, Art thou then the Son of God? And he said unto them, Ye say that I am. And they said, What need we any further witness? for we ourselves have heard of his own mouth... And the whole multitude of them arose, and led him unto Pilate. (Luke 22:54,63-71;23:1)

John

Then the band and the captain and officers of the Jews took Jesus, and bound him, And led him away to Annas first; for he was father in law to Caiaphas, which was the high priest that same year. Now Caiaphas was he, which gave counsel to the Jews, that it was expedient that one man should die for the people. And Simon Peter followed Jesus, and so did another disciple: that disciple was known unto the high priest, and went in with Jesus into the palace of the high priest. But Peter stood at the door without. Then went out that other disciple, which was known unto the high priest, and spake unto her that kept the door, and brought in Peter. Then saith the damsel that kept the door unto Peter, Art not thou also one of this man's disciples? He saith, I am not. And the servants and officers stood there, who had made a fire of coals; for it was cold: and they warmed themselves: and Peter stood with them, and warmed himself. The high priest then asked Jesus of his disciples, and of his doctrine. Jesus answered him, I spake openly to the world; I ever taught in the synagogue, and in the temple, whither the Jews always resort; and in secret have I said nothing. Why askest thou me? ask them which heard me, what I have said unto them: behold, they know what I said. And when he had thus spoken, one of the officers which stood by struck Jesus with the palm of his hand, saying, Answerest thou the high priest so? Jesus answered him, If I have spoken evil, bear witness of the evil: but if well, why smitest thou me? Now Annas had sent him bound unto Caiaphas the high priest...Then led they Jesus from Caiaphas unto the hall of judgment: and it was early; and they themselves went not into the judgment hall, lest they should be defiled; but that they might eat the passover. (John 18:12-24,28)

Analysis of the Trial before the Sanhedrin

It is easy to see the differences when the passages are read in a parallel manner. Here are the highlights of the differences shown in the following examinations of the story elements.

Story Element: *Who was Jesus taken to first?*

Mark

Caiaphas

Matthew

Caiaphas

Luke

Caiaphas

John

Annas [2]

Story Element: *Did Jesus go to his trial alone?*

Mark

Yes

Matthew

Yes

Luke

Yes

John

---

[2] *And led him away to Annas first; for he was father in law to Caiaphas, which was the high priest that same year. (John 18:13)* This is the point to ponder. If the other accounts say that Jesus went straightaway to Caiaphas then the question is, *"Do we throw out John's account or the other three gospels?"* Remember, the Word of God is supposed to be perfect. There are those scholars who concede that the New Testament contains scribal errors but also contend those errors are small and contribute nothing to the overall meaning or narrative of the New Testament. This is not the case here. This is a major difference but there are other mistakes which make this one almost not worth mentioning.

No, an unnamed disciple goes with him [3]

Story Element: *Was Jesus beaten before the High Priest questioned him?*
Mark

No, afterward

Matthew

No, afterward

Luke

Yes

John

No, but he was struck during the questioning

Story Element: *What did Jesus say to the person trying him?*
Mark

And Jesus said, I am: and ye shall see the Son of man sitting on the right hand of power, and coming in the clouds of heaven.

Matthew

Jesus saith unto him, Thou hast said: nevertheless I say unto you, Hereafter shall ye see the Son of man sitting on the right hand of power, and coming in the clouds of heaven.

Luke

And he said unto them, If I tell you, ye will not believe: And if I also ask you, ye will not answer me, nor let me go. Hereafter shall the Son of man sit on the right hand of the power of God. Then said they all, Art thou then the Son of God? And he said unto them, Ye say that I am.

John

The high priest then asked Jesus of his disciples, and of his doctrine. Jesus answered him, I spake openly to the world; I ever taught in the synagogue, and in the temple, whither the Jews always resort; and in secret have I said nothing. Why askest thou me? ask them which heard me, what I have said unto them: behold, they know what I said. And when he had thus spoken, one of the officers which stood by struck Jesus with the palm of his hand, saying, Answerest thou the high priest so? Jesus answered him, If I have spoken evil, bear witness of the evil: but if well, why smitest thou me?

Story Element: *What happened after the initial trial?*
Mark

And they all condemned him to death. Some began to spit on him, and to cover his face, and to buffet him, and to say unto him, Prophesy: and the servants did strike him with the palms of their hands... And straightway in the morning the chief priests held a

---

3 Was this Judas? If not, who was he? There is no hint anywhere else in the New Testament that any disciple was at the trial of Jesus. So again, the New Testament doesn't disappoint, it leaves you hanging.

consultation with the elders and scribes and the whole council, and bound Jesus, and carried him away, and delivered him to Pilate.

Matthew

They answered and said, He is guilty of death. Then did they spit in his face, and buffeted him; and others smote him with the palms of their hands, Saying, Prophesy unto us, thou Christ, Who is he that smote thee?...When the morning was come, all the chief priests and elders of the people took counsel against Jesus to put him to death: And when they had bound him, they led him away, and delivered him to Pontius Pilate the governor.

Luke

And they said, What need we any further witness? for we ourselves have heard of his own mouth... And the whole multitude of them arose, and led him unto Pilate.

John

Now Annas had sent him bound unto Caiaphas the high priest...Then led they Jesus from Caiaphas [4] *unto the hall of judgment: and it was early; and they themselves went not into the judgment hall, lest they should be defiled; but that they might eat the passover.* [5]

The Trial before Pilate

Mark

And Pilate asked him, Art thou the King of the Jews? And he answering said unto him, Thou sayest it. And the chief priests accused him of many things: but he answered nothing. And Pilate asked him again, saying, Answerest thou nothing? behold how many things they witness against thee. But Jesus yet answered nothing; so that Pilate marvelled. Now at that feast he released unto them one prisoner, whomsoever they

---

4   What are we to make of the narrative we find here? Jesus goes first to Annas. Is John presenting him as having the trial instead of the High Priest? The other gospels indicate that Caiaphas is the High Priest. John makes a confusing mess of his account. In contrast, in all of the synoptic gospels, the entire narrative of Annas trying Jesus is mysteriously missing. It continues to get worse from here on. All of the things that Jesus said to Caiaphas in the other gospels are simply not important enough to John for him to show here. Jesus says nothing to Caiaphas about the destruction of the Temple and rebuilding it. I find that absolutely shocking, to put it mildly. Christians never question these accounts for some reason. I believe that in their minds, they assemble the separate gospels into some sort of "super gospel" combining all four accounts into some impenetrable story that fills gaps in each gospel with elements from another.

5   Who is this passage speaking about when it uses the phrase, *"they themselves"*? It is speaking about the entirety of the Sanhedrin. John presents this ridiculous animation of Pilate running back and forth between Jesus and the Sanhedrin which remain outside the judgment hall. Pilate confers with the Jews then runs in to Jesus to ask him a question and then runs back out to the Jews again. John does this to present the idea that the Jews are unable to go into a place where gentiles are in order to remain pure enough to eat the Passover meal but they are willing to put a innocent man to death. Of course, in the other gospels everyone has already eaten the Passover.

desired. And there was one named Barabbas, which lay bound with them that had made insurrection with him, who had committed murder in the insurrection. And the multitude crying aloud began to desire him to do as he had ever done unto them. But Pilate answered them, saying, Will ye that I release unto you the King of the Jews? For he knew that the chief priests had delivered him for envy. But the chief priests moved the people, that he should rather release Barabbas unto them. And Pilate answered and said again unto them, What will ye then that I shall do unto him whom ye call the King of the Jews? And they cried out again, Crucify him. Then Pilate said unto them, Why, what evil hath he done? And they cried out the more exceedingly, Crucify him. And so Pilate, willing to content the people, released Barabbas unto them, and delivered Jesus, when he had scourged him, to be crucified. And the soldiers led him away into the hall, called Praetorium; and they call together the whole band. And they clothed him with purple, and platted a crown of thorns, and put it about his head, And began to salute him, Hail, King of the Jews! And they smote him on the head with a reed, and did spit upon him, and bowing their knees worshipped him. And when they had mocked him, they took off the purple from him, and put his own clothes on him, and led him out to crucify him. (Mark 15:2-20)

Matthew

And Jesus stood before the governor: and the governor asked him, saying, Art thou the King of the Jews? And Jesus said unto him, Thou sayest. And when he was accused of the chief priests and elders, he answered nothing. Then said Pilate unto him, Hearest thou not how many things they witness against thee? And he answered him to never a word; insomuch that the governor marvelled greatly. Now at that feast the governor was wont to release unto the people a prisoner, whom they would. And they had then a notable prisoner, called Barabbas. Therefore when they were gathered together, Pilate said unto them, Whom will ye that I release unto you? Barabbas, or Jesus which is called Christ? For he knew that for envy they had delivered him. When he was set down on the judgment seat, his wife sent unto him, saying, Have thou nothing to do with that just man: for I have suffered many things this day in a dream because of him. But the chief priests and elders persuaded the multitude that they should ask Barabbas, and destroy Jesus. The governor answered and said unto them, Whether of the twain will ye that I release unto you? They said, Barabbas. Pilate saith unto them, What shall I do then with Jesus which is called Christ? They all say unto him, Let him be crucified. And the governor said, Why, what evil hath he done? But they cried out the more, saying, Let him be crucified. When Pilate saw that he could prevail nothing, but that rather a tumult was made, he took water, and washed his hands before the multitude, saying, I am innocent of the blood of this just person: see ye to it. Then answered all the people, and said, His blood be on us, and on our children. Then released he Barabbas unto them: and when he had scourged Jesus, he delivered him to be crucified. Then the soldiers of the governor took Jesus into the common hall, and gathered unto him the whole band of soldiers. And they stripped him, and put on him a scarlet robe. And when they had platted a crown of thorns, they put it upon his head, and a reed in his right hand: and they bowed the knee before him, and mocked him, saying, Hail, King of the Jews! And they spit upon him, and took the reed, and smote him on the head. And after that they had mocked him, they took the robe off from him, and put his own raiment on him, and led him away to crucify him. (Matthew 27:11-31)

Luke

And they began to accuse him, saying, We found this fellow perverting the nation, and forbidding to give tribute to Caesar, saying that he himself is Christ a King. And Pilate asked him, saying, Art thou the King of the Jews? And he answered him and said, Thou sayest it. Then said Pilate to the chief priests and to the people, I find no fault in this man. And they were the more fierce, saying, He stirreth up the people, teaching throughout all Jewry, beginning from Galilee to this place. When Pilate heard of Galilee, he asked whether the man were a Galilaean. And as soon as he knew that he belonged unto Herod's jurisdiction, he sent him to Herod, who himself also was at Jerusalem at that time. And when Herod saw Jesus, he was exceeding glad: for he was desirous to see him of a long season, because he had heard many things of him; and he hoped to have seen some miracle done by him. Then he questioned with him in many words; but he answered him nothing. And the chief priests and scribes stood and vehemently accused him. And Herod with his men of war set him at nought, and mocked him, and arrayed him in a gorgeous robe, and sent him again to Pilate. And the same day Pilate and Herod were made friends together: for before they were at enmity between themselves. And Pilate, when he had called together the chief priests and the rulers and the people, Said unto them, Ye have brought this man unto me, as one that perverteth the people: and, behold, I, having examined him before you, have found no fault in this man touching those things whereof ye accuse him: No, nor yet Herod: for I sent you to him; and, lo, nothing worthy of death is done unto him. I will therefore chastise him, and release him. (For of necessity he must release one unto them at the feast.) And they cried out all at once, saying, Away with this man, and release unto us Barabbas: (Who for a certain sedition made in the city, and for murder, was cast into prison.) Pilate therefore, willing to release Jesus, spake again to them. But they cried, saying, Crucify him, crucify him. And he said unto them the third time, Why, what evil hath he done? I have found no cause of death in him: I will therefore chastise him, and let him go. And they were instant with loud voices, requiring that he might be crucified. And the voices of them and of the chief priests prevailed. And Pilate gave sentence that it should be as they required. And he released unto them him that for sedition and murder was cast into prison, whom they had desired; but he delivered Jesus to their will. And as they led him away, they laid hold upon one Simon, a Cyrenian, coming out of the country, and on him they laid the cross, that he might bear it after Jesus. And there followed him a great company of people, and of women, which also bewailed and lamented him. But Jesus turning unto them said, Daughters of Jerusalem, weep not for me, but weep for yourselves, and for your children. For, behold, the days are coming, in the which they shall say, Blessed are the barren, and the wombs that never bare, and the paps which never gave suck. Then shall they begin to say to the mountains, Fall on us; and to the hills, Cover us. For if they do these things in a green tree, what shall be done in the dry? (Luke 23:2-31)

John

Pilate then went out unto them, and said, What accusation bring ye against this man? They answered and said unto him, If he were not a malefactor, we would not have delivered him up unto thee. Then said Pilate unto them, Take ye him, and judge him according to your law. The Jews therefore said unto him, It is not lawful for us to put any man to death: That the saying of Jesus might be fulfilled, which he spake, signifying what death he should die. Then Pilate entered into the judgment hall again, and called Jesus, and said unto him, Art thou the King of the Jews? Jesus answered him, Sayest thou this thing of thyself, or did others tell it thee of me? Pilate answered, Am I a Jew? Thine own nation and the chief priests have delivered thee unto me: what hast thou done? Jesus answered, My kingdom is not of this world: if my kingdom were of this world, then would my servants fight, that I should not be delivered to the Jews: but now is my kingdom not from hence. Pilate therefore said unto him, Art thou a king then? Jesus answered, Thou sayest that I am a king. To this end was I born, and for this cause came I into the world, that I should bear witness unto the truth. Every one that is of the truth heareth my voice. Pilate saith unto him, What is truth? And when he had said this, he went out again unto the Jews, and saith unto them, I find in him no fault at all. But ye have a custom, that I should release unto you one at the passover: will ye therefore that I release unto you the King of the Jews? Then cried they all again, saying, Not this man, but Barabbas. Now Barabbas was a robber. Then Pilate therefore took Jesus, and scourged him. And the soldiers platted a crown of thorns, and put it on his head, and they put on him a purple robe, And said, Hail, King of the Jews! and they smote him with their hands. Pilate therefore went forth again, and saith unto them, Behold, I bring him forth to you, that ye may know that I find no fault in him. Then came Jesus forth, wearing the crown of thorns, and the purple robe. And Pilate saith unto them, Behold the man! Then the chief priests therefore and officers saw him, they cried out, saying, Crucify him, crucify him. Pilate saith unto them, Take ye him, and crucify him: for I find no fault in him. The Jews answered him, We have a law, and by our law he ought to die, because he made himself the Son of God. When Pilate therefore heard that saying, he was the more afraid; And went again into the judgment hall, and saith unto Jesus, Whence art thou? But Jesus gave him no answer. Then saith Pilate unto him, Speakest thou not unto me? knowest thou not that I have power to crucify thee, and have power to release thee? Jesus answered, Thou couldest have no power at all against me, except it were given thee from above: therefore he that delivered me unto thee hath the greater sin. And from thenceforth Pilate sought to release him: but the Jews cried out, saying, If thou let this man go, thou art not Caesar's friend: whosoever maketh himself a king speaketh against Caesar. When Pilate therefore heard that saying, he brought Jesus forth, and sat down in the judgment seat in a place that is called the Pavement, but in the Hebrew, Gabbatha. And it was the preparation of the passover, and about the sixth hour: and he saith unto the Jews, Behold your King! But they cried out, Away with him, away with him, crucify him. Pilate saith unto them, Shall I crucify your King? The chief priests answered, We have no king but Caesar. Then delivered he him therefore unto them to be crucified. And they took Jesus, and led him away. (John 18:29-19:16)

Analysis of the Trial before Pilate

Some of the most glaring contradictions are sometimes the most difficult to see. This is especially true in the eyes of Christians. As I have stated before Christians try to blend all of the events together to create a "super gospel" that smooths things over and acts as a unifying agent. I have tried to cut through the muck and mess of the New Testament to reveal how this method is fatally flawed. I have endeavored to bring to light the problems in the New Testament to show that no matter how hard one labors to create a unified view, their efforts will be in vain. We now come to a particularly strange portion in the gospels. As you will see this section will reveal many things that most Christians have missed in their leisurely reading of the New Testament.

CHAPTER 10

Story Element: *Does Jesus appear before Herod?*
Mark

No mention of Herod

Matthew

No mention of Herod

Luke

Yes, Jesus is first brought before Pilate then sent to Herod then back to Pilate, again. Pilate and Herod become friends

John

No mention of Herod

Story Element: *Does Jesus remain silent during his trials?* [6]
Mark

No

Matthew

No [7]

Luke

No

John

No

Story Element: *What does Jesus say when he is tried by Pilate?*
Mark

And Pilate asked him, Art thou the King of the Jews? And he answering said unto him, Thou sayest it.

Matthew

And Jesus stood before the governor: and the governor asked him, saying, Art thou the King of the Jews? And Jesus said unto him, Thou sayest.

---

6 Many Christians believe that Jesus is the suffering servant that Isaiah 53 speaks of. If you skipped the previous chapter in this book entitled, "Isaiah 53: Linchpin or Nail in the Coffin?" then you need to go back and read it carefully. If you did read it then you are aware of my arguments that prove beyond a reasonable doubt that Jesus is not that "Servant". The point that I want to make here is that Jesus did not remain silent at his trials as Christians believe the servant of Isaiah 53 did. I want to convey that Jesus did say much at his trials and what he says varies widely between the gospel accounts.

7 Matthew makes the statement, *And when he was accused of the chief priests and elders, he answered nothing.* This of course is not true because even Matthew's account has Jesus responding. Jesus actually prophecies that, *Thou hast said: nevertheless I say unto you, Hereafter shall ye see the Son of man sitting on the right hand of power, and coming in the clouds of heaven.* This is a veiled and empty threat because none of those present at his trial saw this happen during their lifetimes. Even if Christians believe that Jesus is indicating that they will see him at his second coming they are mistaken because the New Testament indicates that the *rest of the dead* or the *wicked dead* are not raised until after a thousand years after Christ's return (Revelations 20:5), so they will not be resurrected before the Second Coming.

Luke

And Pilate asked him, saying, Art thou the King of the Jews? And he answered him and said, Thou sayest it.

John

Then Pilate entered into the judgment hall again, and called Jesus, and said unto him, Art thou the King of the Jews? Jesus answered him, Sayest thou this thing of thyself, or did others tell it thee of me? Pilate answered, Am I a Jew? Thine own nation and the chief priests have delivered thee unto me: what hast thou done? Jesus answered, My kingdom is not of this world: if my kingdom were of this world, then would my servants fight, that I should not be delivered to the Jews: but now is my kingdom not from hence. Pilate therefore said unto him, Art thou a king then? Jesus answered, Thou sayest that I am a king. To this end was I born, and for this cause came I into the world, that I should bear witness unto the truth. Every one that is of the truth heareth my voice. ... Then saith Pilate unto him, Speakest thou not unto me? knowest thou not that I have power to crucify thee, and have power to release thee? Jesus answered, Thou couldest have no power at all against me, except it were given thee from above: therefore he that delivered me unto thee hath the greater sin.

Story Element: *Does Pilate scourge Jesus?*

Mark

Yes

Matthew

Yes

Luke

Pilate says he is going to but the narrative skips the scourging and proceeds directly to the crucifixion

John

Yes

Story Element: *Does Jesus say that he is the King of the Jews?*

Mark

By implication only [8]

Matthew

By implication only

Luke

By implication only

John

---

8 Mark has Jesus say that he is a king by circumlocution. By Pilate uttering the question, *"Art thou the King of the Jews?"* and Jesus responding, *"Thou sayest it,"* Mark tries to imply that Pilate gives credibility to his kingship.

By implication only

Story Element: *Does Pilate wash his hands?*

Mark

No

Matthew

Yes

Luke

No

John

No

Conclusions about the Trials

Here are my conclusions about Pilate's trial of Jesus

- Matthew basically copied Mark but adds a couple of interesting tidbits. Matthew has Pilate literally wash his hands of the entire matter. This is how Matthew depicts Pilate's actions.

  "When Pilate saw that he could prevail nothing, but that rather a tumult was made, he took water, and washed his hands before the multitude, saying, I am innocent of the blood of this just person: see ye to it."

  Matthew did this to remove any blame on the Romans and place it squarely on the Jews. The way Matthew portrays Pilate doesn't match the historical facts. Pilate was no patsy. To the contrary, he was removed later from Jerusalem because he was so vicious and cruel. Matthew is the only one that recorded this story. Why would Matthew write something like this? The answer is Jesus must be declared righteous and his murderers must be the Jews.

  This is a perversion of a requirement found in the Torah that applies to certain sacrifices. As Matthew sees it, Jesus is being offered up as a sin sacrifice, which must be examined and found to be without any physical spots or defects. In like manner, Matthew believes that Jesus must be perfect also but not only physically. He must be found to be sinless. The problem is that Matthew's thoughts on this are not actually biblical. These requirements being imposed on Jesus were added to existing requirements. Nowhere does it say a gentile can examine the sin sacrifice. To the contrary a priest must examine it. Also it is not allowable for a gentile to kill the sacrifice, which also must be accomplished by the priest. Besides, Jesus says, "no man takes his life, I lay it down," violating the requirement for the priest to slay the sin sacrifice. If no one killed Jesus and he instead caused himself to die, how is this different than suicide? Either way, in all counts Jesus is not found to be a "perfect sacrifice."

  When Matthew concocts these requirements, he violates the command that God gave forbidding adding to or diminishing from the Torah. What would make someone that was so devoted to obeying the Torah come up with these ideas? Perhaps the New Testament itself answers this question. Jesus berates the teachers of Israel for teaching the commands of men, rather than those of God. Combine that with the ignorance that I mentioned earlier in this book and you have the perfect mix to create a "cloaked apostasy" that was pervasive in the time of Jesus. Men ignorant of the written Torah, including Jesus, had been taught incorrectly for so long that they could not tell truth from lies. Over time, heresies crept in and became entwined in the beliefs of certain sects of Judaism giving rise to certain systems of thought such as what we see in Matthew's accounts. Maybe Matthew was only trying to make sense of what had happened to Jesus by piecing together bits of what he had learned over his lifetime in order to explain the unexpected events that took place to Jesus. What's wrong with a little tweaking as long as you can get other people to believe in Jesus? Matthew has Pilate's men take Jesus and have him whipped, stripped and dressed in a robe then lead out to be crucified. The story is much the same as Mark's account.

- Luke adds an additional trial that is not found in any other gospel. In Luke's gospel, Jesus is also sent to Herod, who is glad to see Jesus. Luke has Herod looking forward to seeing Jesus perform a miracle. Luke inserts the idea that Herod and Pilate, although enemies in the past, became really great friends because they both were unified by the condemnation of Jesus. That's so nice, isn't it? Luke also has Herod mock Jesus, put him in a gorgeous robe and send him back to Pilate. Did Jesus leave his clothes with Herod and go back to Pilate in the robe? This is a detail that escapes many because we read in Matthew,

*And they **stripped him (of the gorgeous robe?)**, and **put on him a scarlet robe**. And when they had platted a crown of thorns, they put it upon his head, and a reed in his right hand: and they bowed the knee before him, and mocked him, saying, Hail, King of the Jews! And they spit upon him, and took the reed, and smote him on the head. And after that they had mocked him, **they took the robe off from him**, and **put his own raiment on him**, and led him away to crucify him.*

Now for a show of hands. How many believe Pilate scourges Jesus? He doesn't. Of course, this is a big problem for Jesus because he prophesied to his disciples in Luke's account the following.

*Then he took unto him the twelve, and said unto them, Behold, we go up to Jerusalem, and all things that are written by the prophets concerning the Son of man shall be accomplished. For he shall be delivered unto the Gentiles, and shall be mocked, and spitefully entreated, and spitted on: And they **shall scourge him**, and put him to death: and the third day he shall rise again. And they understood none of these things: and this saying was hid from them, neither knew they the things which were spoken. (Luke 18:31-34)*

What is to be made of this missing scourging in Luke? Remember, this is the New Testament and this is supposed to be without error. Notice also how this passage indicates that the disciples didn't understand what Jesus was saying and that they didn't even remember these things. Luke also indicates that Jesus didn't carry the cross but Simon, a Cyrenian, did. Wouldn't that cause a problem with the whole *foreshadowing* of Isaac carrying the wood up Mount Moriah? Did Abraham have someone else carry the wood for Isaac? I am guessing that Luke hadn't read that part of Genesis yet. We will have to wait til the next section to see if the other gospel writers had read their Torah.

- In his account, John creates an even more absurd scenario expanding the short conversation between Pilate and Jesus to an actual discussion of the matter. Everything John gets his hands on he has to turn into a huge production. Here is the discussion.

Then Pilate entered into the judgment hall again, and called Jesus, and said unto him, Art thou the King of the Jews? Jesus answered him, Sayest thou this thing of thyself, or did others tell it thee of me? Pilate answered, Am I a Jew? Thine own nation and the chief priests have delivered thee unto me: what hast thou done? Jesus answered, My kingdom is not of this world: if my kingdom were of this world, then would my servants fight, that I should not be delivered to the Jews: but now is my kingdom not from hence. Pilate therefore said unto him, Art thou a king then? Jesus answered, Thou sayest that I am a king. To this end was I born, and for this cause came I into the world, that I should bear witness unto the truth. Every one that is of the truth heareth my voice. Pilate saith unto him, What is truth? And when he had said this, he went out again unto the Jews, and saith unto them, I find in him no fault at all. But ye have a custom, that I should release unto you one at the passover: will ye therefore that I release unto you the King of the Jews?

Unbelievably, Jesus denies that his kingdom is earthly, contrary to all of the prophecies in the Hebrew Bible that clearly show that the end-times-king will reign over the whole earth from Jerusalem. If Jesus rules in the hearts of men, doesn't that mean that Jesus rules on Earth making his kingdom *earthly*? If Christians actually read and believed the Hebrew Bible they would be able to scrutinize these fallacies and come to the truth but they are taught that they really don't need that "Old Testament" because their heritage is the *New and improved Testament*. John has Jesus make the statement, *"if my kingdom were of this world, then would my servants fight."* Isn't this what Peter did when they were in the garden earlier? The understanding was that the Messiah would take the throne and deliver his people, not die for people's sins. Couple this with the fact that Peter has no idea about the Messiah having to die in Matthew 16:21, 22 and you begin to see the problems here. Peter was ready to fight to bring Jesus' kingdom into reality. Also, at one time, Jesus tells his disciples to buy swords in Luke 22:36.

Then said he unto them, But now, he that hath a purse, let him take it, and likewise his scrip: and he that hath no sword, let him sell his garment, and buy one. (Luke 22:36)

Why would Jesus tell them to buy a sword if he knew later that he would tell them, *"he who lives by the sword, dies by the sword"?* Are you beginning to see the schizophrenia?

John also says that Barabbas was a robber but Luke says that Barabbas, "Who for a certain sedition made in the city, and for murder, was cast into prison." So, was Barabbas a common thief or was he guilty of sedition and murder?

Evidently, John had never read Luke or vice versa or perhaps they didn't know the facts.

The Crucifixion

Mark

And they compel one Simon a Cyrenian, who passed by, coming out of the country, the father of Alexander and Rufus, to bear his cross. And they bring him unto the place Golgotha, which is, being interpreted, The place of a skull. And they gave him to drink wine mingled with myrrh: but he received it not. And when they had crucified him, they parted his garments, casting lots upon them, what every man should take. And it was the third hour, and they crucified him. And the superscription of his accusation was written over, THE KING OF THE JEWS. And with him they crucify two thieves; the one on his right hand, and the other on his left. And the scripture was fulfilled, which saith, And he was numbered with the transgressors. And they that passed by railed on him, wagging their heads, and saying, Ah, thou that destroyest the temple, and buildest it in three days, Save thyself, and come down from the cross. Likewise also the chief priests mocking said among themselves with the scribes, He saved others; himself he cannot save. Let Christ the King of Israel descend now from the cross, that we may see and believe. And they that were crucified with him reviled him. And when the sixth hour was come, there was darkness over the whole land until the ninth hour. And at the ninth hour Jesus cried with a loud voice, saying, Eloi, Eloi, lama sabachthani? which is, being interpreted, My God, my God, why hast thou forsaken me? And some of them that stood by, when they heard it, said, Behold, he calleth Elias. And one ran and filled a spunge full of vinegar, and put it on a reed, and gave him to drink, saying, Let alone; let us see whether Elias will come to take him down. And Jesus cried with a loud voice, and gave up the ghost. And the veil of the temple was rent in twain from the top to the bottom. And when the centurion, which stood over against him, saw that he so cried out, and gave up the ghost, he said, Truly this man was the Son of God. There were also women looking on afar off: among whom was Mary Magdalene, and Mary the mother of James the less and of Joses, and Salome; (Who also, when he was in Galilee, followed him, and ministered unto him;) and many other women which came up with him unto Jerusalem. And now when the even was come, because it was the preparation, that is, the day before the sabbath, Joseph of Arimathaea, an honourable counsellor, which also waited for the kingdom of God, came, and went in boldly unto Pilate, and craved the body of Jesus. And Pilate marvelled if he were already dead: and calling unto him the centurion, he asked him whether he had been any while dead. And when he knew it of the centurion, he gave the body to Joseph. And he bought fine linen, and took him down, and wrapped him in the linen, and laid him in a sepulchre which was hewn out of a rock, and rolled a stone unto the door of the sepulchre. And Mary Magdalene and Mary the mother of Joses beheld where he was laid. (Mark 15:21-47)

Matthew

And as they came out, they found a man of Cyrene, Simon by name: him they compelled to bear his cross. And when they were come unto a place called Golgotha, that is to say, a place of a skull, They gave him vinegar to drink mingled with gall: and when he had tasted thereof, he would not drink. And they crucified him, and parted his garments, casting lots: that it might be fulfilled which was spoken by the prophet, They parted my garments among them, and upon my vesture did they cast lots. And sitting down they watched him there; And set up over his head his accusation written, THIS IS JESUS THE KING OF THE JEWS. Then were there two thieves crucified with him, one on the right hand, and another on the left. And they that passed by reviled him, wagging their heads, And saying, Thou that destroyest the temple, and buildest it in three days, save thyself. If thou be the Son of God, come down from the cross. Likewise also the chief priests mocking him, with the scribes and elders, said, He saved others; himself he cannot save. If he be the King of Israel, let him now come down from the cross, and we will believe him. He trusted in God; let him deliver him now, if he will have him: for he said, I am the Son of God. The thieves also, which were crucified with him, cast the same in his teeth. Now from the sixth hour there was darkness over all the land unto the ninth hour. And about the ninth hour Jesus cried with a loud voice, saying, Eli, Eli, lama sabachthani? that is to say, My God, my God, why hast thou forsaken me? Some of them that stood there, when they heard that, said, This man calleth for Elias. And straightway one of them ran, and took a spunge, and filled it with vinegar, and put it on a reed, and gave him to drink. The rest said, Let be, let us see whether Elias will come to save him. Jesus, when he had cried again with a loud voice, yielded up the ghost. And, behold, the veil of the temple was rent in twain from the top to the bottom; and the earth did quake, and the rocks rent; And the graves were opened; and many bodies of the saints which slept arose, And came out of the graves after his resurrection, and went into the holy city, and appeared unto many. Now when the centurion, and they that were with him, watching Jesus, saw the earthquake, and those things that were done, they feared greatly, saying, Truly this was the Son of God. And many women were there beholding afar off, which followed Jesus from Galilee, ministering unto him: Among which was Mary Magdalene, and Mary the mother of James and Joses, and the mother of Zebedee's children. When the even was come, there came a rich man of Arimathaea, named Joseph, who also himself was Jesus' disciple: He went to Pilate, and begged the body of Jesus. Then Pilate commanded the body to be delivered. And when Joseph had taken the body, he wrapped it in a clean linen cloth, And laid it in his own new tomb, which he had hewn out in the rock: and he rolled a great stone to the door of the sepulchre, and departed. And there was Mary Magdalene, and the other Mary, sitting over against the sepulchre. Now the next day, that followed the day of the preparation, the chief priests and Pharisees came together unto Pilate, Saying, Sir, we remember that that deceiver said, while he was yet alive, After three days I will rise again. Command therefore that the sepulchre be made sure until the third day, lest his disciples come by night, and steal him away, and say unto the people, He is risen from the dead: so the last error shall be worse than the first. Pilate said unto them, Ye have a watch: go your way, make it as sure as ye can. So they went, and made the sepulchre sure, sealing the stone, and setting a watch. (Matthew 27:32-66)

Luke

And there were also two other, malefactors, led with him to be put to death. And when they were come to the place, which is called Calvary, there they crucified him, and the malefactors, one on the right hand, and the other on the left. Then said Jesus, Father, *forgive them; for they know not what they do. And they parted his raiment, and cast lots. And the people stood beholding. And the rulers also with them derided him, saying, He saved others; let him save himself, if he be Christ, the chosen of God. And the soldiers also mocked him, coming to him, and offering him vinegar, And saying, If thou be the king of the Jews, save thyself. And a superscription also was written over him in letters of Greek, and Latin, and Hebrew, THIS IS THE KING OF THE JEWS. And one of the malefactors which were hanged railed on him, saying, If thou be Christ, save thyself and us. But the other answering rebuked him, saying, Dost not thou fear God, seeing thou art in the same condemnation? And we indeed justly; for we receive the due reward of our deeds: but this man hath done nothing amiss. And he said unto Jesus, Lord, remember me when thou comest into thy kingdom. And Jesus said unto him, Verily I say unto thee, To day shalt thou be with me in paradise. And it was about the sixth hour, and there was a darkness over all the earth until the ninth hour. And the sun was darkened, and the veil of the temple was rent in the midst. And when Jesus had cried with a loud voice, he said, Father, into thy hands I commend my spirit: and having said thus, he gave up the ghost. Now when the centurion saw what was done, he glorified God, saying, Certainly this was a righteous man. And all the people that came together to that sight, beholding the things which were done, smote their breasts, and returned. And all his acquaintance, and the women that followed him from Galilee, stood afar off, beholding these things. And, behold, there was a man named Joseph, a counsellor; and he was a good man, and a just: (The same had not consented to the counsel and deed of them;) he was of Arimathaea, a city of the Jews: who also himself waited for the kingdom of God. This man went unto Pilate, and begged the body of Jesus. And he took it down, and wrapped it in linen, and laid it in a sepulchre that was hewn in stone, wherein never man before was laid. And that day was the preparation, and the sabbath drew on. And the women also, which came with him from Galilee, followed after, and beheld the sepulchre, and how his body was laid. And they returned, and prepared spices and ointments; and rested the sabbath day according to the commandment. (Luke 23:32-56)*

John

And he bearing his cross went forth into a place called the place of a skull, which is called in the Hebrew Golgotha: Where they crucified him, and two other with him, on either side one, and Jesus in the midst. And Pilate wrote a title, and put it on the cross. And the writing was, JESUS OF NAZARETH THE KING OF THE JEWS. This title then read many of the Jews: for the place where Jesus was crucified was nigh to the city: and it was written in Hebrew, and Greek, and Latin. Then said the chief priests of the Jews to Pilate, Write not, The King of the Jews; but that he said, I am King of the Jews. Pilate answered, What I have written I have written. Then the soldiers, when they had crucified Jesus, took his garments, and made four parts, to every soldier a part; and also his coat: now the coat was without seam, woven from the top throughout. They said therefore among themselves, Let us not rend it, but cast lots for it, whose it shall be: that the scripture might be fulfilled, which saith, They parted my raiment among them, and for my vesture they did cast lots. These things therefore the soldiers did. Now there stood by the cross of Jesus his mother, and his mother's sister, Mary the wife of Cleophas, and Mary Magdalene. When Jesus therefore saw his mother, and the disciple standing by, whom he loved, he saith unto his mother, Woman, behold thy son! Then saith he to the disciple, Behold thy mother! And from that hour that disciple took her unto his own home. After this, Jesus knowing that all things were now accomplished, that the scripture might be fulfilled, saith, I thirst. Now there was set a vessel full of vinegar: and they filled a spunge with vinegar, and put it upon hyssop, and put it to his mouth. When Jesus therefore had received the vinegar, he said, It is finished: and he bowed his head, and gave up the ghost. The Jews therefore, because it was the preparation, that the bodies should not remain upon the cross on the sabbath day, (for that sabbath day was an high day,) besought Pilate that their legs might be broken, and that they might be taken away. Then came the soldiers, and brake the legs of the first, and of the other which was crucified with him. But when they came to Jesus, and saw that he was dead already, they brake not his legs: But one of the soldiers with a spear pierced his side, and forthwith came there out blood and water. And he that saw it bare record, and his record is true: and he knoweth that he saith true, that ye might believe. For these things were done, that the scripture should be fulfilled, A bone of him shall not be broken. And again another scripture saith, They shall look on him whom they pierced. And after this Joseph of Arimathaea, being a disciple of Jesus, but secretly for fear of the Jews, besought Pilate that he might take away the body of Jesus: and Pilate gave him leave. He came therefore, and took the body of Jesus. And there came also Nicodemus, which at the first came to Jesus by night, and brought a mixture of myrrh and aloes, about an hundred pound weight. Then took they the body of Jesus, and wound it in linen clothes with the spices, as the manner of the Jews is to bury. Now in the place where he was crucified there was a garden; and in the garden a new sepulchre, wherein was never man yet laid. There laid they Jesus therefore because of the Jews' preparation day; for the sepulchre was nigh at hand. (John 19:17-19:42)

Analysis of the Crucifixion

Modern Christians have a picture in their minds that what they believe shows a true depiction of what happened during the crucifixion. Can Christian's beliefs stand up to close scrutiny? Most Christians won't attempt to compare what they believe against the actual record of the gospels. If you are a Christian, I urge you to do this now.

There are many aspects of the crucifixion that must be examined in this section. I am only concerned with the most important elements in order to try to make this as brief as possible.

Story Element: *When was Jesus crucified?*

Mark

The day after the Passover meal

9:00 in the morning

And it was the **third hour**, and they **crucified him.**(Mark 15:25)

Matthew

The day after the Passover meal

Time of day not specified

Luke

CHAPTER 10

The day after the Passover meal

Time of day not specified

John

When the Passover lambs were being sacrificed (the day before Passover)

12:00 Noon (Three hours later than Mark)

And it was the preparation of the passover, **and about the sixth hour**: and he saith unto the Jews, Behold your King!

But they cried out, Away with him, away with him, crucify him. Pilate saith unto them, Shall I crucify your King? The chief priests answered, We have no king but Caesar.

Then delivered he him therefore unto them to be crucified. And they took Jesus, and led him away.(John 19:14-16)

Story Element: *Did Jesus carry his own cross?*

Mark

No

Matthew

No

Luke

No

John

Yes

Story Element: *What was written on the placard over Jesus' cross?*

Mark

The King of the Jews

Matthew

This is Jesus the King of the Jews

Luke

This is the King of the Jews

John

Jesus of Nazareth the King of the Jews

Story Element: *What did Jesus say while he was on the cross?*

Mark

And at the ninth hour Jesus cried with a loud voice, saying, Eloi, Eloi, lama sabachthani? which is, being interpreted, My God, my God, why hast thou forsaken me?

Matthew

Now from the sixth hour there was darkness over all the land unto the ninth hour. And about the ninth hour Jesus cried with a loud voice, saying, Eli, Eli, lama sabachthani? that is to say, My God, my God, why hast thou forsaken me?

Luke

Besides what he says to the thieves this is all that Luke records:

And when Jesus had cried with a loud voice, he said, Father, into thy hands I commend my spirit: and having said thus, he gave up the ghost.

John

He saith unto his mother, Woman, behold thy son! Then saith he to the disciple, Behold thy mother! And from that hour that disciple took her unto his own home. After this, Jesus knowing that all things were now accomplished, that the scripture might be fulfilled, saith, I thirst. Now there was set a vessel full of vinegar: and they filled a spunge with vinegar, and put it upon hyssop, and put it to his mouth. When Jesus therefore had received the vinegar, he said, It is finished: and he bowed his head, and gave up the ghost.

Story Element: *What interaction was there between the two thieves and Jesus?*

Mark

Mark only offers this information about the thieves:

And with him they crucify two thieves; the one on his right hand, and the other on his left. And the scripture was fulfilled, which saith, And he was numbered with the transgressors.

There is no interaction between the thieves and Jesus recorded

Matthew

Then were there two thieves crucified with him, one on the right hand, and another on the left... The thieves also, which were crucified with him, cast the same in his teeth.[9]

Both thieves reviled Jesus

Luke

And one of the malefactors which were hanged railed on him, saying, If thou be Christ, save thyself and us. **But the other answering rebuked him, saying, Dost not thou fear God, seeing thou art in the same condemnation?** And we indeed justly; for we receive the due reward of our deeds: but this man hath done nothing amiss. And he said unto Jesus, Lord, remember me when thou comest into thy kingdom. And Jesus

---

9   What are we to make of this strange phrase "cast the same in his teeth" that Matthew uses? It is the terrible translation that disguises what the Greek words actually mean. The Greek word *oneidizo* is used ten times in the New Testament and is translated as *upbraid* three times, *reproach* three times, *revile* twice, and *suffer reproach* once, *cast in (one's) teeth* once here. For some reason the translators are trying to obscure the meaning because they knew this is a clear contradiction to Luke's account. Luke has one of the *thieves* ridiculing Jesus and not the other but Matthew has both of them ridiculing Jesus. John avoids this problem by only mentioning the two thieves in passing without even giving any details of what transpired.

said unto him, Verily I say unto thee, To day shalt thou be with me in paradise.

Only one of the thieves reviled Jesus

John

Other than the following statement:

Where they crucified him, and two other with him, on either side one, and Jesus in the midst.

Nothing else recorded

Story Element: *Where were the followers of Jesus during the crucifixion?*

Mark

Afar off

Matthew

Afar off

Luke

Afar off

John

Close enough to have a important but confusing conversation

Story Element: *When was the curtain torn in the Temple?*

Mark

After Jesus died

Matthew

After Jesus died

Luke

When the sun was darkened before Jesus died

John

Not Mentioned

Story Element: *Was there an earthquake when Jesus died?*

Mark

No

Matthew

Yes

Luke

No

John

No

Story Element: *What does the Centurion say in regard to Jesus?*

Mark

And when the centurion, which stood over against him, saw that he so cried out, and gave up the ghost, he said, <u>Truly this man was the Son of God.</u>

Matthew

Now when the centurion, and they that were with him, watching Jesus, saw the earthquake, and those things that were done, they feared greatly, saying, <u>Truly this was the Son of God.</u>

Luke

Now when the centurion saw what was done, he glorified God, saying, <u>Certainly this was a righteous man.</u>

John

The Centurion is not mentioned, only a soldier.

But one of the soldiers with a spear pierced his side, and forthwith came there out blood and water. And he that saw it bare record, and his record is true: and he knoweth that he saith true, that ye might believe.

Story Element: *Was Jesus' side pierced with a spear?*

Mark

No

Matthew

No

Luke

No

John

Yes

Story Element: *What other strange events happened when Jesus died?*

Mark

None recorded

Matthew

An earthquake occurred and the rocks rent and the graves were opened; and many bodies of the saints which slept arose, And came out of the graves after his resurrection, and went into the holy city, and appeared unto many. [10]

---

10 It is unclear why these saints would wait in their graves for three days to appear in Jerusalem instead of doing it immediately. What is even more unclear is why no historians write anything about this event. Not one author in the New Testament, except Matthew, wrote

Luke

None recorded

John

None recorded

Story Element: *When did Joseph ask Pilate for Jesus' body?*

Mark

*And now when the **even was come**,[11] because it was the preparation, that is, the day before the sabbath, Joseph of Arimathaea, an honourable counsellor, which also waited for the kingdom of God, came, and went in boldly unto Pilate, and craved the body of Jesus.*

Matthew

Matthew agrees with Mark

*When the **even was come**, there came a rich man of Arimathaea, named Joseph, who also himself was Jesus' disciple: He went to Pilate, and begged the body of Jesus.*

Luke

Sometime after Jesus' death

John

Sometime after Jesus' death

Story Element: *Did Joseph anoint Jesus' body?*

Mark

No

Matthew

No

Luke

No

John

---

anything about this. The New Testament indicates that Jesus is the firstfruits in 1 Corinthians 15:20: *But now is Christ risen from the dead, and become the firstfruits of them that slept.* Actually these saints were raised first making them the firstfruits of the resurrection not Jesus as Paul states.

11 This means that Jesus remained on the cross until it was dark. This interferes with the Christian teaching that Jesus was in the tomb before it got dark. This means that the first day of Jesus' "three days and three nights" did not happen until after the first full night. If Jesus was already risen when the women got to the tomb while it was still dark as in John's account then there are only two full days, no partial days and three nights. This is still accounting for using the erroneous concept Christians have developed that in Jewish thought that any part of a day can be counted as a full day. Therefore Jesus did not fulfill the one sign that he promised, the sign of Jonah. This also makes Jesus a false prophet.

Yes

Story Element: *What did the women do after Jesus was buried?*

Mark

And Mary Magdalene and Mary the mother of Joses beheld where he was laid.

Matthew

And the women also, which came with him from Galilee, followed after, and beheld the sepulchre, and how his body was laid. And they returned, and prepared spices and ointments; and rested the sabbath day according to the commandment.

Luke

And laid it in his own new tomb, which he had hewn out in the rock: and he rolled a great stone to the door of the sepulchre, and departed. And there was Mary Magdalene, and the other Mary, sitting over against the sepulchre.

John

Not mentioned

Story Element: *What did the Scribes and Pharisees do to secure the tomb?*

Mark

Not mentioned

Matthew

Now the next day, that followed the day of the preparation, the chief priests and Pharisees came together unto Pilate, Saying, Sir, we remember that that deceiver said, while he was yet alive, After three days I will rise again. Command therefore that the sepulchre be made sure until the third day, lest his disciples come by night, and steal him away, and say unto the people, He is risen from the dead: so the last error shall be worse than the first. Pilate said unto them, Ye have a watch: go your way, make it as sure as ye can. So they went, and made the sepulchre sure, sealing the stone, and setting a watch.

Luke

Not mentioned

John

Not mentioned

Conclusions about the Crucifixion

I find it strange that no names of any witnesses are mentioned and also that God's test of the truth being established by two or more witnesses is ignored. As a matter of fact, almost every testimony is in dispute in all of these accounts. This type of testimony would not prove anything in a court of law despite what Lee Strobel[12] says.

If three eye witnesses testified in court that an accident happened on Monday, you

---

12 Author of many Christian books, such as the *Case for Christ*.

might believe that it did happen on a Monday but if a fourth witness testified that it was Sunday when the accident occurred, there would be a problem. You would probably say that the fourth eyewitness was wrong. This is similar to what is going on here in the gospels with one big difference that Christian apologists would like you to forget. The difference being that not one of these authors claims to be an eyewitness.

Most Christians don't realize that we don't know who actually wrote these books. It is only Church tradition that assigns names to the four gospels. Remember, John has Jesus crucified while the lambs are being slaughtered the day before the passover but the other gospels have Jesus eating the Passover and crucified the day after. Someone is lying. I find it even more strange that the author of the gospel that teaches outright that Jesus is God, John, is also the one gospel that differs the most from the other three. Mark, as well as Matthew, and Luke have the disciples and the women standing far off but John again stands alone. He has them standing close enough to have a polite conversation. All this is recorded in the passages at the beginning of this section. Read them again for yourself. All this time, Christians have had in the back of their minds that all the gospels contain all of the truth when it comes down to the crucifixion, but when you really compare them the problems jump out at you. I really hate to beat a dead horse but these books are all we have when it comes to knowing anything about the life of Jesus. If we had four and only four accounts of Adolf Hitler's or Winston Churchill's life that contained discrepancies and contradictions like these gospels do, would we be sure that we knew anything about his life at all? Most people would say the accounts couldn't be trusted but with the gospels, Christians, of course, are ecstatic to make an exception.

It seems that the god of the Christians didn't do such a thorough job here in his revelation. There is more. Mark has darkness cover the earth and the curtain of the temple is torn, of course. Matthew and Luke agree but not John. John doesn't mention any darkness or the curtain. John is too busy stretching Hebrew scriptures like Spandex to make them fit Jesus. Mark also has Joseph of Arimathaea ask Pilate for Jesus' body. He buys fine linen, takes Jesus down, wraps him in the linen, and put him in the sepulchre. Matthew, again, agrees and also Luke. John again is the odd man out. He has Joseph along with Nicodemus also put a hundred pounds of spices on Jesus with the linen.

There is one more strange detail about this part of the story. Mark says,

"when the even was come, because it was the preparation, that is, the day before the sabbath, Joseph of Arimathaea, an honourable counsellor, which also waited for the kingdom of God, came, and went in boldly unto Pilate, and craved the body of Jesus"

and Luke says,

"When the even was come, there came a rich man of Arimathaea, named Joseph, who also himself was Jesus' disciple: He went to Pilate, and begged the body of Jesus."

These passages indicate that Jesus is still hanging on the cross when the evening comes. This means that Jesus is hanging on the cross, dead, on the Sabbath. When the evening comes so does the Sabbath because the Jewish day begins at sundown. Here is the problem. This means that Jesus was not in the tomb before nightfall. John's account says the following regarding this,

"The Jews therefore, because it was the preparation, that the bodies should not remain

upon the cross on the sabbath day, (for that sabbath day was an high day)."

John's portrayal seems to be indicating that Jesus was placed in the tomb before the evening. I say this because of John's extra detail about buying the spices and applying them. If Joseph had waited til he had permission to take the body he would have had to purchase them before sundown and the beginning of the Sabbath. To back up this idea, I submit that Luke also states that the women,

"returned, and prepared spices and ointments; and rested the sabbath day according to the commandment."

This is the reason why they were returning to the tomb as we will see in the next section. This is because, supposedly in the synoptic gospels, Jesus' body had not been anointed with spices because of the hurry to put his body in the tomb. They must anoint him to complete the ritual.

This is a contradiction because a hundred pounds of spices were wrapped up with the linen in John's account. Because of the fact that the women rested the day after the crucifixion proves there is no doubt the day Jesus was crucified on was followed by the evening of a Sabbath. It seems that Mark and Matthew both have Jesus on the cross on the Sabbath but Luke and John have him in the tomb before the Sabbath. Up to this point in our analysis, it had seemed that John couldn't get his story straight but now it seems that two of the synoptic gospels have a new problem to deal with but we will not discuss this *Resurrection Dilemma* until we are well into the next section.

Matthew is the only gospel to contain the story of the guards posted at the tomb. It is hard to overlook that this is missing in the other narratives. Perhaps Matthew was trying to show rumors that Jesus' body was stolen couldn't have been true. Another element that Matthew is the only one to tell us about is an earthquake.

Matthew is the only gospel to say anything about this strange occurrence,

"And the graves were opened; and many bodies of the saints which slept arose, And came out of the graves after his resurrection, and went into the holy city, and appeared unto many."

We are told here that many bodies of dead saints arose but evidently they hid in their graves for three days and nights until Jesus arose. Who is among them? We know the name of the man that had his ear cut off by Peter. We know the name of the man that carried Jesus' cross but nobody thought to get the name of one of these risen saints? This certainly would have been recorded by someone but not even Peter mentions this in his sermons to the great crowds to whom he preached. What I also find strange is that Jesus is considered the first fruits of the resurrection by Paul. He makes no indication in the least that he knows anything regarding this *zombie uprising* as many have called it.

But now is Christ risen from the dead, and become the firstfruits of them that slept. (1 Corinthians 15:20)

But every man in his own order: Christ the firstfruits; afterward they that are Christ's at his coming. (1 Corinthians 15:23)

Luke has Jesus have a lucid conversation with one of the thieves. He also has Jesus say more than in any other gospel. He doesn't question God as he does in Mark and

Matthew or seem to be in any type of mental anguish. John follows Luke's lead here. There is no calling on God, asking why he has forsaken him. John doesn't have Jesus do this either.

John's account has Jesus only say a couple of things while on the cross. He says, *"Woman, behold thy son!"*, *"Behold thy mother!"*, *"I thirst"*, and *"It is finished."* John which throughout his gospel has Jesus giving incredibly long discourses has Jesus offer only these four short utterances.

Can you trust these accounts? If you think that you can, I urge you to go back and read them again.

The Resurrection

Mark

And when the sabbath was past, Mary Magdalene, and Mary the mother of James, and Salome, had bought sweet spices, that they might come and anoint him. And very early in the morning the first day of the week, they came unto the sepulchre at the rising of the sun. And they said among themselves, Who shall roll us away the stone from the door of the sepulchre? And when they looked, they saw that the stone was rolled away: for it was very great. And entering into the sepulchre, they saw a young man sitting on the right side, clothed in a long white garment; and they were affrighted. And he saith unto them, Be not affrighted: Ye seek Jesus of Nazareth, which was crucified: he is risen; he is not here: behold the place where they laid him. But go your way, tell his disciples and Peter that he goeth before you into Galilee: there shall ye see him, as he said unto you. And they went out quickly, and fled from the sepulchre; for they trembled and were amazed: neither said they any thing to any man; for they were afraid. (Mark 16:1-8)

Now when Jesus was risen early the first day of the week, he appeared first to Mary Magdalene, out of whom he had cast seven devils. And she went and told them that had been with him, as they mourned and wept. And they, when they had heard that he was alive, and had been seen of her, believed not. After that he appeared in another form unto two of them, as they walked, and went into the country. And they went and told it unto the residue: neither believed they them. Afterward he appeared unto the eleven as they sat at meat, and upbraided them with their unbelief and hardness of heart, because they believed not them which had seen him after he was risen. And he said unto them, Go ye into all the world, and preach the gospel to every creature. He that believeth and is baptized shall be saved; but he that believeth not shall be damned. And these signs shall follow them that believe; In my name shall they cast out devils; they shall speak with new tongues; They shall take up serpents; and if they drink any deadly thing, it shall not hurt them; they shall lay hands on the sick, and they shall recover. So then after the Lord had spoken unto them, he was received up into heaven, and sat on the right hand of God. And they went forth, and preached every where, the Lord working with them, and confirming the word with signs following. Amen. (Mark 16:9-20)

Matthew

In the end of the sabbath, as it began to dawn toward the first day of the week, came Mary Magdalene and the other Mary to see the sepulchre. And, behold, there was a great earthquake: for the angel of the Lord descended from heaven, and came and rolled back the stone from the door, and sat upon it. His countenance was like lightning, and his raiment white as snow: And for fear of him the keepers did shake, and became as dead men. And the angel answered and said unto the women, Fear not ye: for I know that ye seek Jesus, which was crucified. He is not here: for he is risen, as he said. Come, see the place where the Lord lay. And go quickly, and tell his disciples that he is risen from the dead; and, behold, he goeth before you into Galilee; there shall ye see him: lo, I have told you. And they departed quickly from the sepulchre with fear and great joy; and did run to bring his disciples word. And as they went to tell his disciples, behold, Jesus met them, saying, All hail. And they came and held him by the feet, and worshipped him. Then said Jesus unto them, Be not afraid: go tell my brethren that they go into Galilee, and there shall they see me. Now when they were going, behold, some of the watch came into the city, and shewed unto the chief priests all the things that were done. And when they were assembled with the elders, and had taken counsel, they gave large money unto the soldiers, Saying, Say ye, His disciples came by night, and stole him away while we slept. And if this come to the governor's ears, we will persuade him, and secure you. So they took the money, and did as they were taught: and this saying is commonly reported among the Jews until this day. Then the eleven disciples went away into Galilee, into a mountain where Jesus had appointed them. And when they saw him, they worshipped him: but some doubted. And Jesus came and spake unto them, saying, All power is given unto me in heaven and in earth. Go ye therefore, and teach all nations, baptizing them in the name of the Father, and of the Son, and of the Holy Ghost: Teaching them to observe all things whatsoever I have commanded you: and, lo, I am with you alway, even unto the end of the world. Amen. (Matthew 28:1-20)

Luke

Now upon the first day of the week, very early in the morning, they came unto the sepulchre, bringing the spices which they had prepared, and certain others with them. And they found the stone rolled away from the sepulchre. And they entered in, and found not the body of the Lord Jesus. And it came to pass, as they were much perplexed thereabout, behold, two men stood by them in shining garments: And as they were afraid, and bowed down their faces to the earth, they said unto them, Why seek ye the living among the dead? He is not here, but is risen: remember how he spake unto you when he was yet in Galilee, Saying, The Son of man must be delivered into the hands of sinful men, and be crucified, and the third day rise again. And they remembered his words, And returned from the sepulchre, and told all these things unto the eleven, and to all the rest. It was Mary Magdalene, and Joanna, and Mary the mother of James, and other women that were with them, which told these things unto the apostles. And their words seemed to them as idle tales, and they believed them not. Then arose Peter, and ran unto the sepulchre; and stooping down, he beheld the linen clothes laid by themselves, and departed, wondering in himself at that which was come to pass. And, behold, two of them went that same day to a village called Emmaus, which was from Jerusalem about threescore furlongs. And they talked together of all these things which had happened. And it came to pass, that, while they communed together and reasoned, Jesus himself drew near, and went with them. But their eyes were holden that they should not know him. And he said unto them, What manner of communications are these that ye have one to another, as ye walk, and are sad? And the one of them, whose name was Cleopas, answering said unto him, Art thou only a stranger in Jerusalem, and hast not known the things which are come to pass there in these days? And he said unto them, What things? And they said unto him, Concerning Jesus of Nazareth, which was a prophet mighty in deed and word before God and all the people: And how the chief priests and our rulers delivered him to be condemned to death, and have crucified him. But we trusted that it had been he which should have redeemed Israel: and beside all this, to day is the third day since these things were done. Yea, and certain women also of our company made us astonished, which were early at the sepulchre; And when they found not his body, they came, saying, that they had also seen a vision of angels, which said that he was alive. And certain of them which were with us went to the sepulchre, and found it even so as the women had said: but him they saw not. Then he said unto them, O fools, and slow of heart to believe all that the prophets have spoken: Ought not Christ to have suffered these things, and to enter into his glory? And beginning at Moses and all the prophets, he expounded unto them in all the scriptures the things concerning himself. And they drew nigh unto the village, whither they went: and he made as though he would have gone further. But they constrained him, saying, Abide with us: for it is toward evening, and the day is far spent. And he went in to tarry with them. And it came to pass, as he sat at meat with them, he took bread, and blessed it, and brake, and gave to them. And their eyes were opened, and they knew him; and he vanished out of their sight. And they said one to another, Did not our heart burn within us, while he talked with us by the way, and while he opened to us the scriptures? And they rose up the same hour, and returned to Jerusalem, and found the eleven gathered together, and them that were with them, Saying, The Lord is risen indeed, and hath appeared to Simon. And they told what things were done in the way, and how he was known of them in breaking of bread. And as they thus spake, Jesus himself stood in the midst of them, and saith unto them, Peace be unto you. But they were terrified and affrighted, and supposed that they had seen a spirit. And he said unto them, Why are ye troubled? and why do thoughts arise in your hearts? Behold my hands and my feet, that it is I myself: handle me, and see; for a spirit hath not flesh and bones, as ye see me have. And when he had thus spoken, he shewed them his hands and his feet. And while they yet believed not for joy, and wondered, he said unto them, Have ye here any meat? And they gave him a piece of a broiled fish, and of an honeycomb. And he took it, and did eat before them. And he said unto them, These are the words which I spake unto you, while I was yet with you, that all things must be fulfilled, which were written in the law of Moses, and in the prophets, and in the psalms, concerning me. Then opened he their understanding, that they might understand the scriptures, And said unto them, Thus it is written, and thus it behoved Christ to suffer, and to rise from the dead the third day: And that repentance and remission of sins should be preached in his name among all nations, beginning at Jerusalem. And ye are witnesses of these things. And, behold, I send the promise of my Father upon you: but tarry ye in the city of Jerusalem, until ye be endued with power from on high. And he led them out as far as to Bethany, and he lifted up his hands, and blessed them. And it came to pass, while he blessed them, he was parted from them, and carried up into heaven. And they worshipped him, and returned to Jerusalem with great joy: And were continually in the temple, praising and blessing God. Amen. (Luke 24:1-53)

CHAPTER 10
John

The first day of the week cometh Mary Magdalene early, when it was yet dark, unto the sepulchre, and seeth the stone taken away from the sepulchre. Then she runneth, and cometh to Simon Peter, and to the other disciple, whom Jesus loved, and saith unto them, They have taken away the Lord out of the sepulchre, and we know not where they have laid him. Peter therefore went forth, and that other disciple, and came to the sepulchre. So they ran both together: and the other disciple did outrun Peter, and came first to the sepulchre. And he stooping down, and looking in, saw the linen clothes lying; yet went he not in. Then cometh Simon Peter following him, and went into the sepulchre, and seeth the linen clothes lie, And the napkin, that was about his head, not lying with the linen clothes, but wrapped together in a place by itself. Then went in also that other disciple, which came first to the sepulchre, and he saw, and believed. For as yet they knew not the scripture, that he must rise again from the dead. Then the disciples went away again unto their own home. But Mary stood without at the sepulchre weeping: and as she wept, she stooped down, and looked into the sepulchre, And seeth two angels in white sitting, the one at the head, and the other at the feet, where the body of Jesus had lain. And they say unto her, Woman, why weepest thou? She saith unto them, Because they have taken away my Lord, and I know not where they have laid him. And when she had thus said, she turned herself back, and saw Jesus standing, and knew not that it was Jesus. Jesus saith unto her, Woman, why weepest thou? whom seekest thou? She, supposing him to be the gardener, saith unto him, Sir, if thou have borne him hence, tell me where thou hast laid him, and I will take him away. Jesus saith unto her, Mary. She turned herself, and saith unto him, Rabboni; which is to say, Master. Jesus saith unto her, Touch me not; for I am not yet ascended to my Father: but go to my brethren, and say unto them, I ascend unto my Father, and your Father; and to my God, and your God. Mary Magdalene came and told the disciples that she had seen the Lord, and that he had spoken these things unto her. Then the same day at evening, being the first day of the week, when the doors were shut where the disciples were assembled for fear of the Jews, came Jesus and stood in the midst, and saith unto them, Peace be unto you. And when he had so said, he shewed unto them his hands and his side. Then were the disciples glad, when they saw the Lord. Then said Jesus to them again, Peace be unto you: as my Father hath sent me, even so send I you. And when he had said this, he breathed on them, and saith unto them, Receive ye the Holy Ghost: Whose soever sins ye remit, they are remitted unto them; and whose soever sins ye retain, they are retained. But Thomas, one of the twelve, called Didymus, was not with them when Jesus came. The other disciples therefore said unto him, We have seen the Lord. But he said unto them, Except I shall see in his hands the print of the nails, and put my finger into the print of the nails, and thrust my hand into his side, I will not believe. And after eight days again his disciples were within, and Thomas with them: then came Jesus, the doors being shut, and stood in the midst, and said, Peace be unto you. Then saith he to Thomas, Reach hither thy finger, and behold my hands; and reach hither thy hand, and thrust it into my side: and be not faithless, but believing. And Thomas answered and said unto him, My Lord and my God. Jesus saith unto him, Thomas, because thou hast seen me, thou hast believed: blessed are they that have not seen, and yet have believed. And many other signs truly did Jesus in the presence of his disciples, which are not written in this book: But these are written, that ye might believe that Jesus is the Christ, the Son of God; and that believing ye might have life through his name. (John 28:1-31)

CHAPTER 10

Analysis of the Resurrection

When someone hears different accounts that people tell regarding an incident they often will try to combine the events described into a super account in order to make everything come together into a coherent picture. Sometimes this is possible. Let me give you an example.

Three people witness an accident. One may say they saw a red car come down the street and strike another car stopped at the stoplight. The second person indicates they saw a brown car hit a car at the light. The third and final witness says that the car that hit the stopped vehicle was distracted by a jaywalker that passed in front of them before they hit the stopped car. All witnesses in this case are all telling about the same story and are telling the truth. There are no contradictions that have been told by the witnesses. There is a disagreement as to the color of the car because one person thought the car was a brown instead of red and two witnesses omit the fact of the jaywalker but there are no contradictions.

Sometimes, there are witnesses that give information that may not be true because their account contains contradictions. This is an example.

The police are looking for someone that robbed a local gas station. One man says he was walking up to the gas station from his car at about three o'clock. He saw the lone gunman run out of the door and jump into a white work truck with two other men in it. They sped off and headed east. A second witness was in the back of the store picking out some drinks for his children waiting in his car outside. He saw two men rob the attendant and flee. Through the dirty window, he saw the two men get into two different trucks and head off to the north together.

There could be many reasons why these two witnesses believed what they saw was the truth but let's be frank here and say that at least one of them isn't correct. Most people assume that one person is correct in what they saw and the other is not. Perhaps they both have elements that they are probably correct about. To be truthful, both of them might be incorrect in what they saw. There is no possible way to combine these accounts and make one true account of what actually happened. What would happen if a third and fourth witness were introduced. Suppose one witness said the event happened on Thursday and the other said it happened on Friday, both can't be telling the truth.

This is the type of situation found in the gospel's telling of the resurrection and maybe in a much larger context, the entire life of Jesus. There is a high burden of proof in a secular court of law but shouldn't there be a higher standard in the New Testament?

One thing to remember is that none of the gospel writers say at anytime that they are actual eyewitnesses to any event in the life of Jesus. They have used someone else's information and/or hearsay to construct their account. Conversely, there are gospel writers that did claim to be eyewitnesses that wrote their accounts down. The contents of these non-canonical gospels are often so outlandish that none but the most irrational people would consider them trustworthy such as the gospel of Peter for instance, where a gigantic Jesus and a walking-talking cross emerge from the tomb when Jesus arose from the dead.

Christians will read the differing accounts of the resurrection and figure out that there is something terribly wrong. Instead of seriously studying the stories, they try to congeal them into one solid mass to solve the problems and contradictions. They will try to blur the differences in the accounts and make them fit together. It only makes things worse. Christian apologists will twist, change, combine and ignore elements in the accounts to make the stories fit together somehow. Let's see what's wrong with the stories that makes all this wrestling necessary.

Story Element: *When did people first go to the tomb?*

Mark

At the rising of the sun

Matthew

As it began to dawn

Luke

Very early in the morning

John

When it was yet dark

Story Element: *Were the women going to anoint Jesus' body?*

Mark

Yes

Matthew

No

Luke

Yes

John

No

Story Element: *Who went to the tomb first?*

Mark

Mary Magdalene, Mary the mother of James and Salome

Matthew

Mary Magdalene, and the other Mary

Luke

Mary Magdalene, Joanna, Mary the mother of James, and other women

John

Mary Magdalene

Story Element: *Were guards at the tomb?*

Mark

No

Matthew

Yes

Luke

No

John

No

Story Element: *Was the stone rolled away from the tomb?*

Mark

Already rolled away

Matthew

There is a great earthquake and an angel was seen coming down from heaven, rolls away stone and sits on it

Luke

Already rolled away

John

Already rolled away

Story Element: *Any unusual happenings surrounding the resurrection?*

Mark

No

Matthew

Great Earthquake / Guards frightened and become as dead men

Luke

No

John

John is the most different account. Mary Magdalene comes to the tomb finds the stone rolled away and immediately leaves to go tell the disciples

Story Element: *Do they see anyone at the tomb?*

Mark

One young man sitting on right side in long white garment

Matthew

One angel, countenance like lightning, raiment white as snow

Luke

Two men stood beside them in shining garments

John

Mary Magdalene sees two angels in white sitting inside the tomb, one at the head and one at the feet but not until Peter and the other disciple leave. This is after the initial visit.

Story Element: *What do the angels say to those present?*

Mark

Be not affrighted: Ye seek Jesus of Nazareth, which was crucified: he is risen; he is not here: behold the place where they laid him. But go your way, tell his disciples and Peter that he goeth before you into Galilee: there shall ye see him, as he said unto you.

Matthew

Fear not ye: for I know that ye seek Jesus, which was crucified. He is not here: for he is risen, as he said. Come, see the place where the Lord lay. And go quickly, and tell his disciples that he is risen from the dead; and, behold, he goeth before you into Galilee; there shall ye see him: lo, I have told you.

Luke

Why seek ye the living among the dead? He is not here, but is risen: remember how he spake unto you when he was yet in Galilee, Saying, The Son of man must be delivered into the hands of sinful men, and be crucified, and the third day rise again.

John

Woman, why weepest thou?

Story Element: *Does Jesus make an appearance at the tomb?*

Mark

No, not in the best earliest manuscripts but he does appear to Mary Magdalene in the edited version of Mark

Matthew

No, only after they leave the tomb

Luke

No

John

Yes but not until the angel appears to Mary Magdalene which occurs after the disciples arrive at and leave the tomb

Story Element: *Who does he appear to?*

Mark

Mary Magdalene

Matthew

He appears to Mary Magdalene and the other Mary as they are on the way to tell the disciples but not actually at the tomb

Luke

No appearance at the tomb

John

Mary Magdalene

Story Element: *What happens during this appearance?*

Mark

Not mentioned

Matthew

They held him by his feet and *worshiped him*

Luke

No appearance at the tomb

John

*Jesus says unto her, "***Touch me not***; for I am not yet ascended to my Father: but go to my brethren, and say unto them, I ascend unto my Father, and your Father; and to my God, and your God."*

Story Element: *Who do they tell?*

Mark

No one but in the *edited version of Mark,* Mary tells an unidentified group of people

Matthew

The disciples

Luke

The eleven

John

Mary went to the disciples and was accompanied to the tomb by Peter and "*the other disciple*"

Story Element: *Where does Jesus say to meet him?*

Mark

Galilee

Matthew

Galilee

Luke

Not mentioned

John

Not mentioned

Story Element: *Were there appearances after the tomb but before he met the disciples, and to whom?*

Mark

Yes, to two others in "another form." [13]

Matthew

No

Luke

Yes, to two others

John

No

Story Element: *What did Jesus say to these two?*

Mark

Nothing worth reporting

Matthew

Luke

"O fools, and slow of heart to believe all that the prophets have spoken: Ought not Christ to have suffered these things, and to enter into his glory?" And beginning at Moses and all the prophets, he expounded unto them in all the scriptures the things concerning himself.

John

Story Element: *Did Jesus appear to them in Galilee?*

Mark

Unknown [14]

---

13 This Greek word used here is "hetera" where we get our word "hetero". Its true meaning is "different" as in the usage of "heterosexual". The word "another" is deceptive. The correct word to use here is "different" not "another." If I have a dollar in one hand and I say that I have "another" dollar in my pocket you would expect it to look the same as the one in my hand. If I say I have a "different" dollar in my pocket when I pull it out you expect it to be strange or not like the one in my hand. The author here is saying that the form he appeared in was not exactly the same. This would also agree with the source that Matthew used that stated the two travelers did not recognize him although he had been with them before the resurrection for what some believe to be a time-span longer than three years.

14 The Galilee is more than sixty miles away from Jerusalem. It seems improbable that Jesus appeared to them there that same day as the other accounts indicate because the disciples

CHAPTER 10   185

Matthew

Yes, they went to Galilee but some doubted at his appearance

Luke

No, they remained in Jerusalem

John

Unknown

Story Element: *How many disciples did Jesus first appear to together?*

Mark

11[15]

Matthew

11, This also is described as the first appearance and nothing is said about Thomas being absent

Luke

11

John

10

Story Element: *What occurred at this appearance?*

Mark

Go ye into all the world, and preach the gospel to every creature. He that believeth and is baptized shall be saved; but he that believeth not shall be damned. And these signs shall follow them that believe; In my name shall they cast out devils; they shall speak with new tongues; They shall take up serpents; and if they drink any deadly thing, it shall not hurt them; they shall lay hands on the sick, and they shall recover.

Matthew

Jesus came and spake unto them, saying, All power is given unto me in heaven and in earth. Go ye therefore, and teach all nations, baptizing them in the name of the Father, and of the Son, and of the Holy Ghost: Teaching them to observe all things whatsoever I have commanded you: and, lo, I am with you alway, even unto the end of the world. Amen.

Luke

---

could not have traveled between the two places in less than a day.

15 No mention is made about Thomas being absent. This reference must be to Jesus' first appearance to the disciples because Jesus scolds them for not believing. If this was a second or later appearance Jesus would not have to scold them because they would have already seen him previously. If Thomas was not present then Judas must have been present to make a total of eleven disciples. If it is impossible in your mind for Judas to be there because he has committed suicide then you must find another way to deal with the resulting contradiction.

Jesus said, *"Peace be unto you." But they were terrified and affrighted, and supposed that they had seen a spirit. And he said unto them, "Why are ye troubled? and why do thoughts arise in your hearts? Behold my hands and my feet, that it is I myself: handle me, and see; for a spirit hath not flesh and bones, as ye see me have." And when he had thus spoken, he shewed them his hands and his feet. And while they yet believed not for joy, and wondered, he said unto them, "Have ye here any meat? " And they gave him a piece of a broiled fish, and of an honeycomb. And he took it, and did eat before them. And he said unto them, "These are the words which I spake unto you, while I was yet with you, that all things must be fulfilled, which were written in the law of Moses, and in the prophets, and in the psalms, concerning me." Then opened he their understanding, that they might understand the scriptures, And said unto them, "Thus it is written, and thus it behoved Christ to suffer, and to rise from the dead the third day. And that repentance and remission of sins should be preached in his name among all nations, beginning at Jerusalem. And ye are witnesses of these things. And, behold, I send the promise of my Father upon you: but tarry ye in the city of Jerusalem, until ye be endued with power from on high."*

John

Peace be unto you. And when he had so said, he shewed unto them his hands and his side. Then were the disciples glad, when they saw the Lord. Then said Jesus to them again, Peace be unto you: as my Father hath sent me, even so send I you. And when he had said this, he breathed on them, and saith unto them, Receive ye the Holy Ghost: Whose soever sins ye remit, they are remitted unto them; and whose soever sins ye retain, they are retained. But Thomas, one of the twelve, called Didymus, was not with them when Jesus came.

Story Element: *What evidence does Jesus offer to convince the disciples that he had been crucified?*

Mark

None

Matthew

None

Luke

Behold my hands and my feet, that it is I myself: handle me, and see; for a spirit hath not flesh and bones, as ye see me have. And when he had thus spoken, he shewed them his hands and his feet.[16] *And while they yet believed not for joy, and wondered, he said unto them, Have ye here any meat? And they gave him a piece of a broiled fish, and of an honeycomb. And he took it, and did eat before them.*

It seems that Luke did not know about the wound in Jesus' side!

John

Then the same day at evening, being the first day of the week, when the doors were shut where the disciples were assembled for fear of the Jews, came Jesus and stood in

---

16 Unlike in John's account, Jesus does not mention the wound in his side. John is the only account that mentions any aspect of Jesus being pierced in his side.

the midst, and saith unto them, Peace be unto you. And when he had so said, he shewed unto them his hands and his side.

Story Element: *Does Jesus make an additional appearance to the disciples and what does he say to them at this appearance?*

Mark

No

Matthew

No

Luke

No

John

Yes, *Then Jesus said to Thomas, "Reach hither thy finger, and behold my hands; and reach hither thy hand, and thrust it into my side: and be not faithless, but believing." And Thomas answered and said unto him, "My Lord and my God." Jesus saith unto him, "Thomas, because thou hast seen me, thou hast believed: blessed are they that have not seen, and yet have believed."*

Story Element: *When does Jesus ascend to heaven?*

Mark

Ascends to heaven immediately after **first** appearance to disciples.

Matthew

Not mentioned

Luke

Ascends to heaven immediately after **first** appearance to disciples

John

Ascends to heaven immediately after **second** appearance to disciples.

Story Element: *Other Details*

Mark

Instead of waiting for empowerment from on high the disciples went forth and preached everywhere.

Matthew

No ascension being recorded leaves this gospel incomplete and corresponds to the fact that the original gospel of Mark was also incomplete with no resurrection sightings and no ascension.

Luke

John

The strange statement in this account, "For as yet they knew not the scripture, that he must rise again from the dead," seems to mean something different than the statement that they did not remember and had to be reminded by the angel in Luke's account

Conclusion

If you spend any amount of time examining these accounts you would have to see the problems that are found in the gospel stories. I had to ask myself if any of these stories could be trusted. This is the only information that we have about Jesus. If God wanted us to be confident about the information that we received why did he preserve it in this manner? The Jews don't hold any of these accounts as being truth but the Hebrew Scriptures present the picture that always has the nations coming to Jews for the truth. The Jews aren't going to come to the nations for the truth as Christianity teaches.

In conclusion, I believe that any reasonable person can see that the only accounts that the Church has preserved in their Canon cannot be trusted and leaves us with a confusing portrait of the events surrounding the death, burial and supposed resurrection of Jesus.

CHAPTER 11

Will the Real Messiah Step Forward?

Christians will be quick to spout that Jesus is *the Messiah*, but few will be able to tell you about the passages in the Hebrew Bible that clearly describe the Messianic age. These passages describe the end-times-king and the conditions that surround him, but don't portray a man that sounds much like Jesus. Here is one passage that few if any Christians will point you to during a serious discussion about God's end-times King.

And there shall come forth a rod out of the stem of Jesse, and a Branch shall grow out of his roots: And the spirit of the LORD shall rest upon him, the spirit of wisdom and understanding, the spirit of counsel and might, the spirit of knowledge and of the fear of the LORD; And shall make him of quick understanding in the fear of the LORD: and he shall not judge after the sight of his eyes, neither reprove after the hearing of his ears: But with righteousness shall he judge the poor, and reprove with equity for the meek of the earth: and he shall smite the earth with the rod of his mouth, and with the breath of his lips shall he slay the wicked. And righteousness shall be the girdle of his loins, and faithfulness the girdle of his reins. The wolf also shall dwell with the lamb, and the leopard shall lie down with the kid; and the calf and the young lion and the fatling together; and a little child shall lead them. And the cow and the bear shall feed; their young ones shall lie down together: and the lion shall eat straw like the ox. And the sucking child shall play on the hole of the asp, and the weaned child shall put his hand on the cockatrice' den. They shall not hurt nor destroy in all my holy mountain: for the earth shall be full of the knowledge of the LORD, as the waters cover the sea. And in that day there shall be a root of Jesse, which shall stand for an ensign of the people; to it shall the Gentiles seek: and his rest shall be glorious. And it shall come to pass in that day, that the Lord shall set his hand again the second time to recover the remnant of his people, which shall be left, from Assyria, and from Egypt, and from Pathros, and from Cush, and from Elam, and from Shinar, and from Hamath, and from the islands of the sea. And he shall set up an ensign for the nations, and shall assemble the outcasts of Israel, and gather together the dispersed of Judah from the four corners of the earth. The envy also of Ephraim shall depart, and the adversaries of Judah shall be cut off: Ephraim shall not envy Judah, and Judah shall not vex Ephraim. But they shall fly upon the shoulders of the Philistines toward the west; they shall spoil them of the east together: they shall lay their hand upon Edom and Moab; and the children of Ammon shall obey them. And the LORD shall utterly destroy the tongue of the Egyptian sea; and with his mighty wind shall he shake his hand over the river, and shall smite it in the seven streams, and make men go over dryshod. And there shall be an highway for the remnant of his people, which shall be left, from Assyria; like as it was to Israel in the day that he came up out of the land of Egypt. (Isaiah 11:1-16)

Let's look at what the passage says about the end-times-king. Then we will examine what this passage says about the Messianic Age, which is the broader context.

- The phrase, *"the spirit of the LORD shall rest upon him, the spirit of wisdom and understanding, the spirit of counsel and might, the spirit of knowledge and of the fear of the LORD"* might sound like a good description of Jesus at first glance. Does the Hebrew Bible even once indicate that the spirit of the fear of God rests on the Almighty? This is an unknown concept in the Hebrew Bible. The phrase *"And shall make him of quick understanding in the fear of the LORD"* is translated differently by the Jews. They render it, *"And he will be animated by the fear of the Lord."*

  If you are like most Christians that believe that Jesus is God then how exactly do you answer the question, *"Does God fear Himself?"* Even if you use the explanation that fear actually means a healthy respect then how do you answer the obvious question, *"Does God respect Himself?"* Christians don't realize that *"healthy respect"* is not an accepted definition of the Hebrew or English word *"fear,"* but rather a personal twisting of the word to include concepts it doesn't naturally include. One may have a *healthy respect* for the environment but one would **not** say they have *"fear"* of the environment. This concept of having a *"healthy respect"* has nothing to do with the *fear* mentioned in Isaiah or anywhere else.

- The passage says, *"he shall not judge after the sight of his eyes, neither reprove after the hearing of his ears: But with righteousness shall he judge the poor, and reprove with equity for the meek of the earth: and he shall smite the earth with the rod of his mouth, and with the breath of his lips shall he slay the wicked. And righteousness shall be the girdle of his loins, and faithfulness the girdle of his reins."* This section is indicating that this king will use the Torah or God's teaching to be the measuring stick for his judgment of the people. He will be a righteous Spirit-filled man and he will be faithful to God in all his actions.

  It is important to remember that it does not indicate anywhere in this passage that the end-times-king is God Himself.

Now let's break down the conditions that exist when the end-times-king rules in Jerusalem. In the Hebrew Bible, we do not find an emphasis on the end-times-king but instead we find one on the Messianic Age. When I use this terminology, I mean the time when God has set the end-times-king on his throne. Some Jewish rabbis have theorized that the Messianic Age started when the Temple was destroyed and symbolically the Messiah was born.[1]

In the Isaiah 11 passage, we see some details of the Messianic Age emerge. Here are the elements and conditions revealed in this beautiful passage.

- *"The wolf also shall dwell with the lamb, and the leopard shall lie down with the kid; and the calf and the young lion and the fatling together; and a little child shall lead them. And the cow and the bear shall feed; their young ones shall lie down together: and the lion shall eat straw like the ox."*

---

1 The anticipation of the arrival of the Messiah became realized in the Jewish people.

There will be universal peace. No longer will the animals be afraid of man and we will live peacefully with them. Not since the time of Noah has this been the case. Christians must realize that this has not come to pass despite their belief that their *Messiah* has come.

- **"They shall not hurt nor destroy in all my holy mountain: for the earth shall be full of the knowledge of the LORD, as the waters cover the sea."**

Again, we see that universal peace and the knowledge of God will be the norm. Not only did this **not** come into being but Jesus actually stated why he didn't bring peace with him.

Think not that I am come to send peace on earth: I came not to send peace, but a sword. For I am come to set a man at variance against his father, and the daughter against her mother, and the daughter in law against her mother in law. And a man's foes shall be they of his own household. He that loveth father or mother more than me is not worthy of me: and he that loveth son or daughter more than me is not worthy of me. (Matthew 10:34-37)

To me, this was one of the most puzzling passages in the New Testament. Here we have Jesus actually saying that he will be the one that will cause strife in families. Wouldn't God want there to be honor between children and their parents and love between all? I have heard Christians say that Jesus will bring peace later. The New Testament presents a slightly different picture. When Jesus returns, he will bring destruction to the earth.

- **"And it shall come to pass in that day, that the Lord shall set his hand again the second time to recover the remnant of his people, which shall be left, from Assyria, and from Egypt, and from Pathros, and from Cush, and from Elam, and from Shinar, and from Hamath, and from the islands of the sea. And he shall set up an ensign for the nations, and shall assemble the outcasts of Israel, and gather together the dispersed of Judah from the four corners of the earth."**

God will gather His people from wherever they are to their home in Israel. This has yet to happen.

- **"The envy also of Ephraim shall depart, and the adversaries of Judah shall be cut off:"**

No longer will others be envious of the Children of Israel. The Palestinians will finally live in peace next to Israel. Anyone who thinks this situation exists today hasn't read a newspaper lately.

- **"Ephraim shall not envy Judah, and Judah shall not vex Ephraim."**

There will not be fighting between the Israeli people. At the present time there are many political parties in Israel that struggle with each other. That will come to an end as well as fighting between social factions.

- **"And the LORD shall utterly destroy the tongue of the Egyptian sea;**

and with his mighty wind shall he shake his hand over the river, and shall smite it in the seven streams, and make men go over dryshod. And there shall be an highway for the remnant of his people, which shall be left, from Assyria; like as it was to Israel in the day that he came up out of the land of Egypt."

Conditions will exist like those that enabled the Israelites to leave Egypt and enter the promised land. They will even be able to walk across dry land as they walked across the Jordan to enter into the land of milk and honey.

The Messianic Age is characterized by the actualization of events foretold in certain prophetic passages. Although some Jews anxiously await the *Messiah* himself, it is not because they expect him to be God in the flesh as most Christians do. They await the *Messiah* because his arrival is proof that God's favor has arrived to rest on the Jewish people and the entire world. Let's look at another Hebrew Scripture passage that both the Jews and Christian accept as pointing to the *Messiah* and the *Messianic age.*

The hand of the LORD was upon me, and carried me out in the spirit of the LORD, and set me down in the midst of the valley which was full of bones, And caused me to pass by them round about: and, behold, there were very many in the open valley; and, lo, they were very dry. And he said unto me, Son of man, can these bones live? And I answered, O Lord GOD, thou knowest. Again he said unto me, Prophesy upon these bones, and say unto them, O ye dry bones, hear the word of the LORD. Thus saith the Lord GOD unto these bones; **Behold, I will cause breath to enter into you, and ye shall live:** *And I will lay sinews upon you, and will bring up flesh upon you, and cover you with skin, and put breath in you, and ye shall live; and ye shall know that I am the LORD. So I prophesied as I was commanded: and as I prophesied, there was a noise, and behold a shaking, and the bones came together, bone to his bone. And when I beheld, lo, the sinews and the flesh came up upon them, and the skin covered them above: but there was no breath in them. Then said he unto me, Prophesy unto the wind, prophesy, son of man, and say to the wind, Thus saith the Lord GOD; Come from the four winds, O breath, and breathe upon these slain, that they may live. So I prophesied as he commanded me, and the breath came into them, and they lived, and stood up upon their feet, an exceeding great army. Then he said unto me, Son of man, these bones are the whole house of Israel: behold, they say, Our bones are dried, and our hope is lost: we are cut off for our parts. Therefore prophesy and say unto them, Thus saith the Lord GOD; Behold,* **O my people, I will open your graves, and cause you to come up out of your graves, and bring you into the land of Israel.** *And ye shall know that I am the LORD, when I have opened your graves, O my people, and brought you up out of your graves, And shall put my spirit in you, and ye shall live, and* **I shall place you in your own land:** *then shall ye know that I the LORD have spoken it, and performed it, saith the LORD. The word of the LORD came again unto me, saying, Moreover, thou son of man, take thee one stick, and write upon it, For Judah, and for the children of Israel his companions: then take another stick, and write upon it, For Joseph, the stick of Ephraim, and for all the house of Israel his companions: And join them one to another into one stick; and they shall become one in thine hand. And when the children of thy people shall speak unto thee, saying, Wilt thou not shew us what thou meanest by these? Say unto them, Thus saith the Lord GOD;* **Behold, I will take the stick of Joseph, which is in the hand of Ephraim, and the tribes of Israel his** *fellows, and will put them with him, even with the stick of Judah, and make them one stick, and they shall be one in mine hand. And the sticks whereon thou writest shall be in thine hand before their eyes. And say unto them, Thus saith the Lord GOD; Behold, I will take the children of Israel from among the heathen, whither they be gone, and will gather them on every side, and bring them into their own land: And I will make them one nation in the land upon the mountains of Israel; and one king shall be king to them all: and they shall be no more two nations, neither shall they be divided into two kingdoms any more at all: Neither shall they defile themselves any more with their idols, nor with their detestable things, nor with any of their transgressions: but I will save them out of all their dwellingplaces, wherein they have sinned, and will cleanse them: so shall they be my people, and I will be their God. And David my servant shall be king over them; and they all shall have one shepherd: they shall also walk in my judgments, and observe my statutes, and do them. And they shall dwell in the land that I have given unto Jacob my servant, wherein your fathers have dwelt; and they shall dwell therein, even they, and their children, and their children's children for ever: and my servant David shall be their prince for ever. Moreover I will make a covenant of peace with them; it shall be an everlasting covenant with them: and I will place them, and multiply them, and will set my sanctuary in the midst of them for evermore. My tabernacle also shall be with them: yea, I will be their God, and they shall be my people. And the heathen shall know that I the LORD do sanctify Israel, when my sanctuary shall be in the midst of them for evermore. (Ezekiel 37)*

After I had read this passage a dozen or so times, I noticed a huge contrast to the New Testament's teachings about the *Messiah*. This *Messiah* actually called *David my servant* is said to be king over them. I don't want to make more of the name *David* than I should but it is very interesting that this *Servant David* is crowned after the resurrection of the dead. Could this be the resurrected David, son of Jesse? We can't know for sure now.

Everything else that is done here in this passage is done by God Himself. It does not indicate that the *Messiah* does any of these miraculous things. The following is a list of the highlights of this passage.

- *"Behold, I will cause breath to enter into you, and ye shall live... O my people, I will open your graves, and cause you to come up out of your graves, and bring you into the land of Israel... I shall place you in your own land."*

    This refers to giving new life to the Children of Israel. This is the Resurrection of the dead.

- *"Behold, I will take the stick of Joseph, which is in the hand of Ephraim, and the tribes of Israel his fellows, and will put them with him, even with the stick of Judah, and make them one stick, and they shall be one in mine hand. And the sticks whereon thou writest shall be in thine hand before their eyes. And say unto them, Thus saith the Lord GOD; Behold, I will take the children of Israel from among the heathen, whither they be gone, and will gather them on every side, and bring them into their own land: And I will make them one nation in the land upon the mountains of Israel"*

    Here God is indicating that Judah (the Jewish people) and Israel (the lost tribes) will become one unified people again. Christians overlook this important fact. This did not occur during the time of Jesus. Christians must ignore the pesky facts that point to Jesus being a false messiah because if they dwell on them, it will cause them to doubt their belief, and that can't possibly be allowed to happen.

- *"One king shall be king to them all... And David my servant shall be king over them."*

God does not say here that He Himself will be the king. He actually uses *David*. God has many wonderful names but *David* isn't one that I recall. There are only two possibilities here.

1. This is literally David, the son of Jesse, resurrected from the dead. This would negate Jesus being Christianity's messiah-king. Or

2. This is not literally David, son of Jesse but is someone in the line of David. Being that Christianity teaches that Jesus did not have an earthly father and could not be of the tribe of Judah and the house of David this could not apply to him. Patriarchal decent determines which tribe you are associated with according to Numbers 1:18.

And they assembled all the congregation together on the first day of the second month, and they declared their pedigrees after their families, by the house of their fathers, according to the number of the names, from twenty years old and upward, by their polls.

Because Jesus had no physical father, he had no pedigree and could not be associated with any tribe. Unfortunately, for Christians, this also negates Jesus from being this *David* that this passage speaks about. Christians shoot themselves in their foot when they insist that Jesus was virgin born and has no earthly father. See chapter 6.

- *"Neither shall they defile themselves any more with their idols... I will save them out of all their dwellingplaces, wherein they have sinned, and will cleanse them."*

This is another thing that Jesus did not accomplish. Christians are blind to things like this. They gloss over obvious prophecies like this, yet change the Words of God to make Jesus fit into verses that are not actual prophecies such as in Isaiah 7:14, when they make Jesus born of a virgin.

- *"They shall also walk in my judgments, and observe my statutes, and do them."*

Although the remnant of Israel does keep God's commands, this is speaking of all of Israel.

- *"They shall dwell therein, even they, and their children, and their children's children for ever... multiply them."*

This dispels Christianity's notion that all of Jesus' followers will go to live in the clouds somewhere in a place called *Heaven*. Instead, God will put Israel in their land and they will have children and grandchildren. This verse doesn't say anything about *Heaven*.

- *"Moreover I will make a covenant of peace with them; it shall be an everlasting covenant with them."*

This is the New Covenant (actually *Renewed*) that Jeremiah spoke of. When Christians read this they should realize that this is the closest thing to a slap upside one's head Jesus will ever get. How ridiculous it was for Jesus to think that he could enact the covenant when none of the prerequisites had been fulfilled. The covenant must be made with Judah and Israel after they are reunited.[2] Jesus' institution of the New Covenant is meaningless and Christians should be embarrassed when they realize what this passage shows about Jesus' credibility.

- *"Will set my sanctuary in the midst of them for evermore... And the heathen shall know that I the LORD do sanctify Israel, when my sanctuary shall be in the midst of them for evermore"*

This passage is the cherry on the top. I could have skipped over these statements but I wanted to drive the point home until it pierced the heart of Christianity. These statements clearly show that the Temple of God will be built again after the end-times-king is sitting on a throne in Jerusalem. It is here in black and white. Now, at this point, most Christians would just shrug their shoulders, wondering what the problem is that I would bother to bring this up. Here is the problem with this passage. It contradicts John's book of Revelation. Revelation 21:22 makes the following claim about the New Jerusalem:

- *And I saw no temple therein: for the Lord God Almighty and the Lamb are the temple of it.*[3]

Did John not know what the Hebrew Scriptures said about the *Messianic Age* and that God said his *Temple* would be there forever? How could the scholars that canonized the Christian Bible miss such a horrendous contradiction? Is it because they started with the New Testament and didn't have any regard for what the Hebrew Scriptures said about the matter?

Who are you going to believe?

Either Jesus is or is not *The Messiah* or *end-times-king*. On one side of the argument you have the Christian holding on with dear life to the New Testament with all of its contradictions and mistakes. The Christian will say that the New Testament is based on the Hebrew Scriptures. Unfortunately... it disagrees with the Hebrew Scriptures, in many places.

On the other side of the argument, you have God's original revelation about this end-times-king. It emphasizes the role of God, not a *messiah*, in bringing this *Messianic*

---

[2] *Israel* or the *lost tribes* were still not regathered. This makes the institution of the New Covenant impossible til they are brought back to their land. This is the time-line of the prophets of the Hebrew Scriptures.

[3] Of course, John says things that are much more outlandish things in the next verse. *And the city had no need of the sun, neither of the moon, to shine in it: for the glory of God did lighten it, and the Lamb is the light thereof. (Revelation 21:23)*

Age into reality. The New Testament turns everything upside down and places supreme importance on Jesus as *the Messiah*.

After examining what the Hebrew Bible states the limited role of the end-times-king is and you compare it to the overwhelming differences found in the New Testament, you will have to decide if you trust what the God of the Hebrew Bible says or what the writers of the New Testament wrote.

I think the choice is clear.

If you trust in Jesus, and you are willing to discount the Words of God and how He revealed Himself in the Hebrew Scriptures, then you must choose Jesus.

The alternative is to accept the Hebrew Scriptures as the only Word of God, and realize that belief in any *messiah* has no part in your relationship with *The Almighty*.

Choose wisely, as your eternity is at stake.

CHAPTER 12

Conclusions

To write a comprehensive conclusion to the things that I have presented in this book would probably double its size. Therefore I will try to be brief.

In this book, we have learned many things about the Hebrew Bible's concept of *messiah* but now it becomes necessary to draw some much needed conclusions. We must close out this discussion and depart on the path we choose to go from here. I hope that if I have not convinced you that Christianity is actually principally founded on a terrible error then, at least, I have caused you to analyze your beliefs.

As I see things, I have proven conclusively that if you believe for whatever reason that the Hebrew Bible teaches that there would be a *messiah* or *anointed* man that would come and die for your sins that you are sadly mistaken. If you believe that God can ignore your wickedness and sees only Jesus' righteousness when He looks at you, then you are uneducated about what the Hebrew Bible teaches.

At this point, if you have been paying close attention and your intent is to discover the truth, the time has come for you to make a choice of the way you will go. There are two paths that you could use to depart from this point in your life. One path recognizes and pursues the One True God and the other does not. It is as simple as that. These are some conclusions we must put forward.

If you worship a man that you believe to be *anointed* and you believe he was God in human flesh then you are on the wrong path. If you rely on a man to save you from the judgment of God then, again, you are on the wrong path.

If you rely on a certain man being sent to die in order to demonstrate that God wants us to return to him then, once again, you are on the wrong path. This system of belief is opposed to the truths of the Hebrew Bible.

Let's break this down logically and as simply as we can:

- Nowhere in the Hebrew Scriptures are Jews or gentiles told that they must believe in an *anointed* person when he appears. You will **know** the identity of the end-times-king rather than have to **believe** in him because where knowledge is, there will be no belief necessary. You will see him with your own two eyes or view him on your wide-screen television sitting on his throne in Jerusalem.

- God tells us in the Torah not to follow anyone that commands us to follow another way than He has already commanded. This command was given in

Deuteronomy, not in the Book of Revelations. Therefore this confirms that the Torah is the basis for a relationship with the Almighty.

- Even if a prophet successfully predicts the future or performs miracles he must maintain faithfulness to the *Torah* or *Instructions*. Because of this, no miracles, signs, fulfilled prophecy, nor even stories of a resurrection can give validity to a prophet if he teaches a new way to know God. This cannot be emphasized enough. This is how God said a prophet was to be tested. This test also applies to the prophet known as Jesus of Nazareth. Jesus taught his followers a new way and because of this, he invalidates the entire purpose of the New Testament which is to bring a different way to know God through him. It is your responsibility to follow the Instructions of God, in the Hebrew Bible, if you agree with them or not.

- The story of Jesus teaches us that: he came out of nowhere; claimed to be *anointed*; and he demanded that the world must believe that he is *anointed* (Mark 16:16). The belief in his anointing is required in order to have eternal life. If you choose not to believe you will burn in hell instead. Does this follow any scenario that can be found in the Hebrew Bible? The New Testament makes no attempt to show evidence that Jesus at anytime was anointed with the special oil that God Himself said was necessary to be used in anointing a messiah.[1]

- At times, the Gospel of Jesus is confused. Some New Testament passages indicate that you must believe that Jesus is the Christ (John 20:31) while others tell us that belief on the name of the son is essential (1 John 3:23) while Jesus himself indicates that obeying the commandments of God is foundational to obtain eternal life (Matthew 19:16,17). It seems to me that on an important subject like this, there must be agreement between the authors but there is not.

In the Hebrew Bible, there is complete agreement. Love for God and obedience to the *Torah* or *Instructions* of God is preeminent. All of the authors and prophets are in complete agreement throughout the entirety of the Hebrew Bible and not one foretells of any requirement of belief in any *Messiah*. As a matter of fact, the last prophet of the Hebrew Bible makes an astounding statement in the last verses of his book.

Remember ye the law of Moses my servant, which I commanded unto him in Horeb for all Israel, with the statutes and judgments. Behold, I will send you Elijah the prophet before the coming of the great and dreadful day of the LORD: And he shall turn the heart of the fathers to the children, and the heart of the children to their fathers, lest I come and smite the earth with a curse. (Malachi 4:4-6)

---

[1] In Exodus 30:22-38, God tells Moses about the requirements of a special anointing oil that is not to be made by ordinary Israelites. To make this oil is cause to be cut off from God's people. There is no mention of Jesus being anointed with this oil. There is an attempt to have Jesus anointed for his burial, not for his kingship. This was done by a woman not a priest or prophet with spikenard which is not **EVEN** a component of the anointing oil found in the Torah. See Mark 14:3 and John 12:3.

This is testimony to the fact that the last words of the Hebrew Bible point to the Law of Moses and not to *any messiah*. If God had wanted us to ignore the Torah and look to a man for salvation, he would have told us so. Also in this passage, we see the promise of Elijah being sent to turn the hearts of the children to their fathers and the fathers to the children but this has not happened yet.[2]

- Christianity teaches the New Testament holds that Jews are condemned for not accepting or believing that Jesus is their messiah (Mark 16:16) despite the facts that prove he isn't. In the end, the Jews will be vindicated when God makes Himself known to the whole world in order to deliver them from their enemies. At that time, He will set his end-times-king on his throne in Jerusalem. The nations will come to the Jews and ask to be taught the Torah in order to dispel the lies that they have inherited as we see here.

O LORD, my strength, and my fortress, and my refuge in the day of affliction, the Gentiles shall come unto thee from the ends of the earth, and shall say, Surely our fathers have inherited lies, vanity, and things wherein there is no profit. Shall a man make gods unto himself, and they are no gods? (Jeremiah 16:19,20)

Thus saith the LORD of hosts; In those days it shall come to pass, that ten men shall take hold out of all languages of the nations, even shall take hold of the skirt of him that is a Jew, saying, We will go with you: for we have heard that God is with you. *(Zechariah 8:23)*

The Hebrew Scriptures never depict the gentiles teaching the Jews truth about their God.

- The end-times-king will fear God and offer a sin offering on an altar for all of Israel and himself. This proves that the end-times-king is not sinless as Christians believe Jesus was.

It is difficult for me to fathom the number of people that have been persecuted or even killed for not believing in Jesus by those claiming to be more righteous than them. The number of families that have been divided because of differing beliefs about Jesus must be staggering. Is this what God would want?

Let's hear God's own final answer on the question on whether or not we are to believe in or accept a man that comes to us and tells us a new way to have a better relationship with Him.

If there arise among you a prophet, or a dreamer of dreams, and giveth thee a sign or a wonder, And the sign or the wonder come to pass, whereof he spake unto thee, saying, Let us go after other gods, which thou hast not known, and let us serve them; Thou shalt not hearken unto the words of that prophet, or that dreamer of dreams: for the LORD your God proveth (is testing) you, to know whether ye love the LORD your God with all your heart and with all your soul. Ye shall walk after the LORD your God, and fear him, and keep his commandments, and obey his voice, and ye shall serve him, and

---

2 Instead of Elijah having come we see that the New Testament depicts John the Baptist as coming, "*in the spirit of Elijah.*" The priests approach John and ask him if he is Elijah but John indicates that he is not Elijah. (See John 1:19-26)

cleave unto him. And that prophet, or that dreamer of dreams, shall be put to death; because he hath spoken to turn you away from the LORD your God, which brought you out of the land of Egypt, and redeemed you out of the house of bondage, to thrust thee out of the way which the LORD thy God commanded thee to walk in. So shalt thou put the evil away from the midst of thee. If thy brother, the son of thy mother, or thy son, or thy daughter, or the wife of thy bosom, or thy friend, which is as thine own soul, entice thee secretly, saying, Let us go and serve other gods, which thou hast not known, thou, nor thy fathers; Namely, of the gods of the people which are round about you, nigh unto thee, or far off from thee, from the one end of the earth even unto the other end of the earth; Thou shalt not consent unto him, nor hearken unto him; neither shall thine eye pity him, neither shalt thou spare, neither shalt thou conceal him: But thou shalt surely kill him; thine hand shall be first upon him to put him to death, and afterwards the hand of all the people. And thou shalt stone him with stones, that he die; because he hath sought to thrust thee away from the LORD thy God, which brought thee out of the land of Egypt, from the house of bondage. And all Israel shall hear, and fear, and shall do no more any such wickedness as this is among you. (Deuteronomy 13:1-11)

We now know that a *messiah* is simply a person anointed with oil and dedicated to a particular purpose, whether a king, a priest or a prophet. Because of this, the question, *"Who is the Messiah?"* is not one that concerns us as much as we originally had thought. This is because in the end when this end-times-king, who is referred to by many as *The Messiah,* is revealed, we will all realize it had nothing to do with any belief in Jesus. The identity of *The Messiah* is God's choice not ours after all. We have absolutely no choice in the matter.

If the Jesus in the New Testament did succeed in drawing part of Israel away from the One True God and caused them to look to him as the *new way* to approach God, then he is truly accursed. Let this be my wake up call to Christians.

God does not look favorably upon those who pity him and his image on the tree and is repulsed by any image of Jesus that men worship. I find it extremely disturbing that Jesus would have equated himself with the bronze serpent that Moses made and lifted up in the desert. That serpent was eventually destroyed by King Hezekiah after Israel began to worship it.

He removed the high places, and brake the images, and cut down the groves, and brake in pieces the brasen serpent that Moses had made: for unto those days the children of Israel did burn incense to it: and he called it Nehushtan. (2 Kings 18:4)

Also the idea that a man can die for another man's sin will be destroyed immediately before the New Covenant is made.

In those days they shall say no more, The fathers have eaten a sour grape, and the children's teeth are set on edge. But every one shall die for his own iniquity: every man that eateth the sour grape, his teeth shall be set on edge. Behold, the days come, saith the LORD, that I will make a new covenant with the house of Israel, and with the house of Judah: (Jeremiah 31:29-31)

If you are following him, it is my sincere desire and prayer that you consider *Leaving Jesus.* Jesus is not a cure all for your life's problems. He is a placebo that only rips someone from real truth, which ends up with real confusion, bitter disappointment and a final destruction. What Jesus does first is get rid of truth, meaning what agrees with reality, God's reality. Once God's truth is gone, all your other consequences fall into place. Instead, turn to the God that had laid out his plan for your life in his Torah[3] while there is still time to learn his ways and spend the rest of your life pleasing him.

---

3   Torah literally translates to *Instruction*. It is the first five books of the Hebrew Scriptures.

Printed in Great Britain
by Amazon